Enhancing English Language Learning in Elementary Classrooms

Study Guide

Allene Grognet, Judith Jameson, Lynda Franco, and Maria Derrick-Mescua

Center for Applied Linguistics, Sunbelt Office
and
Delta Publishing Company
A Division of Delta Systems Co., Inc.
2000

Delta Systems Co., Inc.
1400 Miller Parkway
McHenry, IL 60050-7030

1-800-323-8270
www.delta-systems.com

This printing contains corrections and revisions made after the initial print run. The content and pagination remain the same.

Printed in the United States of America.   12 13 14 15 16 17 18

Enhancing English Language Learning in Elementary Classrooms: A Professional Development Program

ISBN # Complete Program (Manual, Study Guide, Video) 1-887744-47-9
        Trainer's Manual Only 1-887744-50-9
        Study Guide 1-887744-48-7

Preface and Acknowledgments

This book is the combined effort of over 70 years of teaching and professional development experience on the part of four individuals. It comes from working with schools and teachers across the United States, helping them to meet the challenge of their linguistically and culturally diverse elementary classrooms. *Enhancing* is a practical, easy to use, teacher education curriculum for both in-service and pre-service teachers.

Sincere thanks are due to my co-authors, Judy Jameson, Lynda Franco, and Maria Derrick-Mescua, and to Charlotte Kelso, administrative assistant and typist.

Special thanks are also due to the many authors and organizations that have given permission for their work to be used in these materials. Major contributions include:

Christine Sutton and the International Reading Association for "Helping the Nonnative Speaker with Reading," *The Reading Teacher*, May 1989.

Mary W. Olsen and the International Reading Association for "Content Reading Instruction in the Primary Grades: Perceptions and Strategies, "*The Reading Teacher*, December 1991.

The National Clearinghouse for Bilingual Education for the following:

Katherine Davies Samway, *Writers' Workshop and Children Acquiring English as a Non-Native Language* (Program Information Guide No. 10), 1992.

Deborah J. Short, *Integrating Language and Content Instruction: Strategies and Techniques* (Program Information Guide No. 7), 1991.

Emma Violand-Sanchez, Christine P. Sutton, and Herbert W. Ware, *Fostering Home-School Cooperation: Involving Language Minority Families as Partners in Education* (Program Information Guide No. 6), 1991.

Video footage from:

Montgomery County (MD) Public Schools, Office of Global ACCESS Technology

Los Angeles County Schools, ETN (Educational Telecommunications Network)

The Center for Applied Linguistics and The Media Group

CAL has also received permission to use many additional, shorter, materials in this work. Those permissions are acknowledged where the relevant material appears.

Allene G. Grognet
Vice President, Center for Applied Linguistics

Enhancing English Language Learning in Elementary Classrooms

Study Guide

Note to Presenters:
This printing contains corrections and revisions made after the
original print run. The content and pagination remain the same.

Enhancing English Language Learning in Elementary Classrooms

Study Guide

Section 1
Introduction

Introduction

Goal

To understand the need for professional development for teachers working with English language learners and to identify personal priorities to improve one's classroom instruction.

Performance Objectives

• Understand why there is a need for professional development for teachers who work with English language learners.

• Analyze the activities in this section and their usefulness for ELLs.

• Reflect on your personal priorities for learning in this course.

Course Goals, Requirements, and Expectations of Classroom Instruction

Course Goals

- To learn how to plan and deliver instruction to help English language learners understand academic content, develop academic language, and participate in classroom activities.

- To learn how to facilitate ELLs' adjustment to a new culture and how to help all students develop an appreciation for diversity.

- To learn how to advocate for ELLs in the school and community so that these institutions also facilitate their achievement.

Course Requirements

- Attendance and participation (40 hours)
- Five outside assignments (1 hour each)
- Portfolio = Completed Study Guide + 5 Outside Assignments
- Completed Journal

Expectations of Classroom Instruction

1. Instruction should be comprehensible to all learners

2. Learning should be interactive

3. Instruction should be cognitively challenging

4. Instruction should connect school to students' lives and promote cross-cultural understanding

5. Instruction should develop language and literacy across the curriculum

6. The goal of instruction should be achievement of academic standards by all students

Summary Reading

Directions: Read the following passage and write an appropriate title for it in the allotted space.

Title: _____

As teachers look at the students in their classrooms today, they see a scenario much different from the classrooms of their own childhoods. Today 1 in 3 children nationwide is from an ethnic or racial minority group, 1 in 7 [14%] speaks a language other than English at home, and 1 in 15 was born outside the United States. The linguistic and cultural diversity of America's school population has increased dramatically during the past decade, and it's expected to increase even more in the future. While three quarters of Americans now claim European descent, by 2050 only half will. The concept of "minority" group will become obsolete as no group will form a majority.

Educating children from immigrant and ethnic minority group families is a major concern of school systems across the country. For many of these children, US education is not a successful experience. While one tenth of non-Hispanic White students leave school without a diploma, one fourth of African Americans, one third of Hispanics, one half of Native Americans, and two thirds of immigrant students drop out of school.

Confronted with this dismal reality, administrators, teachers, parents, and policy makers urge each other to do something different–change teaching methods, adopt new curricula, allocate more funding. Such actions might be needed, but will be meaningless unless we begin to think differently about these students. In order to educate them, we must first educate ourselves about who they are and what they need in order to succeed. Thinking differently involves viewing these students in new ways that may contradict conventional notions, and coming to a new set of realizations.

Eugene E. Garcia, Ph.D.
University of California, Berkeley

Think-Pair-Share Worksheet

Directions: Use this worksheet to take notes at each stage of the Think-(Write)-Pair-Share activity described by the presenter. The question is: How can teachers think and act differently about English language learners, about teaching ELLs, and about making schools more receptive and supportive of ELLs.

Think-(Write)

Pair

Share

Enhancing English Language Learning in Elementary Classrooms

Study Guide

Section 2
Learning to Read

Learning to Read

Goal

To define strategies to teach reading to ELL students.

Performance Objectives

- Identify the three most important predictors of reading success in students grades K-2.

- Relate the three most important predictors of reading success to all students grades K-6.

- Identify effective strategies to teach reading skills to ELL students.

- Identify implications specific to ELL students learning to read.

- Identify when an ELL student is ready to begin formal reading instruction.

Phonemic Awareness Skills List

1. rhyme/alliteration
    a. rhyme
        Example: Do you see the <u>fat</u> <u>cat</u> sitting on the <u>mat</u>?

    b. alliteration
        Example: <u>T</u>wo <u>t</u>iny <u>t</u>oads <u>t</u>ake <u>t</u>ime <u>t</u>o <u>t</u>alk.

    c. assonance
        Example: I s<u>ee</u> thr<u>ee</u> birds in the gr<u>ee</u>n tr<u>ee</u>.

2. oddity tasks
    a. rhyme
        Example: Which word does not rhyme: *fin, pat, pin*? (pat)

    b. beginning consonants
        Example: Which two words begin with the same sound: *man, hat, mad*?
        (man, mad)

    c. ending consonants
        Example: Which two words end with the same sound: *pig, pan, bag*? (pig, bag)

    d. medial sounds (long vowels)
        Example: Which word does not have the same middle sound: *cake, kite, make*? (kite)

    e. medial sounds (short vowels)
        Example: Which word does not have the same middle sound: *ten, can, pat*? (ten)

    f. medial sounds (consonants)
        Example: Which two words have the same middle sound: *kitten, missing, lesson*?
        (missing, lesson)

3. oral blending
    a. syllables
        Example: Listen to these word parts. Say the word as a whole. *can...dle*–What's
                the word? (candle)

    b. onset/rime
        Example: Listen to these word parts. Say the word as a whole. /p/...at–What's
                the word? (pat)

    c. phoneme by phoneme
        Example: Listen to these word parts. Say the word as a whole. /s//a//d/–
             What's the word? (sad)

4. oral segmentation
    a. syllables
        Example: Listen to this word: *candle*. Say it syllable by syllable. (*can...dle*)

    b. onset/rime
        Example: Listen to this word: *pan*. Say the first sound in the word and then the
             rest of the word. (/p/...an)

    c. phoneme by phoneme (counting sounds)
        Example: Listen to this word: *sat*. Say the word sound by sound. (/s//a//t/)
             How many sounds do you hear? (3)

5. phonemic manipulation
    a. initial sound substitution
        Example: Replace the first sound in *cat* with /m/. (mat)

    b. final sound substitution
        Example: Replace the last sound in *cat* with /n/. (can)

    c. vowel substitution
        Example: Replace the middle sound in *cat* with /o/. (cot)

    d. syllable deletion
        Example: Say *baker* without the *ba*. (ker)

    e. initial sound deletion
        Example: Say *fun* without the /f/. (un)

    f. final sound deletion
        Example: Say *hit* without the /t/. (hi)

    g. initial phoneme in a blend deletion
        Example: Say *stop* without the /s/. (top)

    h. final phoneme in a blend deletion
        Example: Say *fast* without the /t/. (fas)

Activities For Developing Phonemic Awareness

The first four task types should be a part of the curriculum for beginning readers. Students often find success with rhyming, alliteration and oddity tasks activities. It is not essential for students to master each task type before moving on to the next task. Use a variety of appropriately sequenced activities focusing on what students need.

TASK 1 - Rhymes /Alliteration

A. **Rhyme**
Do you see the <u>fat</u> <u>cat</u> sitting on the <u>mat</u>?

B. **Alliteration**
<u>T</u>wo <u>t</u>iny <u>t</u>oads <u>t</u>ake <u>t</u>ime <u>to</u> <u>t</u>alk.

C. **Assonance**
I s<u>ee</u> thr<u>ee</u> birds in the gr<u>ee</u>n tr<u>ee</u>.

Rhyme and Alliteration Activities

1. **DO YOU KNOW?** - Copy the song "Do You Know?" on chart paper. Track the print as you sing to the tune of "Muffin Man." Repeat several times asking students to substitute one syllable rhyming words to replace king and ring. Use post-it notes to record the new rhyming words and place them on the chart.

Do You Know?

Do you know two rhyming words,
Two rhyming words,
Two rhyming words?
Oh, do you know two rhyming words?
They sound a lot alike.

King and ring are two rhyming words,
Two rhyming words,
Two rhyming words.
King and ring are two rhyming words.
They sound a lot alike.

2. **RHYME BOOK** - Paste a different picture at the top of a piece of paper for each student in the class. Have students draw or find pictures from magazines of objects that rhyme with the picture at the top of the page. Gather the pages together and bind to form a class book.

3. **RHYME HUNT** - Go on a rhyme hunt with students around your classroom or schoolyard. Have students find something from their environment that rhymes with a given word (cook, book).

4. **SILLY SENTENCES** - Assist students as they create silly alliterative sentences. Have students illustrate their sentence and combine all pages to form a class book on alliteration. Example: Five funny frogs fell.

5. **SONG/RHYME** - Sing familiar songs such as Row, Row, Row Your Boat. Change the stanza "Merrily, merrily, merrily, merrily" to "Jerrily, jerrily, jerrily, jerrily," etc.

6. **NURSERY RHYME RATTLE -** Say three words, two of which rhyme. Have students identify the rhyming pair. Tell students to listen for rhyming pairs in nursery rhymes such as Jill, hill. Distribute noise makers. Read nursery rhymes. Invite students to make noise whenever they hear the second half of a rhyming pair.

7. **SEEING SOUNDS -** Give each student a hand held mirror. Say words and have students repeat them as they look in the mirror. Point out teeth, tongue, and mouth positions as they say different letter sounds. Have children practice placing their hands in front of their mouth to hear the air expel and placing their hands on their chins to feel mouth positions.

8. **DRAW A RHYME STORY -** Say a rhyme and leave out the last word. Have students draw what they think the last word will be. Example: "When you draw a monster it is said, you always begin with his "HEAD". "This bird can see when he flies, if we draw him two big EYES."

TASK 2 - Oddity Tasks

A. Rhyme
Which word does not rhyme: fin, pat, pin ? (pat)

B. Beginning consonants
Which two words begin with the same sound: man, hat, mad ?

C. Ending consonants
Which two words end with the same sound: pig, pan, bag ?

D. Medial sounds (long vowels, short vowels)
Which word does not have the same middle sound: cake, kite, make ?
Which word does not have the same middle sound: ten, can, pat ?

E. Medial sounds (consonants)
Which two words have the same middle sound: kitten, missing, lesson?

Reprinted with permission from Hillsborough County Public Schools. (August, 1999). *Elementary Language Arts and Reading Frameworks.* Tampa, FL, pp. D20-21.

Oddity Task Activities

1. **PICTURE CARDS -** Create a set of picture cards using drawings or magazine pictures. Display a set: fan, feet, man, mop, six, soap. Mix the cards and have students pick two cards whose picture names begin with the same sound. Try the other variations using picture cards for rhyme, ending consonants and medial vowels.

2. **WHICH DOESN'T BELONG -** Use picture cards to have students determine "which doesn't belong?"

3. **FIND YOUR MATCH -** Make picture cards using large index cards and distribute a card to each student. Have students find their match by locating the classmate whose picture card begins with the same sound, ends with the same sound, or rhymes.

4. **SOUND CONCENTRATION -** Create a set of concentration cards for rhyme, beginning sounds, ending sounds, or medial vowels. Choose one of these categories to be the set of cards used for that game. Spread cards face down on a table. Each player takes a turn by flipping over two cards, saying the name of both pictures and deciding if a match has been made.

5. **STAND, SIT, AND TURN AROUND -** Using students' names, say a sound, such as /b/. Ask all students whose name begins with /b/ to stand up, sit down, turn around, jump and clap or another movement.

6. **HOW DOES IT END? -** Show students a picture card. Have them choose other picture cards that end with the same sound. Continue with other ending sounds.

TASK 3 - Oral Blending

A. Syllables
Listen to these word parts. Say the word as a whole. can...dle – What is the word? (candle)

B. Onset/rime
Listen to these word parts. Say the word as a whole. /p/...at -- What is the word? (pat)

C. Phoneme by phoneme
Listen to these word parts. Say the word as a whole. /s/ /a/ /d/ – What is the word? (sad)

Oral Blending Activities

1. **GUESS IT!** - Teacher orally segments the name of an animal. Students guess the animal's identity. You may want to tell students, "I am thinking of a farm animal. It is a /p/... ig. What am I thinking of?" Continue to play with other animal categories or numbers, colors, classroom objects, etc.

2. **BREAK THE CODE GAME** - Divide the class into teams of up to 5 players. Say a word in parts /m/... ad. The team should respond with the word mad. If that team gets it wrong, give other teams the opportunity to provide the correct answer. Model how to blend word parts together to say the word as a whole. Teams receive one point for each correct answer. Play until a team reaches 10 points.

3. **NAME GAME** - As you line up students for recess or lunch, model blending. Say students' names in parts as you call them to line up. For example, /D/... an.

4. **PUT IT TOGETHER** - Use a classroom puppet for this activity. Tell students they will guess what word the puppet will say after listening to you say a word in parts. If you say /s/ /u/ /n/ students should respond with the word sun. Let the puppet provide feedback and model blending when necessary.

5. **DRAW IT** - Have students fold a sheet of paper into fourths. Orally segment the name of an easily drawn object. Segment by onset and rime if this is the students' first experience with this type of activity, such as /c/...at. Tell students to orally blend word parts and then draw a picture of the word in one section of their paper. In later activities, segment phoneme by phoneme, such as /c/ /a/ /t/.

6. **MYSTERY SENTENCES** - Read aloud sentences from a book or sentences that you made up. Orally segment one word in the sentence.

> *Teacher :* I rode the /b/ /u/ /s/ this morning? What did I ride?
> *Students :* The bus!

Reprinted with permission from Hillsborough County Public Schools. (August, 1999). *Elementary Language Arts and Reading Frameworks.* Tampa, FL, pp. D22-23.

TASK 4 - Oral Segmentation

A. Syllables
Listen to this word: candle. Say it syllable by syllable (can...dle).

B. Onset/rime
Listen to this word: pan. Say the first sound in the word and then the rest of the word. (/p/...an)

C. Phoneme by phoneme (counting sounds)
Listen to this word: sat. Say the word sound by sound. (/s/ /a/ /t/)
How many sounds do you hear? (3)

Oral Segmentation Activities

1. **WHAT'S THE SOUND?** - (sung to the tune "Old MacDonald Had a Farm") Write the song "What's the Sound?" on chart paper. Sing the song several times as you track the print. Invite students to sing along. Replace the words sad and silly with two other words beginning with the same sound.

   What's the sound that these words share?
   Listen to these words.
   Sad and silly are these two words.
   Tell me what you've heard. (sssssssss)

   With a /s/, /s/ here and a /s/, /s/ there,
   Here a /s/, there a /s/, everywhere a /s/ /s/.
   /s/ is the sound that these words share.
   We can hear that sound!

2. **SECRET SOUND** - Tell students that you are going to play a word game. Say three words and have students listen closely and tell what sound is the same in all three words. Be sure the target sound is in the same position (initial, medial, or final). The following word sets may be used:

sun, sick, send	tell, top, tan	ship, shark, shoe
game, plain, late	soap, road, note	sight, ride, life
team, game, home	robe, cab, web	doll, well, hill

3. **I SPY** - Display a favorite picture from a book or use the classroom environment to play I Spy. Tell students "I spy something with my little eye that starts with /s/." Continue to play focusing on different sounds.

4. **ONE POTATO** - Teach students the rhyme "One Potato". Have small groups sit in a circle. As you say the rhyme, pass around an object (potato). The student holding the object at the end of the rhyme states a new word that begins with /p/ since it is the first sound in potato. Repeat the rhyme replacing the word potato with the new word. Continue to play until all students have had an opportunity to make a suggestion.

VARIATION: Play with other food names such as banana /b/, tomato /t/, etc.

> One potato, two potato
> Three potato, four,
> Five potato, six potato
> Seven potato, more.

5. ELKONIN BOXES - Give students a sheet of paper with 3 or 4 connected one inch boxes on it and four chips. Say three or four letter words. Ask children "What sounds can you hear?" Have children put one chip in each box for each sound that they hear. Silent letters do not get chips.

c	a	T
sh	i	P

6. CLAP SYLLABLES - Once students can count words, they are ready to clap syllables. Clap out the number of sounds you hear in each student's name. Then clap words. After you clap a word, decide how many syllables it has.

> **TASK 5 - Phonemic Manipulation**
>
> A. **Initial sound substitution**
> Replace the first sound in cat with /m/. (mat)
>
> B. **Final sound substitution**
> Replace the last sound in cat with /n/. (can)
>
> C. **Vowel substitution**
> Replace the middle sound in cat with /o/. (cot)
>
> D. **Syllable deletion**
> Say baker without the ba. (ker)
>
> E. **Initial sound deletion**
> Say fun without the /f/. (un)
>
> F. **Final sound deletion**
> Say hit without the /t/. (hi)
>
> G. **Initial phoneme in a blend deletion**
> Say stop without the /s/. (top)
>
> H. **Final phoneme in a blend deletion.**
> Say fast without the /t/. (fas)

Phonemic Manipulation Activities

1. **INITIAL SOUND SWITCH -** Have students make new words by replacing the first sound in each word you say with /s/. If you say the word run, students will say sun. Continue to play with these words: hit, well, funny, bun, mad, bend, rat, rope. This game can become more challenging by substituting final consonants and then medial vowels.

2. **SOUND SWITCHEROO -** Say a word and have students listen carefully to the sounds in the word. Play switcheroo with one of the sounds by changing one sound in the beginning, middle, or end of a word. Students will identify the sound that was switched. Example: Say mat and then sat, /m/ was switched with /s/. Use any of the following word pairs: fan/fat, run/sun, hat/hot, pick/pack, ball/bell, leaf/loaf, pig/pin, fish/dish, gate/game, tap/tape, van/ran, zip/lip.

3. **CONSONANT RIDDLES -** Play a consonant riddle game by saying a word. Students will think of a word that rhymes with your word and starts with a particular sound.

   Teacher :   What rhymes with sat and begins with / p /?
   Students: pat

4. **SOUND SPELLING MATCH -** Give each student a set of letter cards: **a, f, h, i, m, n, o, p, s, t, u.**

Step 1:   Using one letter card at a time, model the sound that each letter stands for. Provide an example of a word that begins with that sound. Continue until all letter cards have been taught.

Step 2:   Using all letter cards, review the sound that each letter stands for.

Step 3: Build words with the letter cards. Review the sounds each letter stands for and model how to blend words.

Step 4: Replace sounds in words to create new words. Spell the word sat, blend the word and substitute /s/ with /m/. What word did we make?

This activity may be repeated using other consonants and vowels.

Concepts Of Print Test

☑ *Indicates expectation has been met*

❏ Demonstrates left to right page sequence

❏ Demonstrates awareness of text progression (left/right; top/bottom)

❏ Demonstrates return sweep

❏ Demonstrates voice print match (spoken word to written word)
   with one-to-one matching

❏ Demonstrates awareness that print, not pictures, contains the
   message and that the message remains constant

❏ Begins to read at the beginning of the book and ends at the back of the book

❏ Indicates cover, title, title page, front, and back of a book

Indicates awareness of:
   ❏ a letter
   ❏ a word
   ❏ a first letter
   ❏ a last letter
   ❏ an upper case letter
   ❏ a lower case letter
   ❏ the space between words
   ❏ function of . ? ! " "

Reprinted with permission from Hillsborough County Public Schools. (August, 1999). *Elementary Language Arts and Reading Frameworks.* Tampa, FL, pp. B-14

Activities For Teaching Concepts Of Print

1. **SHARED READING -** During shared reading, point to the words, talk about direction, return sweep, punctuation marks, spaces between words and alphabet letters.

2. **SHARED/INTERACTIVE WRITING -** During shared or interactive writing, discuss where to start writing on the paper. Model left to right and top to bottom progression when writing. Discuss spaces between words, punctuation marks, beginning sounds, words and letters.

3. **GUIDED READING -** During guided reading, students are supported in their efforts to demonstrate print concepts. They should be provided with daily opportunities to practice.

4. **INDEPENDENT WRITING -** During independent writing sessions, students will have the opportunity to demonstrate their knowledge of print concepts.

5. **GUIDED WRITING -** Guided writing opportunities often occur while other students are writing independently and give the teacher additional opportunities to support students in their efforts to apply what they have learned in the area of print concepts.

6. **COUNTING WORDS -** Give each student ten counters in a paper cup (bingo chips, raisins, two colored counters, etc.). Say a sentence at a normal rate. Then repeat the sentence, pausing after each word. Have students put down counters as you slowly say the words in the sentence and then count the counters and decide how many words you said.

7. **SPEECH BUBBLES -** Call attention to speech bubbles contained in a big book. After reading the story, lay a jump rope on the floor in a circle to represent a speech bubble. Let the students take turns making statements for the teacher to record and place in the speech bubble.

8. **PUNCTUATION -** Write sentences from big book stories on tagboard strips. Leave off the punctuation. As a class use:
   - **macaroni** to glue on the sentences as commas or apostrophes
   - **clothespins** to clip on the sentences as quotation marks
   - **punched out dots** to glue on the sentences forming periods or question marks
   - **spaghetti** to glue on the sentences for exclamation marks

9. **WHAT IS A LETTER, WHAT IS A WORD? -** Use Wikki sticks, pipe cleaners or highlighter tape to have students find "a letter" or "a word" during shared or guided reading.

10. **SPACES BETWEEN WORDS -** Emphasize spaces during shared writing by writing each word of a sentence on a separate piece of tagboard and gluing the individual words onto chart paper. Talk about how the individual words go together to make a

sentence. Model how to put the sentence together. Demonstrate how to space between words.

11. **ONE TO ONE WORD MATCHING-** Give students pointers (pencils with eraser tops, tongue depressors, etc.) to point to words on a chart or in a book during shared reading, to "read the room" and to use when reading their guided reading books.

12. **LEFT TO RIGHT -** Cut sentences apart and have students put them back in order using the text as a model.

13. **RETURN SWEEP -** Use Jack Hartman's song tape about return sweep. Let the children pretend they have brooms and "return sweep" along with Jack as he sings.

Reprinted with permission from Hillsborough County Public Schools. (August, 1999). *Elementary Language Arts and Reading Frameworks.* Tampa, FL, pp. D13-14.

Teaching Alphabet Recognition

1.   Assess alphabet recognition. (Identify uppercase and lowercase letters in and out of sequence.)
2.   Expose students to alphabet books.
3.   Teach letter names first. (Begin by using the children's own names.)
4.   Teach the shapes and sounds of the letters.
5.   Focus attention to similarities and differences among letters.
6.   Provide extra support for students having difficulty discriminating letters.
7.   Provide letter-writing practice and independent writing opportunities.
8.   Use multisensory activities.

Activities For Developing Alphabet Recognition

1. ALPHABET CORNER - Set up an area of the room for alphabet exploration and practice. Stock with magnetic letters, stencils, alphabet blocks, picture cards, alphabet stamps, alphabet cookie cutters, sponge letters, alphabet puzzles and games, alphabet flash cards, dry-erase boards, mini chalkboards, alphabet cassettes, magazines, alphabet books, clay, and any other materials you may want to include.

2. ALPHABET CONCENTRATION - Limit the game to 8-12 cards. Make a set of letter cards (one letter for each card, two cards per letter). Objective: Make as many matches as possible. Variations: uppercase letters only, lowercase letters only, mix upper and lowercase letters or match letters to a picture card.

3. TOUCH IT - Place hair styling gel or glue with food color in small plastic zipper bags. Students "write" letter on the outside of the bag then "erase" when ready to form a new letter.

4. NAME SCRAMBLE - Have students use letter cards to spell their names. Scramble the cards and have students reform their name or unscramble the name of a friend. Keep a class name chart handy for this and other activities.

5. LETTER HUNT - Distribute a letter card to each student. Have them find their letter in newspapers or magazines. Find pictures that begin with that letter and glue to the back of the card.

6. ALPHABET WALK - Take students for a walk around the school. Look for and identify learned letters in environmental print.

7. WORD ROUNDUP - Write a series of simple words on the board. Most of the words should begin with the same letter. Read the words aloud and have volunteers circle words that begin with the same letter
EXAMPLE: mad   mom   sad   top   mat

8. **WORD PAIRS -** Write two words on the board such as fat and hat. Read the words aloud. Have students identify the letter that is different in each word.

9. **HIDE AND SEEK -** Hide letter cards around the room. Have students search for them. When a card is found have students return to their seats. Students then share the letter they found as they write it on the board.

10. **DISAPPEARING LETTERS -** Use a small wet sponge or paintbrush to write a letter on a mini chalkboard. Students must identify the letter before it disappears (students may play this game with a partner at a center).

11. **LETTER SNACKS -** Snack ideas for introducing letters:

apples	milk
bananas	noodles/nachos
carrots/cookies	oatmeal cookies
donuts	pizza/peaches
eggs	raisins
French fries	soup/salad
gum	toast/tacos
hamburgers	upside-down cake
ice cream	vegetables
Jell-0/juice	watermelon
Kool-aid	yogurt
lemonade	zucchini bread

12. **ALPHABET CEREAL SORT -** Place a pile of alphabet cereal on a napkin for each child. Sort by letter and count the number of times they found each letter. Create a class graph.

13. **ALPHABET BOOK TAPE -** Make a tape of an alphabet book to place at the listening center. Record activity directions such as "Find the letter **s** on page 8. Write the letter **s**. Find the picture of the sun. Sun begins with the letter **s**."

14. **MAKING LETTERS -** Have children make letters in shaving creme, sand, pudding, playdough, etc.

15. **SORT WORDS -** Sort words according to letters, words that have a "t" in them, words that have two of the same letter, etc.

16. **WIKKI STICKS -** Use Wikki Sticks to circle letters in words in shared or guided reading. Use Wikki Sticks to make letters.

17. **HIGHLIGHTER TAPE –** Use highlighter tape to highlight letters in books or in shared writings.

18. **ALPHABET SONG -** Give each student an alphabet letter. Begin singing the

alphabet song. As students hear their letter sung, they should stand up.

19. **LETTER ACTIONS** - Teach children actions for each consonant. Practice
    them. Once they know some of them, call out a letter and see if the children
    can remember the action. Examples of letter actions:

bounce	gallop	laugh	run	walk
catch	hop	march	sit	yawn
dance	jump	nod	talk	zip

20. **LETTER FORMATIONS** - When teaching students how to form letters, use
    large movements with simple verbal directions. For example, if you are
    teaching the letter d say "around, up and down--d". Have the children make
    and say the letter in the air, on the table with their finger and on paper with a
    pencil.

21. **ALPHABET BEANS** - Using a permanent marker, write an uppercase letter on
    a large, plastic or dry, kidney-shaped bean. Write corresponding lowercase
    letters on the other sides of the beans. Store beans in a can with a plastic lid.
    Students can use them to match upper and lowercase letters.

22. **ADDING MACHINE TAPE** - Have students stamp the alphabet, in order, on
    adding-machine tape. Invite students to shake a can of alphabet beans, spoon
    out five letters, and place them in the correct place on the adding-machine
    tape. Have students shake, scoop, and place beans until the adding-machine
    tape is filled.

Reprinted with permission from Hillsborough County Public Schools. (August, 1999). *Elementary Language Arts and Reading Frameworks.* Tampa, FL, pp. D17-19.

Developmental Continuum In Reading

	AWARENESS & EXPLORATION	EXPERIMENTAL READING/WRITING	EARLY READING/WRITING	TRANSITIONAL READING/WRITING	INDEPENDENT READING/WRITING
Skills:	• Sounds, tones, rhythms • Gestures/paralanguage • Use of symbols of print • Manipulate objects • Alphabetic principles, sounds • Phonemic awareness	• Identify letter shapes, sounds and names • Discrimination of letter shapes • Alphabetic principles • Phonemic awareness • Vocabulary development	• Decoding • Automaticity • Word identification • Sight words • Comprehension	• Decode words • Sight words • Comprehension • Revise, edit, proofread	• Decode words • Fluent reader • Critical evaluation, comprehension • Writing conventions • Correct spelling
Strategies:	• Maintain home language • Listen to rhymes, jingles • Read to and along with child, big books • Retell story • Multiple rereadings • Talk, talk, talk • Word awareness • Print-rich environment • Predictable, patterned text • Alphabet puzzles, blocks • Choral readings • Draw, print • Invented spelling • Ask predictive and analytical questions	• Rereadings • Language experience charts, stories • Dictation of child's story • Practice decoding in meaningful context • Interactive activities/ cooperative groups • Letter naming • Functional reading/ writing • Simple punctation, capitalization • Invented spelling • Ask predictive and analytical questions	• Systematic code instruction with meaningful connected reading • Variety of reading strategies • Independent reading • Familiar text • Metacognitive strategies (predict, self-correct, DRTA) • Integrate reading/writing • Writing for real purposes • Read and retell • Invented spelling • Spelling instruction (patterns, high frequency words) • Authentic assessment • Talk/read to child • Ask predictive and analytical questions	• Read/write for a variety of purposes • Spelling strategies • Word identification strategies (patterns) • Ask predictive and analytical questions	• Read for multiple purposes • Talk, read with child • Independent reading • Parental involvement • Ask predictive and analytical questions

Adapted with permission from NAEYC: A Joint Position Statement by the International Reading Association (IRA) and the National Association for Education of Young Children (NAEYC), Learning to Read and Write: Developmentally Appropriate Practices for Young Children, Adopted 1998. *Young Children*, July 1998, 53 (4): 30-46 (www.naeyc.org).

Enhancing English Language Learning in **Elementary Classrooms**
Study Guide Section 2: **Learning to Read**

Cueing Systems:

ELL Students Require Additional Support in Using Cueing Systems

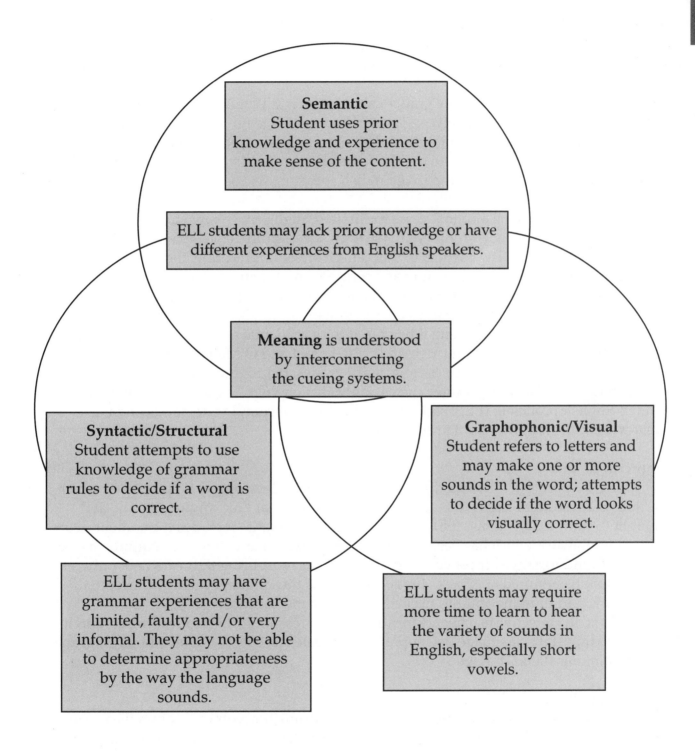

Semantic
Student uses prior knowledge and experience to make sense of the content.

ELL students may lack prior knowledge or have different experiences from English speakers.

Meaning is understood by interconnecting the cueing systems.

Syntactic/Structural
Student attempts to use knowledge of grammar rules to decide if a word is correct.

Graphophonic/Visual
Student refers to letters and may make one or more sounds in the word; attempts to decide if the word looks visually correct.

ELL students may have grammar experiences that are limited, faulty and/or very informal. They may not be able to determine appropriateness by the way the language sounds.

ELL students may require more time to learn to hear the variety of sounds in English, especially short vowels.

Helping the Nonnative English Speaker with Reading

By Christine Sutton
The Reading Teacher, May 1989.

Focusing on 4 critical areas in a language rich environment helps LEP students become proficient readers of English.

Children in the elementary grades can encounter difficulties in reading for reasons as varied as the children themselves. Those whose native language is not English often have problems when reading in English. This is no surprise; yet the response to these reading difficulties frequently is to overlook the obvious and to place the students in remediation classes designed for native English speakers, whose reading problems usually have different causes.

It may take as long as 5 to 7 years for limited English speaking students to gain the command of English needed for them to perform successfully in academic areas (Collier, 1987; Cummins, 1984). The barriers to their effective communication and comprehension, particularly in tasks involving reading and writing, are sometimes hidden by their relatively quicker acquisition of conversational language and mastery of decoding skills in reading. Thus students who *appear* to have command of English may in fact be struggling to communicate and find meaning when faced with academic settings and tasks that are decontextualized and cognitively demanding (Chamot and O'Malley, 1986).

As students reach the upper elementary grades, the cognitive and linguistic demands they face in reading become increasingly challenging. Teachers can help their limited English proficient (LEP) students deal with these complex demands and make greater sense of what they read in several ways.

Four crucial areas

It is helpful to think of reading as a multi-faceted developmental process in which the successful student learns to make those connections that link language, print, and thought (Smith, 1982; Thonis, 1981). Here, the term "thought" includes the student's conceptual framework which has been shaped by experience, education, and culture. In order to comprehend messages encoded in print, the reader must bring to the text not only the decoding skills required to "crack" the code, but also the language facility, conceptual framework, and thinking abilities needed to understand the message.

Thus, the effective teacher addresses all four areas important to reading comprehension—decoding skills, language development/competence, concept/context building, and critical thinking skills/strategies.

Word recognition

For second language learner, oral language acquisition comes through the use of language *in context* (Krashen, 1982; Krashen and Terrell, 1983). Focusing on contextualized language is important in reading development as well (Hudelson, 1984; Krashen, 1981; Thonis, 1981). Students even in the early stages of acquiring English can identify and understand many forms of environmental print (e.g., *men/women, Burger King, EXIT*). The teacher can build upon the students' ability to recognize words in context by integrating print into the classroom environment as well:

- Label items, locations, and activities in the room, on bulletin boards, and on display tables.
- Write directions, schedules, calendar information, names, and work duties on the board and refer to them as the information is discussed orally.
- Use language experience activities to describe events in the classroom. These can be the basis for developing sentence strips and student books (Feeley, 1983).
- Include simple reading/writing activities for beginning level students as reinforcement for language practiced orally. Include copying of language experience information, penmanship, dictation, labeling, vocabulary matching activities, word puzzles, and following simple directions.
- Have students identify words they would like to know in print. This key word approach to the development of sight word vocabulary has been quite effective with LEP learners (Hudelson, 1984).
- Provide students with a place to keep track of important words (e.g., a notebook or word cards). The students can use a combination of cues to remember meaning: English words and native language definition or equivalent.

A discussion on word recognition instruction requires a word about phonics in developing reading competence. Certainly students need to be aware of the grapheme/phoneme connection that ties reading text to oral language and is at the heart of a phonics approach to reading instruction. However, there are some cautions that should be observed when the students are not native English speakers.

- English is not a phonetically consistent language, particularly with respect to vowels. In the words women and fish, for example the sounds represented by the first vowel of each word are identical. English is replete with examples of phonetic irregularities that can confuse the LEP student.
- It is sometimes difficult for LEP students to differentiate sound variations in English, especially if such distinctions do not exist in the native language. It is more difficult still for the student to produce such sound differences in the early stages of language acquisition.
- Phonics drills, like any language drill, may focus on such a narrow aspect of the language process that the total message gets lost. Phonics instruction integrated with other approaches can help students decode print in context.

Language competence

In the process of acquiring a second language, children develop competence by using the language for real communication (Dulay, Burt, and Krashen, 1982). Exposure to whole language activities that integrate listening, speaking, reading, and writing and involve students in interactive communication and experiential learning promote purposeful language that leads to language acquisition.

With respect to reading, there are several things the teacher can do to produce a rich language environment in the classroom:

- Incorporate the Language Experience Approach (LEA) into reading and writing instruction, LEA draws upon both the knowledge and language base of the students and integrates print activities naturally into language development. (For a more detailed description of the use of language experience activities with LEP students, see Coady, 1981; Feeley, 1979, 1983; Moustafa and Penrose, 1985.)

- Expose students to a wide variety of material written in different styles. Include quality works in their entirety. Read aloud to students often so that they experience the flow of the oral language as well. Select well illustrated texts on topics that are familiar and interesting to the students.

- Incorporate creative dramatics, role playing, and dialogues based on scripts that are familiar orally. Such activities provide a ready bridge between oral and print forms of the language.

- Use reading for enjoyment. Include lyrics to familiar music, poetry, riddles, jokes, group poems, choral reading, plays, call and response chants (such as Jazz Chants for Children by Carolyn Graham, New York, NY: Oxford University Press, 1979).

- Provide experience in which language is greatly contextualized (as, for example, a field trip, a science experiment, role playing, planning a class party, solving a puzzle). Use print materials with these activities as a natural extension of the oral language generated: write a class language experience report about the field trip; record information on a science chart; write dialogues or captions for a set of pictures; make lists of party items needed; follow written directions to find a hidden treasure.

- Introduce interactive writing experiences such as pen pal letters or teacher/student dialogue journals to create text that is both interesting and motivating for the participants. Dialogue journals have been especially useful as sources of comprehensive language input and interesting material for students (Peyton, 1986; Shuy, 1985; Staton, 1985).

- Provide reading materials that are well organized, clearly written, and contain illustrations, charts, and diagrams that are easily understood and supportive of the text. The student then can draw upon multiple cues for meaning.

Expanding conceptual framework

Many of us might find reading a textbook on astrophysics or working through the legal language of a contract to be difficult because of the style of writing, the specialized vocabulary, or the unfamiliar concepts presented. Likewise, we might miss the significance of a treatise on Daoism or a reference to the striking of a Hmong man by his prospective mother-in-law because the underlying cultural values and assumptions are foreign to us.

Any reader can have trouble comprehending a reading selection that is outside the realm of his or her experience and knowledge. For the limited English proficient student who is often learning a new culture, a new view of how individuals behave, and a new set of expectations in addition to learning a new language and academic content, the chances for miscommunication and lack of understanding multiply.

Any reading task runs the risk of being outside the realm of the reader's experience and knowledge framework unless care is taken to select materials that relate to the student's background and to help the student understand selections that contain unfamiliar vocabulary, information, or underlying cultural assumptions and values.

Research indicates that readers are better able to understand and remember print selections that reflect their cultural background (Andersson and Barnitz, 1984). Providing LEP students with reading materials that are culturally familiar should aid comprehension because the conceptual schemata needed to make sense of such selections are more likely to be in place. Plan to include in your reading program the following types of materials:

- Folktales and stories from students' native cultures.
- Materials with familiar experiences, characters, and setting (e.g., selections about the student's country, climate, geography, pastimes, health care, recipes, and holidays).
- Familiar values expressed in stories, folklore, maxims, and historical tales.
- Selections containing familiar lexical items such as food, shelter, clothing, tools, transportation, recreation, and other activities from the native culture (items should be presented in context with good illustrations and clearly written text).
- Language experience materials that students have produced individually or in groups to describe events and ideas that are important to them. These materials may be about either the native culture or the new one the student is absorbing.

When an LEP student faces a reading selection that is culturally unfamiliar (as most will be), the teacher can help the student develop a framework for comprehending the text through a variety of prereading and reading activities and strategies:

- Introduce unfamiliar vocabulary (in addition to words identified by the text developers). For example, many LEP students may lack a repertoire of multiple meanings for English words. Thus, use of the word *table* in a science text might be confusing. Similarly a student who has not yet acquired the irregular past tense forms of verbs may not realize that *sit* and *sat* are related.
- Conduct prereading discussions of concepts important to understanding a selection. Present examples that could help students make the connection between these new concepts and ideas they already understand. For example, students might talk about their experience of moving to a new country before reading a social studies lesson on American pioneer life.
- Provide group assignments, allowing students to work with others to process text, discuss ideas, and complete a task that might be overwhelming if done alone. Each student might be asked to read one section of material and write one or two sentences about it; contributions of all can be combined into a longer report.
- Monitor student comprehension through use of questioning and having students talk about what they have read in their own words. For beginners the teacher may have to supply much of the language while the student responds nonverbally or with short answers.

Introducing strategies

Good readers use many strategies and techniques to help themselves understand print texts of various types. LEP students can make use of these same tools if shown what they are and provided with ample opportunities to practice them:

- Help students establish a purpose for reading to direct their attention.
- Familiarize students with the layout and language of different types of reading materials (e.g., story book, science text, drama, magazine article, telephone book, calendar of events); show students how to use chapter headings, charts, diagrams, illustrations, glossaries, summaries, bold type, and other text cues as tools for understanding reading selections.
- Incorporate learning strategies such as imaging, notetaking, integrating new information into existing knowledge framework, making word/idea associations, predicting, and

confirming, and questioning (Chamot and O'Malley, 1986).

- Demonstrate different kinds of reading techniques to be used in different reading situations such as scanning, skimming, reading for main idea, reading for details, rereading to confirm or clarify.
- Introduce summarizing, self monitoring, recalling events in chronological order, retelling in one's own words, outlining, and the use of graphic organizers as pre and postreading text management techniques.
- Provide "real" reading selections used in their appropriate contexts. LEP students frequently are placed in remedial reading classes and receive instruction designed for native English speaking remedial readers whose needs may differ significantly from theirs. Focusing on isolated word attack skills, overuse of phonics drills, or disjointed exercises may impede the integrative processes that link language, print and thinking.
- Foster the higher level thinking skills used by good readers:
  – Introduce problem solving with selections that contain relatively simple language but which require students to process print in thoughtful ways. Examples: Kim is taller than Mai but shorter than Lan. Write the names of the girls in order of height.
  – Pose questions that invite students to analyze, make comparisons, predict, and draw conclusions, such as "Why did thus-and-so happen? How are x and y different? What do you think will happen next?"
  – Increase the teacher wait time after questions to allow students time to process language and to think and reflect about what they have read.
  – Have students create their own problem solving tasks such as math word problems, word puzzles, riddles, and analogies.

By attending to the decoding skills, language development, concept expansion, and thinking processes that are all so critical to learning to read, the teacher can help the student whose English is limited become truly proficient.

Christine Sutton teaches LEP students in the Arlington Public Schools in Arlington, Virginia.

References

Andersson, Billie V., and John G. Barnitz. "Cross-cultural Schema and Reading Comprehension Instruction." Journal of Reading, vol.28 (November 1984), pp. 102-08.

Chamot, Anna Uhl, and J. Michael O'Malley. A Cognitive Academic Language Learning Approach: An ESL Content-Based Curriculum. Rossly, VA: National Clearinghouse for Bilingual Education, 1986.

Coady, James. "Using the Language Experience Approach for Bilingual Instruction." Paper presented at the International Reading Association annual convention, New Orleans, LA, April, 1981.

Collier, Virginia P. "Age and Rate of Acquisition of Cognitive-Academic and Second Language Proficiency." Paper presented at the American Educational Research Association, Washington, DC, April, 1987.

Cummins, James. Bilingualism and Special Education: Issues in Assessment and Pedagogy. Clevedon, England: Multilingual Matters, 1984.

Dulay, Heidi, Marina Burt, and Stephen Krashen. Language Two. New York, NY: Oxford University Press, 1982.

Feeley, Joan, T. "Help for the Reading Teacher Working with LEP Children." The Reading Teacher, vol. 36 (March 1983), pp. 650-55.

Feeley, Joan, T. "A Workshop Tried and True: Language Experience for Bilinguals." The Reading Teacher, vol. 33 (October 1979), pp. 25-27.

Hudelson, Sarah. "Kan Yu Ret and Rayt en Ingles: Children Become Literate in English as a Second Language." TESOL Quarterly, vol. 18 (June 1984), pp. 221-38.

Krashen, Stephen D. "Effective Second Language Acquisition: Insights from Research." In Second Language Classroom: Directions for the 1980's, edited by J.E. Alatis et al. New York, NY: Oxford University Press, 1981.

Krashen, Stephen D., and Tracy D. Terrell. Language Acquisition in the Classroom. Oxford, England: Pergamon Press, 1983.

Moustafa, Margaret, and Joyce Penrose. "Comprehensible Input PLUS the Language Experience Approach: Reading Instruction for Limited English Speaking Students." The Reading Teacher, Vol. 38 (March, 1985), pp. 640-47.

Peyton, Joyce Kreeft. "Literacy through Written Interaction." Passage, vol. 2 (Spring 1986), pp. 24-28.

Shuy, Roger W. "Dialogue Journals and Reading Comprehension." Dialogue, vol. 3 (December 1985), p.23.

Smith, Frank. Understanding Reading, 3rd ed. New York, NY: Holt, Rhinehart & Winston, 1982.

Staton, Jana. "The Teacher's Writings as Text." Dialogue, vol. 3 (December 1985), pp. 5-6.

Thonis, Eleanor W. "Reading Instruction for Language Minority Students."In Schooling and Language Minority Students: A Theoretical Framework. Los Angeles, CA: Evaluation, Dissemination and Assessment Center, California State University, 1981.

Enhancing English Language Learning in Elementary Classrooms

Study Guide

Section 3
Language Acquisition

Section 3
Language Acquisition

Goal

To understand the principles of language learning in order to facilitate the learning of English by ELL students in content classrooms.

Performance Objectives

• Understand the principles, similarities, and differences of first and second language acquisition.

• Describe how the principles of second language acquisition can be used in the mainstream classroom to facilitate language development of ELL students.

• Differentiate social and academic language and describe the implications for school programs.

• Develop activities appropriate to different stages of an ELL student's language development.

• Describe program models for second language students and tell when each is appropriate.

Anticipation Guide: Language Acquisition

Directions: Read each statement and place an A (Agree) or D (Disagree) next to it. Draw from your own knowledge and experience. Then, discuss the items you are least certain about at your table.

_____ 1. A child acquires its first language primarily by imitating adults.

_____ 2. The process of acquiring a second language is more similar to the process of acquiring the first language than it is different.

_____ 3. The best way for a child to learn English in school is to control the vocabulary, syntax, and sequence of grammatical structures that the child is exposed to.

_____ 4. Oral fluency in English is a strong indicator that an English language learner (ELL) will succeed in the classroom.

_____ 5. Once a student has learned the language of instruction, English, his problems in the classroom are largely over and he should be able to handle academic assignments with little difficulty.

_____ 6. Placing a child learning English in a mainstream classroom will ensure that he/she will spend enough time in English to learn the language quickly.

_____ 7. An initial "silent period" can benefit the ELL because it allows him/her an opportunity to process and decode the new language.

_____ 8. Good teachers should suggest to the parents of a child learning English that the parents speak English at home.

Reading On Language Acquisition

Directions: Read the following passage with the questions on the Anticipation Guide in mind. You may revise your responses on the guide if desired.

Chomsky and Krashen

Since 1950, two linguists have exerted especially strong influences on the field. Chomsky asserts that a substantial part of language acquisition must be innate (inborn, like an instinct). Krashen places emphasis on the social and interpersonal aspects of language acquisition; his ideas have revolutionized language classrooms. Since it is unethical to experiment with brain surgery or social deprivation and then study the effects on language acquisition, theorists must rely on observations, naturally occurring experiments, and cross-cultural studies.

Language acquisition is innate

In the late 1950s and 1960s, Noam Chomsky, arguably the most influential theoretical linguist of the 20th century, reasoned that certain aspects of language were innate—that is, they were inborn in the human brain. This view contradicts both the behaviorism of the time and the current social science model. The former explained behavior as stimulus-response learning and the latter explains it as a product of the surrounding culture.

The innateness of language can be visualized as the general outline of a blueprint or electrical wiring diagram that is inborn as "channels" or "circuitry" in the brain. As the child develops, the blueprint is filled in and becomes more detailed, building on the basic structure. Clearly, the original innate blueprint must guide language development in any language to which the child is exposed—a Chinese child, raised in China will learn to speak Chinese; the same child raised by English-speaking parents will learn to speak English.

Chomsky called this concept Universal Grammar. The word grammar in this sense does not mean rules for correctness, but rather general characteristics that all languages possess. For example, all languages have categories of words that name objects and other categories that describe actions, and all languages can express ideas such as number, place, and time. The innate blueprint would help a child develop categories for words and unconscious rules for putting the words together in sentences and conversations. Incidentally, the argument that there are innate aspects of language is not an argument against individual differences. An analogy is lungs: all humans are born with lungs, and all lungs work according to the same basic blueprint, but some lungs are inherently more efficient than others (natural athletes) and other lungs can be trained to be more efficient.

The theoretical construct of Universal Grammar—the innate, generalized blueprint, common to all human brains—is supported by several types of observations:

1. All human cultures, even primitive cultures, have complex, rule-governed language. This observation is consistent with the view that language is a biological adaptation, developed over hundreds of thousands of years, in order to communicate information. The forerunners of language can be seen in animal communication.

2. Children, in natural settings, learn language rapidly and without formal instruction. Their language utilizes thousands of rules that were acquired unconsciously and are transparent to them. Language is so complex that even state-of-the-art computers have difficulty producing it, yet, virtually all children learn language regardless of IQ, social class, formal education, and other social and cultural variables. Middle class Americans think that mothers teach their children language by speaking "Motherese," but other cultures do not speak directly to very young children, and the children still learn to speak on schedule.

3. If children are not exposed to rule-governed, complex language, they will create it. In Hawaii, about 1890, there was a sugar plantation where immigrant laborers came from many different countries and had no common language. The adults developed a makeshift pidgin with a limited vocabulary, few rules, and a limited ability to communicate complex ideas. But children born into this situation created for themselves a fully-developed, standardized, complex language in one generation. (Chomsky would say that they had no choice but to fill in their innate blueprint.) Language creation has also been observed in groups of deaf children with hearing parents.

4. There are several "naturally occurring experiments" such as traumatic injuries to the brain that destroy specific aspects of language such as the ability to put words together into sentences (grammar), but do not affect either knowledge of content words, cognition, or intelligence.

[For more information, see Steven Pinker (1994), *The language instinct*, NY: HarperCollins, especially chapter 2.]

Language acquisition requires comprehensible input

Perhaps the strongest influence on second language teaching and learning in the past 20 years is that of Stephen Krashen. Krashen's theory is based on the assumption that first and second language acquisition take place in very similar ways. This was a new idea as recently as 20 years ago. Prior to Krashen, people often learned second languages through grammar study so the similarity between natural, childhood, first language acquisition and later second language acquisition was not apparent.

The central role in Krashen's theory is played by "comprehensible input." Krashen believes that the language learner needs language "input" which consists of the new language along with clues as to what the language means; without these clues, the learner could hear a lot of language without ever learning to understand it. Without *comprehensible* input, hearing a new language would be like listening to Hungarian on the radio with no way to begin to understand individual words or even topics. Comprehensible input is the type of language that parents naturally supply to their children: it is slower and simpler, it focuses on the here and now, it focuses on meaning over form, and it extends and elaborates on the child's language.

Krashen postulates that the comprehensible input that is most effective is just slightly beyond the learner's current level of competence. Sometimes this concept is written as "i + 1." If the input is either too easy or too difficult, it does not promote improvement as effectively—slightly "stretching" to understand is what promotes improvement. But, Krashen states, parents and teachers need not worry about pinpoint targeting of i + 1 for each language learner. Learners at different levels can each acquire benefit at his own level from a rich, interesting, and positive language acquisition environment.

Second, Krashen believes that there are two distinct ways of developing ability in a language: acquisition and learning. Acquisition is the natural, subconscious process of "soaking up" a language like that of children naturally developing their first language. Learning is a formal, conscious process often involving learning grammar, vocabulary, and rules. Krashen believes that acquisition is overwhelmingly the most important process in developing second language ability. Classrooms with second language learners should provide rich, natural, hands-on language acquisition experiences to facilitate this natural process.

A third key factor in Krashen's theory is that of the affective filter. "Affective comes from the noun "affect." It is a psychological term meaning feeling or emotion. Krashen states that emotions and feelings determine how easily language is acquired. Emotional states such as anxiety, stress, or low self-confidence will "raise the filter" providing an emotional barrier to effective language acquisition. Optimal language acquisition occurs in states of low anxiety and stress and high motivation and self-confidence.

Fourth, language researchers have noted that children acquire (not learn) grammatical structures in a relatively predictable order, e.g., in English -ing forms and plural -s are acquired early, third person singular verb -s and possessive -s are acquired later. The order of acquisition for first and second language learners is similar, but not exactly the same. One of the implications of this observation is to discourage overt error correction because errors will tend to fall away when the learner reaches a certain stage of development, assuming that the learner is in a good environment for language acquisition. (Note that Krashen would NOT encourage teaching a second language based on this order because he believes that formal learning is not a good way to develop language ability. He would encourage placing the learner in a rich language <u>acquisition</u> environment which means the learner would hear and be exposed to lots of rich, natural, complex language from which the learner would begin to unconsciously internalize patterns. By controlling or adjusting the input to contain only certain grammatical structures, the learner's natural acquisition process is undermined.)

And finally, Krashen believes that conscious learning can, under limited circumstances, be used to edit or monitor language output, e.g., to make corrections as we speak or write or after we speak or write. In order to use conscious learning to make corrections, we must have time, be consciously thinking about correctness, be concerned with a limited number of rules, and know the rules. It is impossible to monitor hundreds of language rules when trying to speak or write fluently.

At the risk of oversimplifying, the relationship of these factors could be illustrated as follows: Think of an ELL student. He is presented with *comprehensible input*, and if the *affective filter* is low he can take in the input and use it to aid in *acquiring* new language. Some parts of the language will naturally be acquired before others (*natural order*). When the student produces language, it may contain errors because his language is in an intermediate state of development. In a few circumstances, when he is focusing on correctness, the student can use the *monitor* to make some self-corrections, but this focus will conflict with a focus on fluency and the content of the message.

[For more information, see Steven Krashen. (1981). Bilingual education and second language acquisition theory. In *Schooling and language minority students: A theoretical framework*. Los Angeles: Evaluation, Dissemination, and Assessment Center, California State University.]

Summary

Though Chomsky and Krashen assign central roles to different aspects of language acquisition, the theories are not necessarily in conflict: Comprehensible input could be an important, perhaps the most important, way the innate blueprint of Universal Grammar is filled in.

Language Development Stages

I. Pre-Production

Students are totally new to English; stage may last 1-3 months.
    Can understand more than they can say
    Can actively listen for short periods
    Can respond non-verbally

Questions: Point to….; Do you have the…?; Who has the…?

Tasks: Matching, drawing, acting out

II. Early Production

Students are low beginners in English; stage may last several weeks.
    Can respond with words and phrases

Questions: Is this a…or a…?; Who, what, where, when…?

Tasks: Naming, labeling, listing, categorizing

III. Speech Emergence

Students are beginners in English; stage may last several weeks or months.
    Can participate in small group activities
    Begin to use English more freely

Questions: Why, how…?; Tell me about….; Describe….

Tasks: Role play, small group work

IV. Intermediate Fluency

Students are high beginners, intermediate, or advanced; stage will last several years.
    Can participate in reading and writing activities
    May appear orally fluent, but experience difficulty with high level academics and
        literacy for several years

Questions: Describe, compare….; What do you think about…?;
What would happen if….?

Tasks: Can do most classroom tasks if supported or scaffolded

Adapting A Lesson Using The Three Principles

Directions: Work with a partner to choose ways to adapt the nutrition lesson you saw on the videotape. Think about the lesson as a whole before you record your ideas in each of the categories below.

1. The first principle is "Increase Comprehensibility," that is, ELLs need to understand the content of the lesson even though their understanding of the language is limited. For example, Ms. Amin used stuffed animals and props to demonstrate what she was talking about. Describe one or two other ways you would increase comprehensibility for ELLs.

2. The second principle is "Increase Interaction," that is, ELLs need to use the language they are learning either with the teacher or with other students. Describe one or two ways you would build interaction into this nutrition lesson.

3. The third principle is "Increase Thinking/Study Skills," that is, ELLs need to learn higher order thinking skills even while their language is developing. How could you incorporate thinking skills with limited language into this lesson?

Adapting A Lesson For Stages Of Language Development

Directions: Continue working with your partner to adapt the nutrition lesson for ELLs at different stages of language development. Use the chart on page 43 to guide your work. Remember: you are teaching the *content* of the nutrition lesson and using it as a *vehicle* to develop the student's language. The first stage has been done as an example.

1. Pre-production Stage:

- Student can sort items into junk food and healthy food piles.

- Student can point to or hold up an object (e.g., candy).

- Student can draw a picture illustrating the effects of junk food and another one illustrating the effects of healthy food.

- Student can indicate yes or no in response to questions such as "Is this the candy?"

- Student can follow commands such as "Put the candy next to the soda."

2. Early Production Stage:

3. Speech Emergence Stage:

4. Intermediate Fluency Stage:

VIDEO OBSERVATION FORM

Directions: View the videotaped clips of classrooms and identify teaching strategies that illustrate each of The Three Principles. Take notes on this chart.

	Clip 1	Clip 2	Clip 3
Increase Comprehensibility			
Increase Interaction			
Increase Thinking/Study Skills			

Enhancing English Language Learning in Elementary Classrooms
Study Guide Section 3: Language Acquisition

Summary Of Strategies Implementing The Three Principles

Directions: So far in this course, we have identified several general strategies which help ELLs learn English and succeed in school. With a partner, identify the most important strategies and note each under the principle that it best implements. (Some strategies may be noted in more than one category, but try to identify the principle that the strategy best serves.)

Increase Comprehensibility

Increase Interaction (primarily student to student interaction)

Increase Thinking/Study Skills

Other Ideas to Remember:

Helping ELLs Adjust And Begin To Learn

Directions: Here are some other ways to help English language learners bridge the gap between their first cultures and the school culture, and begin to learn. Review the suggestions and circle a few that you especially want to remember for your classroom.

1. Give the students a "personal space"—a cubby or a desk—and show them where to put supplies, coats, etc.

2. Establish a routine—start the day in a certain way, always write assignments in the same place on the board, have students use a daily planner or assignment notebook to record the assignments

3. Assign buddies—preferably students who speak the same language or are comfortable with ELLs, ask the buddies to show the ELLs the restrooms, cafeteria, playground, etc., and to stay with them for the first few days

4. Include the students in activities—plan lessons so that the ELLs can participate in some way, smile and make eye contact with them often

5. Seat the students so they have access to you and to their peers—seat the ELLs near your work area, but so that they can easily see other students and how they are interacting with each other and with you; seat them so that they have access to other ELLs who speak their language as well as to English speakers if possible

6. Teach the class to treat the ELLs appropriately—encourage them to see the situation from the ELLs' point of view; pronounce the students' names correctly, do not anglicize them unless they ask you to; learn a few phrases in the students' language and a little about the students' country

7. Provide first language support where possible—encourage ELLs to use their native language at appropriate times in the classroom; train bilingual aides to preview lessons in the native language; arrange for a peer tutor; obtain reading materials and software in the native language to support ELLs' learning

8. Connect the home and school cultures—give home assignments that can be done in any language and help the student share in the classroom, e.g., collect family stories, make a family tree, make a personal timeline, make a map of where the families have lived, tell about special holidays, foods, fairy tales

Adapted with permission from Law, B. and Eckes, M. (1990). *The more than just surviving handbook.* Winnipeg, Manitoba: Peguis, pp. 7-22.

Enhancing English Language Learning in Elementary Classrooms
Study Guide Section 3: Language Acquisition

Program Models For English Language Learners

Program Model	Short Description	Classroom Composition	Instructional Objectives
ESOL/ESL Models	The language of instruction is English		
1. **Mainstream Classes (Inclusion)**	Mainstream classes with teacher using ESOL strategies to integrate language and content	Native English-speakers with some ELLs	Academic content, e.g., science
2. **Self-contained ESOL Classes and Sheltered Classes**	ELLs are grouped in special classes so that the teacher can modify instruction/curriculum to meet their needs, e.g., 2nd grade for ELLs; Sheltered Science, Sheltered English	100% ELLs	Both academic content and development of English as a second language
3. **English as a Second Language Classes**	ELLs receive instruction to improve English proficiency; may be pulled out of regular classes	100% ELLs	Development of English as a second language
Bilingual Models			
1. **Two-way Bilingual Programs (Two-way Immersion)**	English-speakers and ELLs are in the same class where some subjects are taught in English and other subjects are taught in the ELLs' native language	Half the students are English speakers and half are ELLs who speak a common language (e.g., Spanish)	Academic content and proficiency in two languages and cross-cultural understanding
2. **Developmental Bilingual (Late-exit bilingual education)**	Some instruction is provided in ELLs' native language so they can "maintain" their language as well as learn English and academics	All are ELLs who speak a common language	Academic content, proficiency in English, and sustained development of native language
3. **Transitional Bilingual Programs (Early-exit bilingual programs)**	Some instruction is provided in ELLs' native language so they can progress academically while learning English; the goal is to support ELLs during their "transition" to an all-English program	All are ELLs who speak a common language	Academic content and proficiency in English

Pros And Cons Of Program Models

Directions: Work with a partner to fill in this chart using the program model descriptions on the previous page.

Program Model	When Most Appropriate?	Pros	Cons
ESOL/ESL Models			
1. Mainstream Classes (Inclusion)			
2. Self-Contained ESOL Classes and Sheltered Classes			
3. English as a Second Language Classes			
Bilingual Models			

Enhancing English Language Learning in Elementary Classrooms
Study Guide Section 3: Language Acquisition

Key Factors For Successful Inclusion

1. Teacher collaboration

2. Common planning time weekly

3. Comprehensive staff development

- After students are placed

- To solve specific problems

- To modify curriculum and instruction to meet student needs

Source: Cindy Naranjo, Project EXCEL Administrator Training Materials, The University of Florida

Outside Assignment #1

Introductory Information: This course includes five, one-hour outside assignments. All assignments must be completed and placed in your portfolio to receive full credit for the course. The first and fifth assignments require you to informally interview an English language learning student and a parent of an ELL student, respectively. Ideally, the parent who will be interviewed is the parent of the student who is interviewed. You may use a translator if necessary.

Directions: Review the types of information that you will need to gather in your interview, then choose an English language learning student (ELL) to be interviewed and obtain any necessary permissions. Arrange for one-on-one time with the student without other distractions or responsibilities. The purpose of this assignment is for you to be able to concentrate on this one student—his/her background, language proficiency, and school experiences and needs. Be sure to put the student at ease and explain why you are talking to him/her before beginning the interview. Elicit information so that you can describe the student in terms of the characteristics below. Reflect on your interview and your learning in this section and then record your responses to these questions:

1. Describe your student's age, grade, country of origin, home language, family situation, and length of time in the US.

2. Describe the student's prior schooling (grades completed, in what country, subjects studied, prior exposure to English, if any, did the student like school? why or why not?).

3. Describe the student's response to school in the US (is it very different from school in the home country? how? does the student like school? is it difficult? what does he/she like in school? what is disliked or difficult?)

(continued, next page)

(Outside Assignment #1, continued)

4. Describe the student's listening and speaking skills in English. What language development stage best describes the student? Justify your response.

5. Describe the student's literacy development (ability to read and write) in the home language and in English.

6. Identify the program model that the student is being served in. Based on your knowledge of the student from this interview, make two or three observations on how the student's teacher could meet this student's specific needs linguistically, personally, and culturally.

Enhancing English Language Learning in Elementary Classrooms

Study Guide

Section 4
Culture

Culture

Goal

To provide participants with a multicultural perspective, knowledge about cultural groups, and the opportunity to reflect on the role of students' home cultures.

Performance Objectives

• Reflect on US cultural values as a first step toward increasing cultural awareness.

• Demonstrate in-depth knowledge of one culture represented in the ELL student population.

• Develop classroom strategies that value all languages and cultures.

• Reflect on the role of students' home cultures in their adaptation to the US.

Culture Study Group Tasks

Purpose: To study one culture, using multiple sources, and to identify information relevant to working with English language learners.

Task 1: Study the culture using multiple resources.

  a. Identify 3-5 key factors in the culture's history/immigration and mark the class Timeline.

  b. Identify features of the language on the class Language Matrix.

  c. Identify/infer positions on the value orientation continuums and mark these points on the class visual.

  d. Discuss cross-cultural teacher-student interactions and expectations. Add 2-3 items to the class chart.

  e. Discuss how parents of ELLs might see American schools and teachers. Add 2-3 items to the class chart.

Task 2: Prepare a five-minute presentation for the class and a supporting poster or display.

  a. Choose <u>a part</u> of what you learned that really interested your small group.

  b. Design the presentation to present <u>a limited aspect</u> of the culture in <u>depth</u>.

  c. Prepare the short presentation and a poster or display. (Presentation may not be longer than 5 minutes.)

Goals Of Second Language And Multicultural Education

1. Teach ELLs to understand US culture.

2. Help ELLs achieve a personal accommodation between their two cultures.

3. Teach all students to value language and cultural diversity.

4. Equitably educate diverse students.

Teaching About Differences *

- Differences exist.

- Differences are good.

- Unjust treatment of differences exists.

- Unjust treatment of differences is wrong.

Adapting Lessons To Include Multicultural Strategies

Directions: Work with a partner to adapt these lesson summaries to be more multicultural. Also identify which of the Goals of Second Language and Multicultural Education your activities *primarily* address. The first lesson is done as an example.

1. *Picture File*: A primary teacher has developed an extensive picture file over the years. The pictures are laminated and she uses them in many types of activities in math, social studies, and language arts.

> The teacher specifically adds pictures that show culturally diverse people throughout the United States and the world, and pictures that break down traditional stereotypes, e.g., a woman carrying groceries on her head in Brooklyn, a man vacuuming the house, an African villager reading a book under a tree, or a parent testifying with a translator at a school board hearing. She also includes images of her own students, their families, and the school staff. She feels this tells children that they, their families, and their school are part of the diversity, not outside of it.
>
> Math: Students create addition, multiplication, division, or subtraction problems using the number of people in the pictures.
>
> Match: Students play a game in which they find a common feature in different pictures and "match" them (e.g., both have vehicles, both have people who look worried, both have people cooking), although these may be in very different conditions (Menkart, 1993).
>
> These lessons primarily address Goal 3.

2. *Cinderella*: In story time, the teacher frequently reads common American fairy tales and other children's stories such as The Three Pigs.

(continued, next page)

SECTION 4

3. *Poverty*: A social studies textbook describes the high level of poverty in Latin America and a US-sponsored program to help Latin American governments address the problem.

4. *Multicultural Fair:* Once a year a school holds a multicultural fair in which different counties show their costumes, foods, and music. One teacher wants to add activities that will help her students understand other cultures more deeply. What can she do?

5. Think of a lesson that you currently teach. Describe it and how you can make it more multicultural in the future.

El Árbol

Directions: Read and reflect on the following, then write your thoughts in your journal. The author was raised in a family that worked in the fields. He later became director of a federal agency and a university professor.

One farm winter in the high plains of Colorado where I was born and raised, my father pointed to an árbol — a cottonwood tree as I recall — near our home. He asked simply "¿ Por qué puede vivir ese árbol en el frio del invierno y en el calor del verano?" (How can that tree survive the bitter cold of winter and the harsh heat of summer?) My father was not a man of many words — he was often characterized by relatives as quiet and shy — but a person who, when he spoke, all listened carefully. I remember struggling to find an answer. I was also characterized as quiet and shy. But I tried to respond to my father. I remember rambling on for some time about how big and strong the tree was and how its limbs and trunk were like the strong arms and bodies of my elder brothers....Then my father kindly provided a different perspective by referring to a common Spanish dicho (proverb): El árbol fuerte tiene raíces maduras (A strong tree has mature strong roots). In articulating this significant analysis that was absent from my youthful ramblings, he made very clear that without strong roots, strong trees are impossible, even though we don't see the roots. What became clear to me at that time was that if you have no roots, how can you withstand the tests of the environment that surely come. For me as an individual with a set of cultural and linguistic roots, if my roots were to die and I was to be stripped of the integrity that lies in those roots, then I would also disappear along with all that is important to me.

For many limited English proficient students in this nation, their roots have been either ignored or stripped away in the name of growing strong. Many have been directed to stop speaking the languages of their homes, to perceive their culture as one less than what it should be, and to assimilate as quickly as possible, so they can succeed in American society. And, unfortunately many have suffered the fate of the rootless tree — they have fallen socially, economically, academically, and culturally.

Eugene Garcia

Reprinted with permission from Eugene E. Garcia and Sandra H. Fradd from Fradd, S. H., and Lee, O. (1998). *Creating Florida's multilingual global workforce: Educational policies and practices for students learning English as a new language.* Tallahassee, FL: Florida Department of Education, p. VII-5.

Enhancing English Language Learning in Elementary Classrooms

Study Guide

Section 5
Writing

Writing

Goal

To consider elementary writing activities with respect to the needs of
ELLs.

Performance Objectives

• Integrate The Three Principles into writing activities.

• Learn to use the writing process and writing conferences with ELLs.

• Examine ELLs' writing to identify what they already know and what
they need to know.

• Reflect on the use of writers' workshop with ELL students.

Video Observation Notes

Instructions:

While watching the video segment, consider the following questions. Use the spaces following each question to take notes.

1. How did the teacher introduce the lesson? What warm-up techniques/
   activities were used?
   Technique/Activity #1

   Technique/Activity #2

2. What techniques/activities did the teacher use while presenting the
   lesson?
   Technique/Activity #1

   Technique/Activity #2

   Technique/Activity #3

(continued, next page)

SECTION 5

3. What do you think the steps in the writing process were?

Focus #1

Focus #2

Focus #3

Focus #4

Focus # 5

Other

Creating and Using Writing Rubrics

What is a rubric?

A rubric is a set of criteria used to evaluate a student's performance. A writing rubric lists the criteria to evaluate student writing and provides a scale to identify how well the writer achieved each of the criteria.

Why use a rubric?

- The rubric makes the evaluation criteria clear to the students so that they know what a good job looks like and they can work toward that. This is especially helpful to less competent writers who need clear indications of how to improve. It is also helpful to ELLs whose educational and cultural backgrounds may value different criteria in writing.

- The rubric makes the evaluation criteria clear to the teacher so that writing scores are more consistent (reliable) over time and less influenced by other factors (more valid).

- Scores based on rubrics show teachers where individual students and the class as a whole need additional instruction.

- Students can learn to develop and use rubrics, helping them to become self-directed learners.

- The rubric helps parents understand how their child is graded.

How can I develop and use rubrics?

There are six main steps to developing and using rubrics. They are summarized below and then discussed in more detail.

1. Clearly specify the writing task or prompt the students will use.
2. Determine the most important criteria for evaluating the writing.
3. Develop a scoring scale for the criteria.
4. Make the rubric clear to the students when the assignment is given.
5. Involve students in developing and using rubrics when possible.
6. Plan learning experiences and instruction to lead to excellent performance.

Clearly specify the writing task or prompt the students will use. Provide written directions (and the rubric) for the task to the students. Go over the task with students and give them the opportunity to ask questions. Give one or two examples of the task.

Determine the most important criteria for evaluating the writing. For example, the Florida statewide writing assessment uses four elements: focus, organization, support, and conventions. Remember that rubrics cannot measure everything; some teachers establish standard rules to be followed for all assignments but not measured by the rubric; for example, papers must be neat, the heading must follow a certain format, the paper must be complete and turned in on time.

Eventually, teachers should give students the rubric to guide their work, but initially, some teachers prefer to simplify the rubric into a checklist, which mirrors the rubric's criteria but is often easier for less experienced students to use. A checklist might include questions such as the following:

- Did you write on the assigned topic? (focus)

- Did you edit and correct your work for spelling, grammar, and punctuation? (conventions)

Develop a scoring scale for the criteria. Usually scoring scales range from 0 to 4 or 0 or 6. The score of 0 is usually reserved for an unscorable paper. Even-numbered scales discourage the scoring of most papers at the mid-point of the scale and force a decision of "just above" or "just below" the mid-point. Although criteria most often receive equal weight, they may be weighted to place emphasis on some characteristics over others; for example, focus and organization could be weighted more heavily than conventions. After determining the criteria and the scoring scale, develop a simple form or checklist to record student achievement of the criteria.

Make the rubric clear to the students when the assignment is given. Give the students a copy of the rubric and discuss it with them. Check with the students at intervals during their work to make sure they are on target. Give students a chance to revise their final draft so that it better meets the criteria of the rubric; for example, hold a conference with the student before he turns in his work and jointly evaluate it using the rubric, then give the student an opportunity to improve his work before turning it in for the official assessment. Use peer feedback based on the rubric.

Involve students in developing and using rubrics when possible. When students face a new task, ask them what a good product will look like and guide them in developing the scoring rubric. This helps students think about new tasks and plan to accomplish them well. Have students evaluate their own work and that of their peers using rubrics. Students are unlikely to write well unless they can first recognize good writing and the criteria that make that writing good. The knowledge necessary to perform well is often the same knowledge required to evaluate competence.

Plan learning experiences and instruction to lead to excellent performance. Rubrics help teachers and students identify exactly what is needed for excellent performance. Teachers can use this information to modify instruction for the whole class and to differentiate instruction for individual students.

Developing good rubrics takes practice and is made easier by teachers working together. It is a necessary step for good writing instruction.

For more information and examples of rubrics with emphasis on the needs of ELLs, see O'Malley, J.M. and Valdez Pierce, L. (1996). *Authentic assessment for English language learners: Practical approaches for teachers.* Addison-Wesley Publishing Company.

Sample Standards for Writing–Third Grade

WRITING

State Standard	Strategy	Benchmark	Ongoing Curriculum
		The student...	The teacher facilitates and provides opportunities for...
Uses writing processes effectively	Prewriting	• prepares for writing by recording thoughts, focusing on central and supporting ideas.	• brainstorming, researching, listing, mapping, webbing and using other graphic organizers. • establishing audience and own purpose: inform and/or entertain. • discussing prompts as one form of writing.
	Drafting and Revising	• focuses on the topic.	• referring to prewriting tools to focus, clarify and extend topic.
		• organizes writing to show beginning, middle and end.	• composing introduction, body and conclusion.
		• uses a variety of sentence structures.	• incorporating simple and complex sentences into writing.
		• writes independently.	• ample time to write for authentic purposes: stories and poems, learning logs and research. • choosing a topic: student initiated, teacher initiated or group negotiated. • feedback during peer and teacher conferences. • identifying strengths within a piece.
	Editing for Conventions for Publication	• produces documents that have been edited for capitalization, punctuation, spelling, indentation and grammar.	• using capitalization of initial word in sentence, the word 'I' and proper nouns. • using punctuation: periods, question marks, exclamation marks, quotation marks and commas in a series, dates and addresses. • identifying misspelled words in a written piece. • using resources to check spelling: word walls, dictionaries, classroom books and spell checkers. • using indentations for paragraphs. • using standard grammar in a written piece: subject/verb agreement, noun/pronoun agreement, singular/plural nouns and complete sentences.
Writes to communicate ideas and information effectively	Writing to Learn	• writes to show comprehension of content and experiences.	• responding to content and experiences in a variety of written formats: learning logs, note-taking, essays, book reports and plays/scripts.
		• organizes information using a variety of strategies.	• determining and using appropriate strategies for organizing information: categorizing, webbing and listing.
	Writing intended for others	• uses legible cursive handwriting.	• forming upper and lower case letters efficiently and legibly.
		• writes to explain.	• writing for a variety of occasions, audiences and purposes.
		• writes to tell a story.	• exposure to rubrics or other self-assessment tools to enhance writing.
		• uses technology to assist in writing.	• using available technology: word processing software, presentation software, electronic media and internet.

Reprinted with permission from Orange County Public Schools. (1997). *Elementary reading and language arts curriculum guide.* Orlando, FL. p. 8EL192d.

Sample Writing Rubric - Third Grade

Writing Elements	SCORE		
	1/2	3/4	5/6
Focus	Slightly related to the topic Extra information not related to topic	Mostly on topic Some extra information not related to topic	Totally on the topic No extra information not related to topic
Organization	No organization Not complete Only one idea No transition words	Tried to organize May lack a sense of completeness Two or more undeveloped ideas or one developed idea Uses simple transition words	Has logical organization Has a sense of completeness Contains 2 or more developed ideas Uses varied transition words
Support	No details or examples Does not use precise language (nouns/verbs) or descriptive words (adjectives/adverbs)	Has details & examples for 1 idea or has a lot of ideas with no details Has some precise language (nouns/verbs) or descriptive words(adjectives/adverbs)	Has 2 or more details or examples to support each idea Uses precise language (nouns/verbs) or descriptive words (adjectives/adverbs)
Conventions	Sentence fragments or run-on sentences Frequent capitalization/punctuation errors Many spelling errors of high frequency words	Generally uses complete sentences Generally uses correct capitalization/ punctuation Generally spells high frequency words correctly	Most sentences are complete Uses correct capitalization/punctuation Uses complex vocabulary which may or may not be spelled correctly

A student scores 0 if his/her paper is not related to the topic, only rewords prompt, refused to write, written in a foreign language, illegible, cannot be read, there is no meaning in the way it is written, or there is not enough writing to tell if student was writing about the topic.

Source: Deborah Stanek and Pam Harris, teachers at Dover Elementary School in Dover, FL, developed this rubric for student use. Reprinted with permission.

SECTION 5

Julio's Report

Julio is a third grade student and an English language learner.

Process of the egg experiment[1]

1   Hello I am Dr. Pérez i would like to tell you about an

2   experiment. It is about an egg and how you can observe how

3   it is changing. the steps are the following.first you need to

4   make a chart so you can results ¿what has happen? You

5   make sure you have all the materials you need to make the

6   experiment. You take a hard boiled egg and put it in the

7   vinegar wait for a moment and write the results ¿what has

8   happen? Now take the other hard boiled egg and put it in

9   the mouthwash and wait a moment and write the results

10 ¿what has hapen? And that is my presentation i hope you

      liked it.

[1]Howard, E and Christian, D. (1997 March). *The Development of Bilingualism and Biliteracy in Two-Way Immersion Studies.* Paper presented at the annual meeting of the American Educational Research Association, Chicago, IL. Reprinted with permission.

What Does Julio *Know* About Writing?

Instructions: Here you are concentrating on describing what the student does know about writing, not on the errors. For each of the sections below, give examples from Julio's writing to illustrate your responses.

1. **Type of writing:** Think about what kind of writing this piece represents and the audience for the writing:
   Expressive writing: to convey feelings or emotions. Letters, journal entries.
   Narrative or fiction writing: to tell a story. Stories, poems, drama with setting, characters, conflict and resolution.
   Expository writing: to present information, to report, to explain, to persuade. Summaries of information, reports.

   a. What type of writing is this; or what is the purpose for this piece of writing?

   b. List what the student knows about making the purpose clear.

2. **Organization:** Think about how the parts and sequence of this piece of writing are organized. *Time sequence, comparison and contrast, cause and effect, steps in a procedure*

   a. How is the writing organized?

   b. Give examples or details to show what the student knows about organizing the parts of this piece of writing.

(continued next page)

3. **Idea development**: Think about the topic of the writing and the details that the student includes.

   a. What does the student know about focusing on a topic and giving details, examples, and descriptions to help the reader understand key ideas? Give examples.

4. **Language**: Think about the student's choice of words and the type of language used.

   a. List some examples of the *vocabulary* that the student uses. Is the vocabulary academic, abstract and formal, or social, specific and informal? Is the vocabulary appropriate for the purpose of the writing?

   b. List some examples of the *sentence* types that the student uses. Are there different types of sentences, or just one or two basic sentence patterns? (*Sentence types: simple, compound, complex*)

5. **Writing conventions**: Think about punctuation, spelling, capitalization, paragraphing.

   a. List what the student knows about the conventions of writing.

Talking To Julio
His comments as a writer; Your comments as a reader

Instructions: *Now look over Julio's lab report again. You will be meeting with Julio to hear his comments as a writer and to give him your reactions as a reader. Write out what you will say, in language that he can understand, about the following:*

Finding out the parts that he likes in his report:

The parts that you liked in his report:

Finding out the parts that he would change in his report:

Some questions that you had as a reader:

Some places where he could make the writing more conventional (punctation, capitalization, etc.):

Teacher's note: **Identify three priorities that you will help Julio work on as a writer:**

Samples Of Student Work

School:

Dover Elementary School is a school in an agricultural area of Florida. The classrooms are multi-age.

Assignments:

The Dover teachers who offered these writing samples gave the following explanations of the purposes and audiences for these pieces of writing:

Assignment #1: (Second/Third Grade) Writing lesson about details that help make a picture for the reader. Students were asked to write a paragraph with details about a place they had visited.

Assignment #2: (Second/Third Grade) After discussing the stegosaurus in reading groups and at science centers, student were asked to write a paragraph about how they thought the dinosaur used the plates on his back.

Assignment #3: (Third/Fifth Grade) This assignment is the first grade 3-5 expository writing of the school year. The class worked paragraph by paragraph on expository form. This is not an edited copy, but a first draft. These students were writing to other students in the class. We 'published' by reading these orally in class.

Students:

L.- a grade 2/3 student - a paragraph about a place she has visited, and a science writing assignment about the stegosaurus

A. - a grade 2/3 student - his science writing assignment about the stegosaurus

R. - a grade 2/3 student - a paragraph about a place she has visited

C. - a grade 3/5 student - expository on her first day of school

Student work is reprinted with permission.

"L"—First Sample

When I was small I uant to the beach I uas omly tuo year old I uant to the beach. And I seen uild dolphines and my dad uas suiming and my uokule was suiming too. And it uas rain and I had to go houe but it uas fun to go to the beach.

"L"—Second Sample

Why do stegosaurus have Plates? Stegosaurus plates sway to keep them cool a long time ago when dinosaurus lived in the forest. Stegosaurus Plates sway to protection them when other dinosaurus attck.

"A"

Stegosaurus is a plant eat he his plates on his back we. Thingck that the plates mack ham cool of he is hat. The plates will mack hem cool agen.

"R"

This summer I went to The Magic Kingdom. We got on air planes my nicese was driveing she went up to the sky. Then my big sister got scared. Then we got on a eallen ride I sat in the front I got so wet. After that we got ice cream. We had a great time.

"C"

I just knew the first day of school would be so awesome! Let me tell you why it was so awesome, I felt comfortable with my teacher, I got the most funny teacher, and I saw my old friends.

I knew Mrs. Dickerson since I was in third grade. I went to reading with Mrs. Dickerson. She is so nice. and I know she is going to be the best teacher.

My friends haven't changed a bit since I last saw them. They had pretty new clothes but they were still Old friends, I was so excited on the first day of school because the first thing I saw was my old friends.

(continued, next page)

My teacher is the most funny teacher. She is so nice but I mean nice she's aways giving the class treats and the most funniest thing about her is that she has purple hair! When she gets in tne sun you can see her purple hair.

Finally, My teacher is the best, my friends are the best, and I got the most funny teacher.

What Does The ELL Student
Know About Writing?

Instructions: Here you are concentrating on describing what the student does know about writing, not on the errors. For each of the sections below, give examples from the student's writing to illustrate your responses.

1. **Type of writing:** Think about what kind of writing this piece represents and the audience for the writing:
   Expressive writing: to convey feelings or emotions. Letters, journal entries.
   Narrative or fiction writing: to tell a story. Stories, poems, drama with setting, characters, conflict and resolution.
   Expository writing: to present information, to report, to explain, to persuade. Summaries of information, reports.

   a. What type of writing is this; or what is the purpose for this piece of writing?

   b. List what the student knows about making the purpose clear.

2. **Organization:** Think about the parts and sequence of this piece of writing. *Time sequence, comparison and contrast, cause and effect, steps in a procedure*

   a. How is the writing organized?

   b. Give examples or details to show what the student knows about organizing the parts of this piece of writing.

(continued next page)

3. **Idea development**: Think about the topic of the writing and the details that the student includes.

   a. What does the student know about focusing on a topic and giving details, examples, and descriptions to help the reader understand key ideas? Give examples.

4. **Language**: Think about the student's choice of words and the type of language used.

   a. List some examples of the *vocabulary* that the student uses. Is the vocabulary academic, abstract and formal, or social, specific and informal? Is the vocabulary appropriate for the purpose of the writing?

   b. List some examples of the *sentence* types that the student uses. Are there different types of sentences, or just a 1-2 basic sentence patterns? (*Sentence types: simple, compound, complex*)

5. **Writing conventions**: Think about punctuation, spelling, capitalization, paragraphing.

   a. List what the student knows about the conventions of writing.

Talking To The ELL Student
His comments as a writer; Your comments as a reader

Instructions: *Now look over the ELL student's report again. You will be meeting with the ELL student to hear his comments as a writer and to give him your reactions as a reader. Write out what you will say, in language that he can understand, about the following:*

Finding out the parts that he likes in his report:

The parts that you liked in his report:

Finding out the parts that he would change in his report:

Some questions that you had as a reader:

Some places where he could make the writing more conventional (punctation, capitalization, etc.)

Teacher's note: **Identify three priorities that you will help the ELL student work on as a writer:**

Writers' Workshop and Children Acquiring English as a Non-Native Language

by Katharine Davies Samway

Acknowledgments

My teaching of writing has been greatly influenced by the work of Donald Graves, Nancie Atwell and Lucy McCormick Calkins, as anyone who is familiar with their work will probably recognize as they read through these pages. I have taken their ideas, tried them out, mulled over them, altered them to fit my teaching situation, and generated my own ways of teaching. I am indebted to them for the practical insights they offered and the stimulus to consider my own solutions and ways of teaching. That may be the greatest gift that one teacher can give another.

I would like to thank Dorothy Taylor, Jennifer Jones-Martinez, Laurel Cress, and Sui-Mui Woo for continually sharing with me their experiences and insights into children's writing development and writers' workshop–you will read their students' writing in the following pages. I also appreciate the insights of Josie Cirone, Ronnie Gruhn, Sharon Roddick, Stephanie Steffey, and Emily Vogler. Lorraine Valdez Pierce was a stimulating person to work with throughout the writing of this publication–I value all that she did as the editor.

Introduction: One Writers' Workshop

The sixth grade students in Ms. Ramirez' Spanish/English bilingual class are catching up with each other after a long weekend. The language that is shared in this classroom is English, but other languages are spoken and

Reprinted from Samway, K. D. (1992). *Writers' Workshop and Children Acquiring English as a Non-Native Language* (Program Information Guide No. 10), National Clearinghouse for Bilingual Education.

respected, including Spanish, Farsi, Lao, and Vietnamese. At the sound of a small bell, the students head for their desks, which are clustered in groups of four around a worn area rug in front of the blackboard. Once she has the attention of all thirty-four students, Ms. Ramirez comments that when reading through the children's writing folders that many of them were writing poetry. She wonders if they realize that poetry doesn't have to rhyme and adds, "Sometimes I felt as if you were limited by the need to find a rhyming word. I thought it might be a good idea to read some poetry that doesn't rhyme and try to figure out what these poets do when writing poetry."

Ms. Ramirez then reads a selection of poems, some written by students from previous years, some written by famous writers, others written by her. English is not the native language of many of her students, and she believes that they need to develop their native language literacy in order to be fully literate. Ms. Ramirez, therefore, encourages her students to write in whatever language they are most comfortable. Most of the poems that she reads are in English, but some are in Spanish and one is in Farsi. Because she does not read Farsi, Ms. Ramirez invites Homah, an Iranian student who had arrived in the United States five weeks earlier, to read it. After Homah has finished, Ms. Ramirez reads the English translation. As she reads each poem, she places a copy on the overhead projector to aid the children in their understanding and to help them see how poets structure their poems. She has made copies of these poems so that the children can begin to put together their own poetry anthologies. She reminds them that they may find it helpful to read other people's poetry and points to a section on the long bookshelf where poetry books are stored.

"I'm gonna write a soccer poem," announces Hugo at the end of this ten-minute mini-lesson. Ms. Ramirez says, "Hugo has just mentioned what he's going to do. Let's do our quick check-in." She then calls out the children's names, and one by one, they briefly say what they are planning to do during writers' workshop. Ms. Ramirez jots down short notations of each child's plans. Several children mention that they will be helping other children who speak very little English: Roberto says that he's going to help Antonio translate his "teaching book" on industrial pollution from Spanish to English; Mary is going to help Thang and Muang with their picture stories; and Freddy will read to Homah from a selection of predictable books that the children have come to love since studying picture books in preparation for tutoring first grade students. Whenever Ms. Ramirez comes to the name of a child whose English is not fluent, she encourages the child to show or point to what s/he will be doing and then verbalizes the child's intentions, e.g., "Muang, will you be working with Mary?" Muang nods and lifts up a sheaf of pictures. "Okay, Muang is going to work on her picture story with Mary." At the end of this quick check-in, the children disperse to different areas of the classroom.

For the next forty minutes the children engage in a variety of activities. Some work on their environmental science reports; others work on stories, letters, memoirs, poems, advertisements for the upcoming bake sale, and comic strips–the children are responsible for deciding on the topic and format for their writing. They are engaged at different stages of the writing process. A couple of children are trying to decide what to write about and Ms. Ramirez reminds them to look at the list of topics in their folders to see if that gives them any ideas. Some children are working on a first draft, while others are working on a second, third, or fourth draft, or editing their writing. Still other children are conferring together about their writing. Several children are reading, doing research for their writing–gathering information, checking into how others write, looking for ideas. One child is at the publication table, putting the finishing touches to a pop-up book she has written for a first grader she tutors once a week. During this forty-minute writing time, Ms. Ramirez circulates around the room conferring with children. Sometimes she just talks briefly with them, asking how things are going or if they need help. At other times she spends a few minutes listening to them as they explain what they are doing or the problems they are encountering, suggesting alternative ways of approaching their writing, or teaching them skills and strategies she sees they need.

During writers' workshop, Ms. Ramirez does not have time to meet with every child, but she makes a point of briefly meeting with the children who understand and speak little English, even though they are all paired with other students who are more fluent English speakers. She pulls up a chair next to these pairs to find out what they are doing, give them an opportunity to talk with her, or make suggestions. The peer tutoring is very effective, and Ms. Ramirez spends time with tutors each week evaluating the success of their work and demonstrating new teaching/learning strategies (e.g., writing picture stories, helping rather than doing for other children).

At the end of this intensive writing time, the class comes together to talk about what they accomplished in that day's writers' workshop, comment on how things went, share finished pieces, and discuss problems they are experiencing. Hugo comments that he didn't have time to write much because he spent a lot of time reading the poetry books, "To see how to do it." Gloria mentions that she had a good conference with Angela and Adam: "They like how I started my soccer story with dialogue, like in *Roll of Thunder, Hear My Cry*. That's where I got the idea 'cuz I thought it was boring before when I just said what happened. They liked that. The dialogue in the beginning." "How did you start it?" Tony asks. Gloria glances down at the sheets of paper in her lap. She clears her throat and reads: "'Get back, get back!' I scream at the fullbacks. A skinny girl is racing down the wing towards me. She's all alone and she's moving the ball towards me and the goal. She's fast. Real fast. I look at the net and position myself." Gloria stops reading. "Ooh, that's good," says Monica, "Did she get a score?" Gloria shakes her head, "No, I looked her in the eye and she missed!" Everyone laughs.

Ms. Ramirez knows from meeting with Thang, Muang, and Mary that Muang has finished her picture story about the birth of her baby sister. She invites Muang to share her finished book. At first Muang is reluctant, but at the urging of Mary and Thang, she comes to the front of the class, sits on the special chair reserved for authors, and with eyes downcast, slowly turns the pages that show in great detail this special event. Mary proudly tells the story for Muang, but at the end, Muang herself speaks up. "This my baby," she whispers as she points to the final frame of a woman holding a tiny baby whose eyes are shut tightly. The class erupts into applause. Muang smiles for the first time. Because it's time for recess, the day's writers' workshop ends with this exchange.

The sketch of this classroom is a composite of many classrooms where children engage in writers' workshop. These classrooms share several characteristics. In them, children:

- write on a regular basis for extended, predictable periods of time;

- are responsible for selecting their own topics;

- confer with each other and with adults about their writing goals, processes, products, problems, and accomplishments;

- write for many audiences–their class peers and teacher, family members, the immediate and wider community, and themselves;

- read a great deal and have many opportunities to talk about reading and writing;

- choose the language that they write in–this is influenced by many factors including their fluency in English, the purpose of their piece, and the needs of their audience; and

- have teachers who are themselves avid readers and writers who share their reading and writing habits, successes, and struggles with their students.

Teachers like Ms. Ramirez did not always have writers' workshops. In fact, in past years many of these teachers rarely focused on writing. In many cases, greater knowledge of the writing process prompted them to redesign their curricula to include time for writing and authentic opportunities for students to develop as writers. Teachers such as Ms. Ramirez have moved toward writers' workshop because of their knowledge about children's writing processes. The purpose of this guide is to introduce writers' workshop to teachers in Grades K-6 who have students acquiring English as a non-native language.

Theory Behind Writers' Workshop

Contrary to learning theories implied or stated in instructional and methodological materials that equate writing with fill-in-the-blank worksheets or patterned writing, it is now known that children acquiring English are capable of much more than is generally expected of them.

Writing as a Meaning-Making Process

Writing is an active, personal, theory-building, theory-testing process that facilitates the making of meaning. Through writing, one can create and clarify meaning. Writing is not simply a mechanism for expressing preconceived, well-formed ideas; instead, it allows one to explore and articulate one's thoughts. Smith (1982) argues that knowing how to write involves being able to delicately integrate global and local conventions with one's own global and local intentions–when we write we try out our theory of the world and in the process discover what we know and think. As a consequence, our own thinking develops through writing. Despite the frequency of writing tasks in school that deny this cognitive function of writing, "a writer's normal task is a thinking task" (Flower & Hayes, 1977, p. 457).

In the process of writing, texts unfold as writers attempt to understand and discover what they want to write about. This is true for both children writing in their native language (Calkins, 1982, 1986; Edelsky, 1986; Graves, 1982,1983b) and children writing in English as a non-native language (e.g., Hudelson, 1989; Samway, 1987a, 1987b; Urzúa, 1987). When exploring their writing with both peers and adults, children's thinking (and subsequently, writing) is enhanced.

Writing as a Recursive Process

Writing is not a simple, static, or linear process of pre-writing, writing and revising. This linear view of writing has given birth to several misguided maxims, including "writers know what they have to say before they say it" (Murray, 1982, p. 26). In the process of writing, new ideas are generated and plans and goals are altered. This phenomenon has been described by Perl (1979, p.17) as:

> a kind of 'retrospective structuring'; movement forward occurs only after one has some sense of where one wants to go.

Even young writers go back and forth in the text (written and pictorial) while composing. They are constantly re-reading and re-evaluating their writing, drawing, and organization, and they make changes accordingly.

Writing as a Development Process

Children's writing development is irregular, regardless of whether they are writing in their native language or in English. Although Edelsky (1982, 1986) found patterns of development for individual children acquiring English, she did not find a developmental pattern that characterized children's writing. Other studies have also indicated great variation in children's writing in terms of both quality and quantity (Hudelson, 1989; Samway, 1987a; Taylor, 1990; Urzúa, 1987).

High levels of oral language development are not necessary for children acquiring English to successfully communicate their thoughts and experiences in writing. Even if they have not yet mastered the English system of syntax and semantics, children are nevertheless able to express their thoughts effectively (Hudelson, 1989; Samway, 1987a; Taylor, 1990; Urzúa, 1987). Writing is a developmental process that is accessible to all children, regardless of their relative proficiency in English.

Writing Processes of Children Acquiring English

Children acquiring English develop as writers in idiosyncratic ways (Hudelson, 1989; Samway, 1987a; Urzúa, 1987). Some children are more fluent speakers, while others are more proficient writers. It is clear that sophisticated oral language development is not necessary for children acquiring English to successfully communicate their thoughts and experiences in writing. In fact, as a result of their exposure to environmental print (e.g., advertising, product packaging, and television), children can write quite early in their English language experience (Hudelson, 1984). This writing growth frequently reflects a development in oral fluency. Students often compensate for their lack of fluency in English by using symbols to express complex thoughts (Taylor, 1990). For example, **Figure 1** illustrates how students who were just beginning to learn English used the X to indicate negation (Box A), the loss of a pet (Box B), and the loss of a vacation (Box C).

We also know that children can write in English before receiving formal reading instruction in the language (Edelsky, 1982; Hudelson, 1984; Hudelson & Serna, 1991), and that this writing may form the basis of their first reading experiences. Children acquiring English are also aware of the need to write in the language that is most accessible to their audience (Hudelson & Serna, 1991). For example, a child may write in English for monolingual English-speaking peers but in Spanish for monolingual Spanish-speaking grandparents. When children are given opportunities to write for authentic, meaning-making, message-sharing purposes, they can accomplish much, even when they are emerging readers and writers and/or writing in a language which they have not yet mastered.

Designing a Writers' Workshop

When planning a writers' workshop for students acquiring English, it may be helpful to remember that this learning event is designed to do the following:

- encourage children to become enthusiastic, experienced writers capable of communicating their ideas in clear and evocative ways;

Figure 1

I do not have any sisters and brothers

When Diana was born the dog got lost.

Then I told him the truth, but he said that I would get a vacation, raise, work for two weeks, and then I would be FIRED!!!

Source: D. Taylor. 1990. "Writing and Reading Literature in a Second Language." In N. Atwell (Ed.), *Workshop 2: Beyond the Basal*. Portsmouth, NH: Heinemann. Reprinted with permission.

- enhance children's knowledge of the craft of writing and give them opportunities to bring that knowledge to discussions about literature (both fiction and non-fiction);

- provide children with opportunities to read and write across the curriculum;

- offer children opportunities to write for real audiences, that is, audiences other than the teacher;

- provide a means to use writing to think and vice versa;

- build a collaborative learning and work environment in which children view each other as valuable resources; and

- show students the relationship between oral and written language.

The classroom procedures indicated on the following pages are intended as suggestions. Every classroom is unique and teachers will therefore need to develop their own procedures to match the experiences and needs of their students. The following factors can influence the scope and/or success of a writers' workshop: classroom set-up and procedures; the roles of the teacher and students; native language literacy; and ESOL classes.

Classroom Set-up

Writing is both a solitary and social act; it requires both quiet time a time to talk. It is important, therefore, that the classroom be set up to accommodate these differing functions. There should be places that are quiet and places where writers can freely communicate with each other. The social aspect of writing is particularly true for young writers–their writing is enhanced by the give and take that occurs when they talk and watch each other at work. Setting the room up with round tables, small rectangular tables, or clusters of four to five desks seems to work best. As some children need a very quiet writing environment, it may be helpful to also establish a secluded writing corner where talking is discouraged. In addition, some teachers designate areas in the room for conferences, such as a corner with pillows or chairs. Teachers may find it helpful to set up classroom work stations for such functions as editing, illustrating, and publishing. These centers can be as simple as a small table, a few chairs, and the appropriate resources stored on shelves or in boxes.

An *editing center* should help children refine the mechanics of their writing. They need reference guides such as dictionaries, thesauruses, and style sheets that explain, for example, the uses of punctuation symbols or features of grammar. It is also helpful to have lists of frequently used words that are added to throughout the year as children become more

SECTION 5

conscious of their vocabulary needs. Children also need to have tools at their disposal that allow them to revise. Cutting and pasting is an efficient way to rearrange texts–scotch tape, scissors, and staplers are invaluable for doing this.

An *illustrating center* should contain a variety of materials (e.g., collage materials, pens, brushes, colored pencils, crayons, paints, different kinds of paper), and reference books or charts describing illustrating techniques and guidelines (e.g., for washes, mosaics). Examples of illustrators' work are also helpful.

A *publishing center* should contain paper of different textures, qualities, sizes, and colors–many print shops will donate or sell for a small fee odd pieces of paper from the ends of rolls. Children often use color and other techniques to express emotions and provide emphasis, both in the text and in the illustrations. Therefore, a publishing center should be equipped with a variety of writing utensils (e.g., pens, pencils, and crayons of different thicknesses, types, and colors). If children are to publish their own writing, they need guidelines for bookmaking or mounting pieces. A computer or typewriter is also very helpful for typing final drafts. Handwritten final drafts, however, can be very attractive. In some schools, children go to a publishing center to illustrate their books. These publishing centers are located in a separate resource and staffed by volunteers from the community.

Classroom Procedures

At the beginning of a writers' workshop, one is likely to hear children briefly stating what they will be doing (whole class check-in). Although the children are often working at their own pace, one will also find the whole class meeting together for a mini-lesson, a time when the teacher gives focused instruction on a particular skill, strategy, or organizational issue. One is certain to see a lot of children writing; some will be beginning or continuing with a first draft, others will be revising their writing and working on a fourth or fifth draft, and still others will be editing their writing. Some writers may be conferring with each other or with the teacher. Others may be searching for a topic to write about, or adding topics to their topic list. Still other children may be doing research (e.g., reading, watching a film, or conducting an interview). Children may be illustrating a piece of writing that is about to be published. Others may be publishing or making final, clean copies; depending on the kind of writing, children may be using a computer to write a final draft, mounting their writing for display on a bulletin board, or making a cover for a book. Toward the end of the writers' workshop, one is likely to see the children all come together for a whole group share where they talk about their writing and writing processes. If a child has just published a piece, the writer may sit in a special chair (the author's chair) to read it–this is an opportunity for the whole class to celebrate in the accomplishments of class members.

If children are to write well, they need to write often. They also need to write at regular, predictable times. This means that writers' workshop cannot occur sporadically. It must be at an agreed-upon time that is well known to the children. Pull-out teachers who meet with students only two to three times a week need to decide on which days to have writers' workshop. Self-contained classroom teachers need to decide on which days and at what times to have writers' workshop. It is best to hold writers' workshop every day, but if this is not possible, teachers may want to aim for at least three times a week, preferably the same days and times each week. Students also need to know what will be predictable about the scheduling of the workshop. For example, once they understand that there will always be a mini-lesson, a brief check-in time at the beginning workshop, and a whole group share at the end of the workshop, children will be able to better prepare themselves for these times.

Other procedures should also be predictable, such as where children's writing is stored. Many teachers keep ongoing writing in manila folders filed in a cardboard storage box that is easily accessible to students; complete drafts of published and/or abandoned pieces can be stored by name in a filing cabinet. Students should be urged to save and date everything they write or draw, even very rough drafts, as these are precious manifestations of their development as writers and thinkers. Children also need to know where to put pieces that need an editing or publishing conference with the teacher.

The Roles of the Teacher and Students

In a writers' workshop, there are potentially as many teachers as there are members of the class. The teacher, however, is the head teacher, as well as a fellow writer and mentor. Through sharing their writing processes and products, teachers are able to demonstrate, inspire, and guide students. It is important to note that there seems to be a connection between the degree to which teachers are themselves writers and the quality of students' writing. It is helpful to spend a few minutes working on one's own writing before circulating around the room to confer with students. Some teachers do their writing on chart paper so that their students can see them at work. Other teachers bring in pieces that they have been working on at home. Teachers need to demonstrate to children what it means to be a writer.

When teachers share a letter to an author or a letter of complaint that they have written, it is very likely that some children will follow suit and write their letters. By sharing a draft of a poem, explaining what they are trying to accomplish, discussing problems they are experiencing in the writing of the poem, and asking for feedback, teachers are letting students know that they know what it is to be a writer. They are also letting students know that they value their reactions and thoughts. When teachers share a letter from an editor informing them that their article will be published, they are letting students share in their exhilaration, while also demonstrating that writing is for real purposes–in this case, to be read by other people whom we may not know.

Children are typically thought of a being fledgling, inexperienced writers. However, even while they are in the process of acquiring English, children are budding teachers and can provide considerable support to each other by offering feedback, seeking feedback on their own writing, and sharing their successes and difficulties as writers. In addition to being responsible for their own writing, students are also responsible for helping each other grow as writers.

Native Language Literacy

Many teachers do not understand the native language(s) of their students, and children in these classrooms often write in English. Sometimes, however, they write in their native language. When teachers appreciate these efforts and encourage them to read their pieces to the class, children are supported as writers and as human beings.

If a teacher can read in the students' native language(s), it is advisable to encourage students to write in the language in which they are most proficient and comfortable; they should not be required to write in a language in which they are not yet comfortable. Children's increasing exposure to English and experience as writers will help them transfer their knowledge of the writing process to English. Children will write in English when they are ready. If the teacher cannot read in the students' native language, s/he can enlist the help of paraprofessionals, tutors, or students to translate.

ESOL Classes

Teachers of English to speakers of other languages (ESOL) may work in a variety of programs, e.g., self-contained classrooms, newcomer centers, and pull-out classes. Although the suggestions provided in this guide for implementing writers' workshop are particularly appropriate for ESOL and bilingual teachers in self-contained classrooms, they can also be implemented by those working in other settings. The scope of the workshop may be affected by the number of children teachers work with at one time, the frequency with which they meet with students, and the length of each session. For example, one pull-out teacher met with her ESOL students from two to four times a week, each session lasting about forty minutes (Taylor, 1990). Because the children attended schools where a great deal of emphasis was placed on reading children's literature, the teacher elected to focus on writing in her classes. Although only two to four children met with her at one time, she was still able to implement a successful writing program. The students wrote in class, conferred with each other and their teacher, and published their books, which were then read by other students. The students frequently solicited feedback on their writing from other students in the ESOL programs, with the teacher acting a conduit. In fact, students' writing became the initial reading experience for students who had just arrived in the country and spoke very little English. The students also corresponded with the teacher in dialogue journals.

Implementing Writers' Workshop

Getting Started

When introducing students to writers' workshop, it may be helpful to take them through the whole writing process in a week, from generating topics to publishing a piece (see **Figure 2**).

Day 1

On the first day, it is useful to begin with a mini-lesson on *generating topics* to introduce the class to the notion that we all have stories to tell (mini-lessons are brief whole-class sessions which focus instruction on a particular feature of writing that students have indicated a need for). Using the blackboard or overhead projector, the teacher lists and briefly discusses four or five topics that s/he knows a lot about and would like to write about (e.g., "the time I had my front teeth knocked out when playing field hockey" or "the time I wanted to write a letter to Kentucky Fried Chicken to ask them why they don't sell roast chicken in the local store"). *Select topics* that will interest the students. In an initial list, include a variety of genres so that children see that writing can have many purposes (e.g., personal anecdote, business letter). After demonstrating how you select topics, ask the students to list topics that they would like to write about; then give them five to ten minutes to write. Children can list their topics in the form of pictures, if necessary. Next, they can spend about ten minutes sharing their topics in pairs or in groups of three, followed by a quick whole group share; this is a way for children to learn from each other and help each other generate topics.

Show students how to select the topic they will write about by eliminating from your own list topics that are too broad or which you don't know enough about. Select one of the topics from your list and begin to write on the overhead or blackboard. Invite the children to select one of their topics and to begin writing on it. Urge students to write on only one side of a sheet of paper and, if writing on lined paper, to write on alternate lines in order to make revising easier. At this stage, the children may write for ten to twenty minutes, depending upon their age, confidence, and ability. While they are writing, move around the room, briefly checking in with children. Complete this introduction to writers' workshop by having children share their reactions to the topic generation and writing time. Some children may read favorite parts of their writing or comment on what they learned from hearing other children's topics.

Figure 2

Day 1	
10 minutes	Mini-lesson on generating writing topics
5-10 minutes	Students generate own lists of topics
10 minutes	Students share their topics in pairs
10-20 minutes	Everyone writes
5-10 minutes	Whole class share
Day 2	
10 minutes	Mini-lesson on writing conferences
10 minutes	Students confer in pairs
5-10 minutes	Debriefing on the conference experience
20 minutes	Everyone writes
5-10 minutes	Whole group share
Day 3	
10-15 minutes	Mini-lesson on revising writing
20-35 minutes	Everyone writes and/or confers
10 minutes	Whole class share
Day 4	
10-15 minutes	Mini-lesson on editing
20-30 minutes	Writing and editing
10-15 minutes	Whole class share
Day 5	
10 minutes	Mini-lesson on publishing
40 minutes	Publishing books
10 minutes	Whole class share

Day 2

On the second day, begin the workshop with a mini-lesson on *writing conferences.* Demonstrate the process with a student and ask the rest of the class to watch and listen closely. Before the student reads the piece aloud, it may be helpful to ask what s/he is trying to accomplish as a writer, what s/he likes best about the piece, or if s/he encountered any problems when writing it. After the student has read the piece, you can comment on what you learned from it and liked best about it. You may also want to ask a couple of clarification questions. End the brief confer-ence (two-to-five-minutes) by asking the student what s/he will do next with the piece. Ask the rest of the children to comment on what they saw you and the student doing (e.g., asking questions, saying what you liked best, talking about favorite parts and why they are favorite parts). After clarifying the role of responders (to support a writer) with the students, have them confer with each other in pairs. After a short debriefing session in which the children comment on how the conferences went, you can all continue writing. After working on your own writing for about five minutes, circulate around the room, quickly checking in with as many children as possible. End the writers' workshop with a five-to-ten-minute whole class share; the children may briefly mention something they learned while writing, read a favorite part, comment on an accomplishment, or raise a difficulty they are experiencing.

Day 3

On the third day, begin with another mini-lesson, this time focusing on *revision strategies*. Children are often not familiar with the revision options that are available to them beyond re-writing, a tedious and often painful task. You can show students how you and other writers revise. Show them how to cut-and-paste, how to use carets (^) to insert something, how to delete with a single line, and how to use symbols and arrows to signal the movement of text. Ask children if they are familiar with other revision strategies; if they mention rewriting, talk about the advantages and limitations of this method. Encourage the children to take another look at their writing to see whether it does what they want it to do. Urge them to revise as they see fit, considering the comments of those who conferred with them. Continue with the writing/revising. After writing for a few minutes, circulate around the room, briefly conferring with children. At the end, have a whole class share for about ten minutes.

Day 4

On the fourth day, begin the session with a mini-lesson on *editing*. Demonstrate with your own writing. Point out that you first need to check to see that your story is clear and says what you want it to say. Then show students how to check for punctuation, capitalization, grammar, word use, and spelling. When checking for spelling, circle all the words you think may be misspelled. Select three or four of these words and try spelling them several different ways in an attempt to find the correct spelling. Encourage the children to edit their own pieces in preparation for publication the next day. Continue writing and editing, and circulate around the room, as on other days. End the session with a whole class share.

Day 5

On the fifth day, begin with a mini-lesson on *publishing*. Select a simple method of book publication, such as stapling sheets of paper in a construction paper cover. Talk about page breaks, illustrations, the front cover, writing a brief autobiographical sketch of the author, and the procedure for making a clean, final copy. This may be a lot of new information, some of which may have to be revisited in the future, but the point is for the children to experience the accomplishment of writing and publishing for a real audience (that is, people who will read their writing for the message it is conveying). Work on publishing students' books, and end the session with a whole class share devoted to celebrating the books that have been completed.

The purpose of this first week's writers' workshop is to give students a taste for writing, to show them what it's like to confer, to write for a real audience, and to be a published writer. This is the only time that children are all doing the same thing at the same time. Once children have been introduced to writers' workshop, they will work at their own pace, engaged in different activities. This first week's writers' workshop may take longer than one week with some classes.

Topic Generation/Selection

One element that often concerns teachers who are new to writers' workshop or are in the habit of assigning writing topics is that children will not know what to write about. Even very young children are able to write on self-selected topics, using invented spelling and pictures to express their thoughts. Most children will have something they want to write about, particularly after being encouraged to think about topics that they are interested in and know something about. This is not to say that a child will not come up blank on occasion.

There is considerable danger in assigning topics if one wishes children to become independent, resourceful writers. Graves (1983) has suggested that assigning topics has the effect of keeping children on writers' welfare. Instead, it is helpful to offer some useful strategies, such as re-reading one's list of writing topics or walking around the room and noticing what other people are writing about. Other suggestions might include conferring with another student about one's dilemma, reading one's dialogue journal to see if there are topics there, or reading a book. In addition, students can be encouraged to list ten good and bad things that have happened to them, to look back in their writing folder to see if there is an unfinished piece that they may want to complete, or to check a list of different kinds of writing that may include the following:

When children are introduced to writers' workshop, it is common for them to write personal memoirs. This is a logical and very important aspect of being a writer as we write best about those things with which we are very familiar. However, children should be exposed to and encouraged to write in many genres, e.g., personal memoirs, poetry, reports, fables, essays, short stories, and letters. As teachers, we need to read from a wide selection of writing, teach about the special features of particular genres, and encourage (not force) children to try different kinds of writing. Teachers can, for example, show how to take a first person narration and rewrite it as a poem or third-person short story.

Many teachers who implement writers' workshops correspond with their students in dialogue journals (see Peyton & Reed, 1990). Sometimes these journals are open-ended and give children the freedom to write about anything, as in the following journal entry by first grader,

Annie, a native Cantonese speaker in a bilingual Chinese/English class. Annie had accompanied her class to see a play about Rumpelstiltskin and wrote about it in her daily journal. The teacher's response to her entry reflects a genuine interest in what she had written:

Annie:

I like are love The pork	I like and love the part
word day marea and I Love The	where they marry and I love the
baby bat The baby is	baby but the baby is
Fek is not The rew wun	fake is not the real one.

Teacher:
How could you tell that the baby was not real? That it was a doll?

Annie:

bea Kus I soll is han cat	because I saw his hand can't
mev and his eaeysis not mev.	move and his eyes not move.

At other times, teachers ask their students to focus their dialogue journal writing on books or what they have learned in a particular class (e.g., math or science). In one pull-out ESOL class, students were investigating conditions for optimal plant growth and recorded their observations in a science dialogue journal. Pedro was able to express humor, even though he had been speaking English for only a short time:

My pea plant don't groon!	My pea plant don't grow!
I am rungri!	I am angry!
I don't no at rapend!	I don't know what happened!
grrrr!!! THE END	Grrrr! The end
My pea plant	My pea plant
(picture)	[picture]
Where is the pea plant?	Where is the pea plant?

A first grade bilingual teacher asked her first grade students, most of whom were recent immigrants to the United States, to write about the books they had been reading. Phuong had read *A Hunting Will Go* and wrote the following entry:

How can a	*How can a*
snake hod	*snake hold*
a cupcake on	*a cupcake on*
his hed tdats seley.	*his head. That's silly.*

Young children have concerns and opinions and should be encouraged to express them in writing. After taking the Comprehensive Test of Basic Skills (CTBS), students in a bilingual first grade class decided to write to the publishers. Carmen wrote an indignant letter pointing out that she's not a number, but a person. She also alluded to her growing knowledge of the physical world:

Dear pepol im not	Dear People, I'm not
an embr im a prsen	a number. I'm a person
if you bit me	If you invite me
I Do not cer	I do not care
pico youll no	because you'll know
Me and my frens	me and my friends
wrok Togethr	work together.
Ill chow you	I'll show you
My book	my book.
Ill chow you	I'll show you
My Batr fly	my butterfly.
Ill chow you	I'll show you
My frends	my friends.
Ill chow you	I'll show you
My Besssssss	my bees.
Ill chow you	I'll show you
My Best Best	my best best
Tings.	things.

Carmen and her peers used writing to express opinions about events that had affected their lives. They also used writing to resolve problems. Carmen had been doing somersaults in the classroom, and her teacher suggested that she think about the wisdom of her actions. Carmen wrote a six-page letter of explanation and apology to Ms. Martinez, excerpts of which follow:

Thes is a chem off me	This is a shame of me.
I wod not like To do it	I would not like to do it
any more i chodof Get a	any more. I should have get a
deTenchon for it	detention for it.
My tings wor Bad.	My things were bad.

I sarey Miss Martines	I'm sorry Miss Martinez.
I shood lisin To You	I should listen to you.
But I did noT no That you	But I did not know that you
Wood Get me in Tro Bol	would get me in trouble
love Carmen	Love Carmen

Audience and Publication

Much writing in school is inauthentic (even in classrooms where the focus is on meaning rather than skills) because children rarely take their pieces to publication. That is, their writing stays in their folders and never has to face a real audience, except perhaps for the biannual or annual collection of stories that the teacher puts together. Children should be writing for many audiences (themselves, their peers, other children, the general public, adults). Not everything needs to be published in book form. Children should be exposed to a variety of publishing modes and then encouraged to select the most appropriate for their purpose. These can include: class and school magazines and newspapers; bulletin boards; displays; books to be checked out of the class, school and local library; books to be shared with children and teachers across the country; competitions; personal and business letter to peers, teachers, administrators, family members, friends, the public; dialogue journals; how-to manuals; charts; and posters. When having a writing conference with children, it is helpful to ask them about their audience (e.g., "Who are you writing this for?"). Or, if a child indicates interest in publishing, ask, "Have you thought about how you might publish this?"

Writing Conference

The purpose of writing conferences should be to help and encourage writers to continue writing. Graves suggests that when teachers confer they should focus on the writer rather than the writing (1983b). That is, instead of trying to alter a piece, to "make it better," we should focus on trying to help the writer acquire strategies that will help him/her in the future. When conferring with a student whose story or report does not seem to be well-developed, teachers often resort to gentle inquisitions that then become commands ("I'd like you to do this with your piece"). Instead, when conferring with children, teachers can ask them what they are hoping to accomplish with their piece (purpose), who it's written for (audience), what they like best or least about the piece (this helps to focus the teacher so that s/he can better help the writer), and if there's anything in particular that they'd like the teacher to pay attention to. In this way, inexperienced writers are given opportunities to reflect upon their purposes, processes, goals, and needs while retaining control of their writing.

Some classrooms display charts reminding children of steps in a writing conference (e.g., read your story, audience comments on what they learned and like best, audience asks questions, author comments on what s/he will do next). However, children often become dependent on permanently displayed guidelines, glancing up at the chart and parroting the suggestions when conferring. Instead of relying on charts, talking about conference strategies with the whole group in mini-lessons, in whole class share sessions, or with small groups in writing conferences can be a very effective way of enhancing children's developing skills as responders to writing.

Conference strategies need to be internalized as a natural part of our lives as writers, readers, and listeners. After asking children to carefully observe a conference in order to note salient features, teachers and students can talk about what people heard and saw. At this time, as the children share their insights orally, the teacher can list them on chart paper, the overhead projector, or the blackboard, adding to his/her own insights if needed (children often refer to the features teachers would like them to notice). Instead of having a rather rigid list of steps in the writing process, the class has a list of conference strategies. If children comment during a small group conference that they had a particularly good conference, the teacher can ask them about it and suggest that they talk about their insights in the whole group share.

Conferences can focus on many issues, including the *content* of the piece (e.g., Is it clear? Does it convey the author's intentions? Does it grab the reader's attention?), *style* (e.g., the format in which it is written, the genre, and who the narrator is), and *editing* (e.g., mechanical or form issues such as spelling, punctuation, grammar, and capitalization). It is advisable to limit the number of issues discussed in a conference to no more than one or two items.

Conferences can involve just students and do not need to be teacher-initiated. Students should be encouraged to confer with each other. Conferences involving a teacher should last for just a few minutes–short, focused moments for teachers to check in with children, offer advice, and/or teach strategies or skills. Children may need to be reminded that a conference can be very helpful at any stage of the writing process.

Conferences may lead to revisions, but that is not the primary purpose. Students need to know that revision is an option, not a requirement. Second grader, Alexis, wrote about an occasion when he almost got run over:

Yastrday I omos gat ran	Yesterday I almost got run
ovr becas I was rag my balk	over because I was riding my bike
in the mire of the stret so I	in the middle of the street so I
was trap in the stret becas	was trapped in the street because
tow cars was won in frat and wan	two cars was one in front and one
was in bak of me and wan	was in back of me and when
my mathre same she cat	my mother saw me she got
so scir and I ran my baik	so scared and I ran my bike
in the siwako	in the sidewalk.

When Alexis brought this story to a conference, the session was dynamic. It was the first time that he had shared his writing in a conference, and the other children in his ESOL pull-out class were captivated. The children commented on what had impressed them most about the story. They asked for details of the incident such as how Alexis got to be in the middle of the street and how he felt being there, incorporating this knowledge into their other comments (e.g., Pepe: "I likeded the part when you got scared, your heart was beating real fast. Boom, boom, boom, boom, boom, boom."). They asked about the story's origins (e.g., Pablo: "Is this true? Is it really, really? Is it true?" and Alexis nodded "Yes"). The conference was successful. Alexis left feeling confident about his writing ("I got more things in my mind," he commented as he left the conference table), but he did not revise it, even though the children and teacher wrote comments on slips of paper. Talking about the story was apparently sufficient for Alexis at this point. Requiring

Enhancing English Language Learning in Elementary Classrooms
Study Guide Section 5: Writing

Alexis to make revisions would have taken control of his writing out of his hands. However, Alexis may not have known *how* to revise his writing and could have benefited from direct instruction on how to cut and paste, use carets (^) and arrows and number sections. This type of contextualized skills teaching can be very helpful.

Contextualized Skills Teaching

Traditionally, teachers have placed considerable focus on mechanical accuracy and the form of writing. By contrast, in writers' workshop, teachers and children focus *initially* on meaning and the message. In early drafts children are not admonished to pay attention to spelling, capitalization, paragraphing, punctuation, or grammatical forms. Instead, they are encouraged to express their meaning as clearly and evocatively as possible. However, issues of form *are* important in writing as they help readers make sense of the message. The most appropriate place to pay attention to these elements of writing is in final, pre-publication drafts, once writers have had a chance to develop their ideas as fully as possible. Contextualized skills teaching is essential in writers' workshop and can be provided in mini-lessons and writing conferences. Mini-lessons can target mechanical issues (e.g., writing conventions and spelling), as well as organizational issues (e.g., procedures and where to publish) and crafting issues (e.g., leads, setting, dialogue, and revision strategies).

Editing

Many teachers spend inordinate amounts of time correcting children's writing, even though children can only learn a few mechanical features at a time. Correcting all errors does not appear to lead to more standardized writing. Instead, focusing on one or two important features appears to be most effective. In writers' workshop, teachers teach skills as needed and then hold children accountable for applying those skills they have been taught. Therefore, before having an editing conference, children must take responsibility for checking their work and seeing if they have the best copy possible. If children have writing folders for work in progress it is helpful to keep one section for listing their writing ideas/ topics and another section for keeping a record of skills taught (see **Figure 3**). In this way, children can refer to their skills list before handing in a piece for publication. Therefore, if Ahmed has been taught the use of "too," quotation marks, sub-headings, irregular past tense forms, and the spelling of several words, and these skills have been noted on his Editing Checklist, his teacher could expect him to check his writing for these features and make the appropriate corrections before handing in a final draft. It should be remembered that the amount and type of self-editing that one expects will be influenced by the age and fluency of the students.

Self-editing should precede either a peer or adult editing conference. It may be helpful to think of the editing process as a series of steps for both students and teachers. These might include the steps indicated below.

Figure 3

3.A. EDITING CHECKLIST (skills I've been taught)

9/17	Capital letters: 1. at the beginning of sentences; 2. names of people and places;
9/28	Cutting and pasting to revise (instead of rewriting)
9/28	Write on one side only
10/9	Punctation: periods (.); questions marks (?); exclamation marks (!)
10/20	Contractions: I've (I have); we'll (we will); don't (do not)
11/2	Overusing "and " (check that you really need it)
11/19	Page breaks for books
11/19	Where to put illustrations in book (to help the story)
12/2	Overuse of "then " (check that you really need it)
	Spelling:
9/17	body, girl, I've, write
9/28	friends, could, else
10/9	because, surprise
10/20	new, knew (sound the same); "My jacket is brand new." I knew it cost $2, so I brought enough money."
11/2	aunt, uncle (family members), ant (insect)
11/19	of, off (sound the same): "He helped me off the ride." "The toy is made of plastic."
12/2	would, should (like could, 9/28)

3.B. WRITING TOPICS (things I'd like to write about)

1. When my girbel dide

2. Lurning to scat

3. My baby bruthr he got bornd

4. My burthday party

5. All about snaks

Self-editing (check and change)

Read your story aloud:

- Does it make sense?

- Are there any excess words?

- Check spelling and circle words you think are misspelled:

  - use resources in the room (e.g., word list in folders, charts, dictionaries, classmates);
  - select several words and try alternate spellings for each.

- Check punctuation: periods, commas, question marks, exclamation marks, quotation marks, and apostrophes.

- Check capitalization: names and first word of a sentence.

- Check paragraphing and/or page breaks.

- Decide what illustrations are needed and where they will go.

Peer Editing Conference (check and suggest)

Invite a classmate to check over the piece. Listen to your classmate's recommendations and decide whether to make the changes s/he suggests.

Adult Editing Conference (direct teaching)

- Read the piece in advance of the conference. Has the author self-edited? If not, send the story back to the author.

- Based on the piece, select one or two skills to focus on (e.g., quotation marks, excess use of "then," adding "ed" for the regular past tense).

- Give brief, direct instruction in the selected skill(s).

- Record the skill(s) taught in the writer's folder. Include the date.

Copyediting (preparation of clean copy for publication)
The following suggestions are intended for teachers who elect to copyedit:

- Depending on many factors (e.g., length of piece, degree of mastery of mechanics, personality of the writer, the needs of the writer, time, and availability of help), this stage may or may not be done with the writer present.

- Teachers need to decide whether to copyedit on the writer's final draft, on a xerox copy of the final draft, or on a separate sheet of paper (this is especially crucial if writers recopy for their published draft). In some cases, the teacher's copyedited version will be the final draft.

Publishing

As stated earlier, not everything a child writes needs to be brought to publication. However, publication is an integral part of writing and children need to have that experience in order to know what it is to be a writer in the fullest sense possible. Although we sometimes write for ourselves only (e.g., in personal journals), most writing is also for other people. Although an intensely personal act, writing is also a public act. Through publishing, children can more easily understand the importance of strong leads, well-developed characters, sufficient information, and conventional spelling, to name just a few of elements of writing that we all struggle with.

Most publications include a biographical sketch of the author. Readers like to know about authors; this is true for all authors, regardless of age. Many students insert biographical sketches at the end of their publications. It is very encouraging for children to get responses from their readers, and a Comments Page attached to a publication can serve the purpose quite well. Children need to see their writing displayed on walls, charts, and bulletin boards, published in newsletters, anthologies and newspapers, or bound as books. Publication need not be an elaborate process–the key is that children's writing must be celebrated and read by others.

Successes and accomplishments must be celebrated. In many writers' workshops, when a piece is published, the author reads it aloud from an author's chair. Student's development and progress also need to be celebrated, such as when they overcome writing problems, experiment with a new genre or technique, or receive responses to their writing in the mail. These celebrations are also wonderful opportunities to expose the rest of the class to more writing options.

Recordkeeping and Assessment

If teachers are to assist children at whatever stage of writing development they are at, they need to have accurate and detailed records of their individual development–their stops and starts, their accomplishments, and what they have been taught. Recordkeeping and assessment are therefore crucial elements in managing a successful writers' workshop. The goal should be to be well-informed about each child's language and literacy development so that teachers can talk with confidence with the child, his/her parents or guardian, another teacher, or an administrator.

Peel-off address labels can be of particular assistance in keeping records. They can be used to keep brief, ongoing records of interactions teachers have with children, of actions they see and comments they hear, of questions they have and of children's answers. At the end of the day, these brief records can be easily transferred to a three-ring binder or to individual folders where each child's records are kept (See **Figure 4**).Stored with these individual anecdotal records are writing samples and other documents such as writing interviews or surveys. Teachers can read through these records periodically, assessing the development of each writer and determining the best way to help him/her develop further.

Figure 4

	Alberto
9/14	Dialogue journal writing. I noticed A. saying each word very slowly as he wrote, as if trying to sound out or listen to the sounds in each word.
9/17	I think he is a risk taker. He has risked speaking English before the whole group several times, saying "Good morning" during roll call, standing up and saying what he's wearing, "My shirt is blue," etc.
9/19	Purposely incorporated "si" in his story. Reading and writing it. Now he's copying my question.
9/30	Reading w/big kids–engaged
10/7	Brought me a paper and asked me to read it. I read "Lo LO.: He looked disappointed so I asked him what it said. He said, "Jo< JO." I had written it on the board this morning.

Records can also be kept of students' daily plans as discussed in the check-in time (see **Figure 5**). In this way, teachers are better able to see if there are patterns in a child's writing and gather information that may help them in assisting the writer. For example, if a teacher notices that a child has been writing about her bird for the past two weeks, it may be advisable to talk with the student to find out whether she is stuck on a topic. It may turn out that she is actually very engaged with her topic and is writing a manual on how to take care of her bird for a neighbor who is going to be looking after it during the spring vacation.

Children also need to take responsibility for keeping records of their writing development, processes, and activities. For example, they can keep records of who they confer with and the outcome of each confer-ence (see **Figure 6**).

Students can also keep a record of what they did during writers' workshop (see **Figure 7**). In this way they can see how they have been spending their time and make observations about how they have pro-gressed as writers.

Figure 5
Sample Writers' Workshop Check-in

	5/5	5/8	5/9	5/12	5/15
Andrés	Conf. Magiver/ revise	Revise Magiver/ class share	Edit Magiver/ illus. (Publish)	Finish binding Magiver	(absent)
Alexis	D2 poem - baseball win	D2 contd. poem - baseball win	Read poetry re. sports/ conf. poem	(absent)	Combine 2 poems re baseball win
Alroy	Topic search/ needs help. Conf.?	Letter to grandma - sick	Type letter to grandma/ picture	D1 story re. grandma & fishing	Conf. re grandma/ fishing
Aviva	Play (funny) re. rock concert	D1 contd. play - rock concert w. Jenny	Conf. re. play (w. Jenny)	Stage direc-tions for play	Research stage directions
Chau	D2 contd. science project research (mysteries of the sea)	D2. contd. science proj./ research	D2 contd. science proj./ conf.?	Conf. re science project	D3/Final? science proj.?

Note: D1 = first draft; D2 = second draft; D3 = third draft; conf. = conference

Figure 6
Student's Record Of Writing Conferences

NAME: Andrés				
DATE	STORY	CONFERENCED WITH	WHAT HAPPENED	WHAT I WILL DO NEXT
May 5	Magiver	Juan Peter Jeannie, Mrs. Anderson	They ask me lot of question	Revise the story.
May 8	Magiver	Class	They liked it and laughed	Edit it. I want to publish it.
May 15	Magiver	Class	I read the book. Peter help with with illustrations.	It goes to library. Think of new story.

Figure 7
Sample Writing Record for Children

Writing Record			Name: Aviva
Date	*Time spent writing*	*What I worked on*	*Comments*
5/5	35 mins.	Funny play abuot rock concert	Jenny wants to write it to
5/8	30 mins.	Looked at other plays in library and wrote D1 play	Now I now how to write plays - I think
5/9	30 mins.	Conf. with Liliana and David	People were confuse we need to work on the stage derecshons
5/12	25 mins.	Did stage derecshuns with Jenny	This is hard!

Summary

Although there is no one single way to implement a writers' workshop, there are some key elements that are integral to the implementation and maintenance of this very important classroom event. As teachers, we must believe that children are capable of being writers, even at young ages or when they are acquiring English. We must provide opportunities for children to demonstrate their growing facility as writers. We must give them time to write, read, and confer. We must teach them strategies for becoming better writers. We must demonstrate the importance of writing by sharing our own writing and writing processes with our students. We must provide a simply and clearly organized learning environment that is print-oriented, respectful of learners, and challenging.

Resources

The following books, journals, and videos should be of help to teachers interested in implementing a writers' workshop. It is not an exhaustive list, but it includes materials that many teachers have found most useful and stimulating. Although many of the materials refer to native speakers of English, we have found the strategies and procedures discussed to be equally appropriate for use with children acquiring English as a non-native language.

Books and Journals

Atwell, N. (Ed.). (1990). *Coming to know: Writing to learn in the intermediate grades.* Portsmouth, NH: Heinemann.

Writing is often taught separately from other aspects of the curriculum. The contributors to this book, teachers of Grades 3–6, write about what happened when they invited their students to integrate their content areas and writing, to write as historians, scientists, and mathematicians.

Atwell, N. (1987). *In the middle: Writing, reading, and learning with adolescents.* Portsmouth, NH: Boynton/Cook. (Available from Heinemann.)
This book is written by a former eighth-grade English teacher who replaced her traditional teaching approaches with extremely successful writing and reading workshops. It is a theoretically sound book offering practical suggestions for teachers at all grade levels, not just the middle school. Atwell writes well and her love of books and writing, as well as her respect for learners, resounds.

Atwell, N. (Ed.). (1990) *Workshop 2: Beyond the basal.* Portsmouth, NH: Heinemann.
Articles in this book are written by teachers in Grades K–8 who have been implementing process approaches in the teaching of reading and writing.

Baskwill, J., & Whitman, P. (1988). *Evaluation: Whole language, whole child.* New York: Scholastic.
This book addresses alternative assessment strategies, many of which are appropriate for writers' workshops (e.g., anecdotal records, interviews, surveys).

Bird, L.B. (1989). *Becoming a whole language school: The Fair Oaks story.* Katonah, NY: Richard C. Owen Publishers.
Fair Oaks School is located in Northern California and serves a predominately language minority community. This book, written primarily by Fair Oaks teachers, describes their odyssey as they moved away from skills-based to meaning-based learning and teaching. Several chapters deal with teachers' experiences with writers' workshop.

Bissex, G. (1980). *GNYS AT WRK: A child learns to read and write.* Cambridge, MA: Harvard University Press.
Bissex has recorded the independent growth of her son as a reader and writer from the preschool years through the intermediate grades. The book is particularly insightful in its discussions of invented spelling and purposes for writing.

Calkins, L.M. (1986). *The art of teaching writing.* Portsmouth, NH: Heinemann.
This is a highly readable book that combines research and practice. Chapters deal with children changing as writers, writing conferences, the role of the teacher, writing across the curriculum, and the connection between reading and writing.

Calkins, L.M. (1983). *Lessons from a child: On the teaching and learning of writing.* Portsmouth, NH: Heinemann.

The growth of children's writing in one elementary school is wonderfully portrayed. Calkins also describes the classroom contexts in which these children grew as writers.

Calkins, L.M., & Harwayne, S. (1991). *Living between the lines.* Portsmouth, NH: Heinemann.

This book builds upon Calkins' earlier book, *The art of teaching writing.* The authors discuss writers' notebooks, the reading/writing connection, conferring, mini-lessons, and recordkeeping, among other topics.

Dyson, A.H. (1989). *Multiple worlds of child writers: Friends learning to write.* New York: Teachers College, Columbia University.

Dyson is a gifted observer of children and writers. In this book she describes how young children in a multiethnic first-grade become writers. It is a richly written book that explores the importance of symbols in the development of literacy.

Edelsky, C. (1986). *Writing in a bilingual program: Habia una vez.* Norwood, NJ: Ablex.

Edelsky argues for authentic writing opportunities. She bases her discussion and recommendations on a longitudinal study she conducted into the writing development of children in a bilingual elementary school.

Gordon, N. (Ed.). (1984). *Classroom experience: The writing process in action.* Portsmouth, NH: Heinemann.

Chapters are written by public school teachers in Grades K–8. The authors describe the changes they went through moving from a skills-based to a process approach to teaching writing.

Graves, D.H. (1990). *Discover your own literacy.* Portsmouth, NH: Heinemann.

How many teachers are responsible for reading and writing development? Of these teachers, how many read and write and share their literacy with students? Graves paints a very compelling picture of the need for more teachers to do this and the benefits of doing so.

Graves, D.H. (1989). *Experiment with fiction.* Portsmouth, NH: Heinemann.

When youngsters write, their fiction, their stories often lack plausibility and cohesion. In this book, Graves gives concrete suggestions for helping children and teachers become better fiction writers. He often refers to his own writing processes and strategies.

SECTION 5

Graves, D.H. (1989). *Investigate nonfiction*. Portsmouth, NH: Heinemann.
Graves shows how we can help youngsters write nonfiction (e.g., letters and reports) that builds upon their knowledge of the world around them.

Graves, D.H. (1983). *Writing: teachers and children at work*. Portsmouth, NH: Heinemann.
This book is intended for teachers who want to establish writers' workshops. It is very practical and highly readable. Topics that are discussed include how to establish a writers' workshop, conferences, when and how to teach skills, how children develop as writers, and how to record children's growth.

Hall, N. (Ed.). (1989). *Writing with reason*. Portsmouth, NH: Heinemann.
The focus of this book is on how children between the ages of three and seven function as authors. Most of the chapters are written by classroom teachers, many of them in England.

Hansen, J. (1987). *When writers read*. Portsmouth, NH: Heinemann.
A maxim in discussions on literacy development is that reading enhances writing. In this book, Hansen documents the influences of reading on children's writing and the equally powerful effects of writing on their reading.

Hansen, J, Newkirk, T., & Graves, D.H, (Eds.). (1985). *Breaking ground: Teachers relate reading and writing in the elementary school*. Portsmouth, NH: Heinemann.
This collection of articles written by teachers and researchers shows how a process approach to reading and writing can be successful. The book includes discussions on how reading and writing can be used in content classes and how skills taught in writing help in reading.

Heard, G. (1989). *For the good of the earth and sun: Teaching poetry*. Portsmouth, NH: Heinemann.
Heard is a poet who has worked extensively with children. This book is a compelling invitation to teachers to immerse children in poetry as readers and writers.

Hudelson, S. (1989). *Write on: Children writing in ESL*. Englewood Cliffs, NJ: Center for Applied Linguistics/Prentice Hall Regents.
This is a comprehensive review of the literature on the writing development and processes of children acquiring English as a non-native language.

Inner London Education Authority (ILEA), Centre for Primary Education. (1988). *The primary language record: Handbook for teachers* (distributed by Heinemann).
This book has some excellent suggestions for informally recording children's language and literacy development.

Language Arts. Published by the National Council of Teachers of English (NCTE), 1111 Kenyon Road, Urbana IL 61801.
This is a monthly journal for teachers in Grades K-8. Articles deal with all facets of language arts teaching and learning; many focus on writing.

Newkirk, T., & Atwell, N. (Eds.). (1986). *Understanding writing: Ways of observing, learning and teaching K-8*. Portsmouth, NH: Heinemann.
The essays in this book have been written by teachers. The book consists of thoughtful discussions of the writing behaviors of the authors' students. Topics include: writing in the early grades; conferring; the interrelatedness of writing, drawing, and reading; and assessment of writing.

Perl, S. & Wilson, N. (1986). *Through teacher's eyes: Portraits of writing teachers at work*. Portsmouth, NH: Heinemann.
The case studies of six writing teachers in Grades 1-12 implementing a process approach to writing comprise the core of this book. Teachers share their doubts, successes, and struggles. The authors remark that the book "is about vision–how teachers see their students, how they act toward them, how they help them become writers."

Peyton, J.K., & Reed, L. (1990). *Dialogue journal writing with nonnative English speakers: A handbook for teachers*. Alexandria, VA: Teachers of English to Speakers of Other Languages (TESOL).
The authors offer a comprehensive overview of what a dialogue journal is, the role of dialogue journals in the classroom, and how to introduce and maintain dialogue journals.

Rigg, P., & Enright, D.S. (Eds.). (1986). *Children and ESL: Integrating perspectives*. Washington, DC: Teachers of English to Speakers of Other Languages (TESOL).
The seven chapters in this book discuss ways in which all facets of language are interconnected. The authors share the belief that language is best learned and taught in an integrated, authentic way. Some of the chapters focus on writing.

Turbill, J. (Ed.). (1982). *No better way to teach writing!* Rozelle, N.S.W., Australia: Primary English Teaching Association (distributed by Heinemann).

This book relates how Australian teachers and children in the elementary grades established a process approach to writing. Although the major focus is on children in the first three grades, teachers of older children also contribute their insights and perspectives. A sequel, *Now, we want to write!*, is also available.

The Quarterly. Published by the National Writing Project and the Center for the Study of Writing, Bay Area Writing Project, School of Education, University of California, Berkeley, CA 94720.

This journal, published four times a year, features articles dealing with many facets of the writing process, including classroom instruction.

Videos

Calkins, L.M. (1987). *The writing workshop: A world of difference.* Portsmouth, NH: Heinemann.

This videotape leads viewers into several classrooms in New York City where children are members of writers' workshops. Viewers observe children and teachers working together, writing, conferring, and talking about their writing.

Graves, D. (1986). *One classroom: A child's view.* Portsmouth, NH: Heinemann.

In this very engaging videotape, a young girl serves as a guide to her classroom during writer's workshop. She introduces viewers to children at work, explains what they are doing, and questions them. She also describes work areas and routines.

References

Calkins, L.M. (1986). *The art of teaching writing.* Portsmouth, NH: Heinemann.

Calkins, L.M. (1982). *A study of children's rewriting.* (NCTE Final Report.) Urbana, IL: National Council of Teachers of English. (ERIC Document Reproduction Service No. ED 229 750).

Edelsky, C. (1982). *Development of writing in a bilingual program.* (NIE Final Report.) Tempe: Arizona State University. (ERIC Document Reproduction Service No. 221 057).

Edelsky, C. (1986). *Writing in a bilingual program: Habia una vez.* Norwood, NJ: Ablex.

Flower, L.S., & Hayes, J.R. (1977). Problem-solving strategies and the writing process. *College English*, 39(4), 449-461.

Graves, D.H. (1982). *A case study observing the development of primary children's composing, spelling and motor behaviors during the writing process.* (Final Report). Washington, DC: National Institute of Education. (ERIC Document Reproduction Service No. 218 653)

Graves, D.H. (1983a). Break the welfare cycle: Let writers choose their topics. In Patricia L. Stock (Ed.), *Fforum [sic]: Essays on theory and practice in the teaching of writing.* Upper Montclair, NJ: Boynton/Cook Publishers.

Graves, D.H. (1983b). *Writing: teachers and children at work.* Portsmouth, NH: Heinemann.

Hudelson, S. (1989). A tale of two children. In D.M. Johnson & D.H. Roen (Eds.), *Richness in writing.* New York: Longman.

Hudelson, S., & Serna, I. (1991, August). *Mira, teacher–Escribí mi nombre en inglés: Beginning to become literate in English in a whole language bilingual program.* Paper presented at the Second Annual International Whole Language Umbrella Conference, Phoenix, AZ.

Murray, D.M. (1982). *Learning by teaching.* Montclair, NJ: Boynton/Cook Publishers.

Perl, S. (1979). Unskilled writers as composers. *New York Education Quarterly*, 10(3), 17-22

Peyton, J.K., & Reed, L. (1990). *Dialogue journal writing with nonnative English speakers: A handbook for teachers.* Alexandria, VA: Teachers of English to Speakers of Other Languages (TESOL).

Samway, K.D. (1987a). Formal evaluation of children's writing: An incomplete story. *Language Arts*, 64(3), 289-298.

Samway, K.D. (1987b). *The writing processes of non-native English speaking children in the elementary grades.* Unpublished doctoral dissertation, University of Rochester.

Smith, F. (1982). *Writing and the writer.* New York: Holt, Rhinehart & Winston.

Taylor, D. (1990). Writing and reading literature in a second language. In N. Atwell (Ed.), *Workshop 2: Beyond the basal.* Portsmouth, NH: Heinemann.

Urzúa, C. (1987). 'You stopped too soon': Second language children composing and revising. *TESOL Quarterly*, 21(2), 279-304.

About the Author

Katherine Davies Samway is an Associate Professor in the College of Education at San Jose State University in California. She has conducted research on the development of literacy in children acquiring English as a second language since 1985. Over the years she has worked with and learned alongside many teachers who have been implementing writers' workshops. Her most recent publication is "Reading the Skeleton, the Heart and the Brain of a Book: An Alternative Reading Program" in *The Reading Teacher*, Vol. 45, No.3.

Enhancing English Language Learning in Elementary Classrooms

Study Guide

Section 6
Math

Math

Goal

To learn to assist ELLs in developing language skills through mathematics instruction.

Performance Objectives

• Identify principles and guidelines which assist ELLs in developing language skills while learning mathematics content.

• Identify effective strategies to develop language learning during mathematics instruction.

• Apply language development strategies to mathematics instruction.

ELL Adapted Math Lesson

Grade 1
Hole Punch Activity

MATERIALS

index cards for each student
one-hole punch for each student
a pencil for each student
overhead projector

OBJECTIVE

Students will demonstrate an understanding of basic addition facts.

PROCEDURE (5 minutes)

1. Teacher provides each student with a hand-held hole punch and an index card.

2. Teacher models using her own hole punch and index card.

3. Using TPR, teacher introduces and reinforces basic vocabulary. Teacher says:
   "Look at my hole punch." (She holds up the hole punch.)
   "Show me your hole punch. Hold up your hole punch." (Students hold up hole punches.)
   "Look at my index card." (She holds up her index card.)
   "Show me your index card. Hold up your index card." (Students hold up index cards.)
   "Show me your hole punch." (She waits, then models by holding up her hole punch.)
   "Show me your index card." (She waits, then models by holding up her index card.)

4. Still using TPR, the teacher continues:
   "Watch me punch three holes in my card." (While the teacher punches, she counts.)
   "One, two, three."

5. Teacher places her punched card on the overhead. The light will shine through the punched holes. She points to the holes and counts, "One, two, three holes."

6. Teacher says:
   "Punch three holes in your card." (Using another card, teacher models while students punch their cards.)

7. Teacher says:
   "Count the holes with me. Count the holes in your card." (She points to the overhead holes.) "One, two, three holes."

8. Teacher moves the punched card on the overhead to the left half of the screen. On the right half of the screen where the light is not covered, she writes the number "3" next to the three holes as she again counts to three.

9. "Look at the three holes in my card. Look at the three holes in your card." (Points and models.)

10. "Watch me punch two holes in my card. Watch me punch two holes under the three holes." (Teacher removes card from overhead and punches two holes in her card under the three holes she previously punched. She replaces the card on the overhead and covers the three holes previously punched with another card so only the two just-punched holes show through.)

11. "Look at the two holes in my card; one, two holes." (Points and counts.)
    "Punch two holes in your card." (Models and counts.)

12. Teacher moves the card to the left of the overhead screen and counts the two holes showing through on the overhead. Teacher writes the numeral "2" to the right of the two holes under the three holes.

13. Teacher removes the index card covering the three holes. She counts:

    "One, two, three holes..." (She points to the numeral "3.")

    "...plus..." (She adds an addition sign to the left of the numeral "2.")

    "...one, two holes." (She points to the numeral "2.")

    "Three plus two..." (She points to each as she says it.)

    "Count all the holes with me. One, two, three, four, five." (Points and counts, repeats.)

14. "Three plus two equals (points to each as she says it, then writes the equals line under the "2" to form the equation) FIVE!" (She writes the numeral "5" under the equation on the right side of the screen.)

15. "Pick up your pencil. Count with me." (Students pick up pencils.)

16. Teacher covers equation on the right of screen. Teacher covers two bottom holes, leaving only the three holes showing through.

    "One, two, three. Write the number 3 on your card." (Teacher uncovers the numeral "3" on the right of the overhead. Then the teacher repeats the last command and models by writing the numeral "3" on her card. She shows what she has written on the card to the class. Students write on their cards.)

"Three plus…" (She uncovers the addition sign and writes one on her card. Students write on their cards.)

(Teacher uncovers the two holes.)

"One, two…" (She writes "2" in her equation and uncovers the "2" on the screen. Students write on their cards.)

"…equals…" (she uncovers the equals sign and writes one on her card. Students write on their cards.)

"…five." (Uncovers, writes and models. Students write.)

17. Students now have a card with three holes punched in a line with two holes punched under them and the simple addition fact 3+2=5 written on it. Follow the procedures to explore two other simple addition facts: 6+3=9 and 4+3=7.

(Total lesson time: 20 minutes.)

FOLLOW-UP LESSON

Teacher reviews, following the above procedures for one equation, then repeats, reducing modeling following the model outlined below:

1. Teacher says: "Six…plus…three."

2. Students punch one line of six holes followed by one line of three holes.

3. Teacher puts punched card on the overhead and says:

   "Six…" (points to and counts six holes)

   "…plus three…" (points to and counts three holes)

   "…equals…one, two, three, four, five, six, seven, eight, NINE!" (points and counts)

   Students will join in counting aloud at their own pace depending on their levels of language proficiency. They should be encouraged to join in when they are ready, but not forced.

4. Teacher and students write equation.

Estimating Handfuls Game

This game practices estimating skills and counting. Gallon-sized plastic zipper storage bags are needed. Each bag should be filled with a variety of small, smooth items such as buttons or marbles. Dried beans or legumes work well since there are such a variety of kinds; navy, lima, lentils, garbanzo, pole, black-eyed, for example.

Following a discussion of the contents of the bags, each student puts his or her hand in a bag and grabs a handful of whatever is in the bag. The students should take care before removing hands from the bags that they can carry intact (without dropping) what is in their hands.

All students return to their seats where they count the objects they have taken. Suggest to students that they divide their objects into groups of 10s for easier calculation. The student writes the total number of objects on a piece of paper.

Next, have all students return all their beans to their hands and tell them to close their hands around the beans. Tell them to notice how the beans feel in their hand. Tell them to squeeze tighter (but not so tight as to damage the contents) and then relax their hand while still holding secure the contents. Tell the students to shake their hands slightly and again notice how the beans feel in their hands.

The students now place their beans in a pile on their desks. Tell them to note the number they wrote down on the paper. Now tell the students they each will put a hand back into the bag to take another handful of beans, and this time they need to try to take MORE beans than the first time.

Students take their handfuls, count out how many they have and write down this number. Have students share their successes. Next, repeat the process having the students attempt to take FEWER beans than the first time.

Finally, give the students a real challenge. Ask the students to put 10 beans in their hands. Notice how 10 beans feel. Now have the students try to take a handful of beans that has 10 MORE beans than their original handful. Then try again to see if students can take 10 FEWER beans than the first time. See which students come closest.

ELL Adapted Math Lesson
Grade 2
Basic Bar Graph Activity

MATERIALS

an apple, an orange, and a banana (other fruit pieces may be added or substituted)
survey sheet (sample follows) for each student and an overhead copy for the teacher
work sheet (sample follows) for each student and an overhead copy for the teacher
a pencil for each child
colored markers or crayons for each child
an overhead and markers

OBJECTIVES

Students will survey the class orally to gather information.
Students will compile information gathered into a bar graph.
Students will explain (in writing or orally) the meaning of the data displayed on their bar graphs.

PROCEDURE

This lesson is a practice, which follows an introductory lesson about bar graphs. The students have looked at bar graphs in a previous lesson and discussed the meaning of the information displayed in those graphs. In this lesson, the students will gather information and create their own bar graphs for display and interpretation.

1. Teacher shows the class the apple, orange and banana. Teacher names each fruit as she picks it up and shows it to the class.

2. Teacher asks individual students if they like the fruit to elicit oral answers:

   Teacher: "Adela, look at this apple. Do you like apples?"
   Adela: "Yes, I like apples." (Teacher accepts any comprehensible answer such as "Yes." or "Yes, I like." and continues by modeling.)

   (Teacher repeats with another student and continues with the remaining two fruits.)

3. Teacher makes a statement:

   Teacher: "I like apples best. Francisco, which fruit do you like best?"
   Francisco: (for example) "I like bananas best." (Teacher accepts comprehensible answer.)
   Teacher: "Francisco likes bananas best. I like apples best."

   Teacher repeats asking a few more students their preference of the three fruits and models acceptable answers.

4. Teacher tells the class that today they will be gathering information and making a bar graph to display what they find out. Teacher asks the class to listen to a question, but to think of their answer only. They will have a chance to say their answer soon. Here is the question:

"Which is your favorite fruit?"

5. Teacher provides each student with a copy of a survey sheet. (See sample provided.) The survey sheet has the name of each child in the class listed with the teacher's name at the top. (Providing sheets with the names in different orders will assist greatly in this activity.)

6. Teacher displays a copy of the survey sheet on the overhead. Teacher asks herself:

"Which is your favorite fruit?"
She provides the answer, "My favorite fruit is an apple."
Teacher checks the "apple" column next to her name.

7. Teacher directs the students to get up and move around the room asking every student in the class, "Which is your favorite fruit." Teacher reminds each student to give the same answer every time she is asked the question. Teacher monitors group activity, directs students to check the correct box and include all students and completes the activity herself checking on her overhead copy.

8. When everyone has been asked, the students return to their seats. Teacher displays her overhead copy, covering it so only the information in one column at a time shows.

9. Teacher directs, "Count how many people say the apple is their favorite fruit." Teacher counts down the column and writes the number at the bottom in the "total" box. Teacher directs students to do the same on their papers.

10. Teacher uncovers the next column and writes the number at the bottom.

11. Teacher uncovers the last column and follows procedures above to have students total the column.

12. Teacher asks questions using "pair share" strategy. (Put students in pairs and have them discuss the answer to the questions before she calls on a student to answer.)

> *Teacher, "Which fruit do students like best?"*
> *"Which fruit do students like least?"*
> *"How many students like apples best?"*
> *"How many students like oranges best?"*

13. Teacher provides graphing sheet and markers or crayons. (See sample provided.) Teacher displays her graphing sheet on the overhead.

14. Teacher asks:

> *"How many students like apples best?"* (Students answer.)

15. Teacher counts UP from the bottom of the "apple" column on the worksheet to the number the class found. She draws a line at the top of that number box. Then she colors in the column (using any choice of color) up to that number to form a bar. Teacher directs students to do the same.

16. Teacher asks:

> *"How many students like bananas best?"* (Students answer.)

17. Teacher directs students to make the bar for the banana column. Then she does the same on her overhead copy.

18. Teacher repeats procedure for the remaining orange column.

Each student now has a completed bar graph of the information gathered in the activity. Teacher asks a student to review the steps followed to complete this activity. (This may be followed up by a written explanation at the teacher's discretion.)

19. Teacher asks,

> *"What do our graphs show us?"* (Students respond in pairs writing their ideas

on a   separate piece of paper.)

The teacher then asks pairs to answer the question. Teacher writes ideas on the board. For example:

> *More students like apples than bananas.*
> *Students like apples best.*

FOLLOW-UP ACTIVITY

The activity following this lesson should repeat the same procedures with five different fruits (for example, a mango, a kiwi, a peach, a cherry, and a grapefruit). This time the students will need less modeling and can get to the information gathering sooner. Display the graphs created along with the explanations of the meanings of the data.

Students should be asked to create their own title for their graphs. They can also be asked to create their own graph sheet by providing them with rulers.

Sample Survey Sheet

Which is Your Favorite?

	APPLE	BANANA	ORANGE
Teacher's Name			
Ana			
Josefa			
Chabeli			
Carlos			
Luis			
Marisol			
Kim			
Quan			
Antonino			
Alexa			
Barney			
TOTAL			

SECTION 6

Sample Graphing Sheet

Our Favorite Fruits

	APPLE	BANANA	ORANGE
18.			
17.			
16.			
15.			
14.			
13.			
12.			
11.			
10.			
9.			
8.			
7.			
6.			
5.			
4.			
3.			
2.			
1.			

Hiding Game

The purpose of this game is to simply provide counting practice in an entertaining, purposeful manner.

The teacher designates an item to be hidden somewhere in the classroom. This object should be large enough for all students to easily see from anywhere in the room. Objects such as a clothespin, a special holiday ornament, or a colored index card will work nicely. The teacher should make certain all students know what the object is. Next, a student is chosen to step out of the room for a minute. Choosing the person can be done in many ways: the teacher can simply choose someone from the group, or it can be done more creatively. Being chosen can be used as a reward for a previous activity or can be "earned" by certain criteria the teacher can invent.

When the person chosen has left the room, the class collaborates to hide the object somewhere in the room. All students in the room should know where the object is hidden. The student waiting outside the room is called back into the room. As soon as the person enters, the class starts counting at a medium volume. As the person moves closer to the location where the object is hidden, the class counts more LOUDLY. As the person moves farther away from the location where the object is hidden, the class counts more *softly*. LOUDLY and *softly* increases or decreases as the person moves around the room as an audible clue to the location of the object until the person finds the designated object.

Mix and Match

This game can be used for addition, subtraction, multiplication or division. The game practices computation skills, oral production, social skills and appropriate interpersonal interaction.

This example is for the practice of addition. The teacher prepares cards for the activity ahead of time. One card has an addition problem (such as 5 + 8) and another card has the sum (in this case 13) written on it. There need to be enough cards for each student to receive one. For a class of 24, for example, there will be 12 problems written on 12 cards and 12 sums written on 12 more cards for a total of 24 cards.

The students should be standing in an open area where they can move around. The teacher randomly hands out all cards. (If there is an odd number of students in the class, the teacher should play too.) Then the students start walking around. Every time they pass a classmate, they exchange cards. Students continue mixing (walking around) and exchanging cards until the teacher asks them to stop (15 to 30 seconds works well) and look at the card they have ended up with.

Next, the students must find their match. Students should be encouraged to talk and call out their numbers. Matches stand together and the teacher checks the matches until all matches are found.

The game continues by mixing and exchanging again until the teacher tells the class to stop and find their new matches. It can be replayed several times, and each round will be new.

Inside/Outside Circle
Addition Facts Practice

PREPARATION

Prepare one set of blue cards and one set of red cards. On each card write a number from one to ten.

THE ACTIVITY

1. Divide the class in half.

2. Provide each student with one blue card and one red card.

3. Direct one half of the class to make a circle facing out. Tell the members of that circle that they are blue.

4. Direct the other half of the class to make a circle around the first facing in. Tell the members of that circle that they are red.

5. Tell the members of the inside and outside circles to match up in pairs facing each other.

6. Tell everyone to show their partner their blue card. The blue circle (the inside one) members must add together the two blue cards and provide the sum. The red partner confirms that the answer is correct.

7. Tell everyone to show their partner their red card. The red circle (the outside one) members must add together the two red cards and provide the sum. The blue partner confirms that the answer is correct.

8. Tell the inside circle to move to the right one person. Everyone now has a new partner, and since everyone has a different number, they also have a new equation to solve.

9. Repeat steps 6, 7, & 8 until the circle has rotated to its starting point. (Alternate who moves, the inside and the outside circles, just to make it more interesting. If the circles always move right or always move left students will get a different partner to work with until the circle is completed.)

Paraphrase Passport Activity

Explain to the class that good listening skills are essential in understanding real-life problems. Explain also that math students need to be able to restate problems, directions, or solutions in order to assist them in solving problems. Tell the class that they will be developing good listening and rephrasing skills through a cooperative activity. Provide the class members with confirmatory statement beginnings to use the first few times this activity is practiced. (The sample topic used here, *what I am good at in math and what I need to improve*, can be changed to restating the directions, suggesting solutions to a problem, and so on.)

Sample confirmatory statement beginnings:

"What I heard you say was…"
"What I understood you to say was…"
"This is what I heard you say…"
"You said…"

Also provide students with suggestions for providing approval statements:

"That's right."
"I agree. You understood me well."
"You are a good listener."
"That's what I meant."
"Yes, that's what I said."

Provide students with suggestions for appropriate redirecting statements when they don't agree with another student's paraphrasing:

"I meant something else. I meant…"
"I see that you misunderstood… What I meant was…"

PROCEDURES

1. Have the members of the class form pairs.

2. Make one member of the pair person "A" and the other member of the pair person "B."

3. Tell everyone in the class to think about what they are good at in math and what they need to improve on in math. Provide the class with a few moments of reflection time.

4. Tell the "A" members of the pairs that they will have 60 seconds to tell their partner about what they are good at in math. Tell the "B" members of the pairs that they are to use good listening skills while "A" is talking. Advise the "B" partners that they will be restating, or paraphrasing , what their partners have told them. Tell the "A" members to

begin speaking.

5. After 60 seconds, tell the group to stop talking. Tell the "B" partners to use their rephrasing skills to confirm what they understood "A" to say. Tell the "A" partners to use appropriate listening skills and provide approval statements when they agree. Tell the "B" members to begin rephrasing.

6. When this cycle is complete, the roles switch. Tell the "B" members of the pairs to tell their partners what they are good at in math. Remind the "A" partners to use good listening skills because they will be paraphrasing what their partners have told them.

7. Have the "A" partners paraphrase what they understood and the "B" partners provide statements of approval when they agree.

8. Repeat the process with a new partner.

SECTION 6

Cooperative Learning in Math

Cooperative Activity	Positive Interdependence	Individual Accountability	Math Class Applications	Other Class Applications
Think-Pair-Share				
Numbered Heads Together				
Mix & Match				
Inside/Outside Circle				
Paraphrase Passport				

SECTION 6

Higher and Lower

This game practices listening and speaking skills and reinforces thinking and reasoning skills.

The teacher secretly writes a number on piece of paper. The teacher can choose the range for the number based on the age and level of the class. The number can be chosen between 1 and 50; or between 1 and 100; or between 1 and 1,000,000.

The teacher begins by asking a student to choose a number between, for example, 1 and 100. The teacher writes the number the student chooses on the board. If the number the teacher has written is higher than the number the student chose, the teacher says, "higher," and writes an arrow pointing up next to the number the student chose. If the number the teacher has written is lower than the number the student chose, the teacher says, "lower," and writes an arrow pointing down next to the number the student chose. The teacher chooses another student to guess a number. The process continues until the number has been pinpointed.

For example, in a game between 1 and 100 when the number is 23, this might be the exchange:

Student:	50
Teacher:	lower (writes an arrow pointing down next to the number 50)
Student:	25
Teacher:	lower (writes an arrow pointing down next to the number 25)
Student:	10
Teacher:	higher (writes an arrow pointing up next to the number 10)
Student:	20
Teacher:	higher (writes an arrow pointing up next to the number 20)
Student:	24
Teacher:	lower (writes arrow down)
Student:	22
Teacher:	higher (writes arrow up)
Student:	23!

Spinning Probability

Grade 5

MATERIALS

Make an overhead of the Prize Spinner on the next page and turn it into a spinner. (To make an overhead spinner, place a tack coming upwards through the center of the spinner circle. Put a paperclip over the tack to make a spinner. Spinner pieces can also be purchased at teacher supply stores.)

PROCEDURE

1. Display the spinner on the overhead.

2. Tell the group that this is a spinner that was used at a carnival to determine the prizes that players would win. Model or demonstrate essential vocabulary by doing it, showing it, or pointing to it (spinner, spin, pencil, book, ball, yo-yo).

3. Use the think-pair-share technique to ask the group the following questions:

   Which do you have more chances of winning, a pencil or yo-yo? [a pencil] How can you tell? [The pencil section of the spinner is bigger than the yo-yo; the pencil section occupies 3/8 of the spinner while the yo-yo section occupies only 1/8; a person has 3 out of 8 chances to win a pencil land 1 out of 8 chances to win a yo-yo.]

   What are your chances of winning a pencil? [3 out of 8 or 37.5%]

   What are your chances of winning a yo-yo? [1 out of 8 or 12.5%]

   Which do you have more chances of winning, a book or a ball? [The chances are the same.]

   What are your chances of winning a book? [2 in 8 or 1 in 4 or 25%] A ball? [2 in 8 or 1 in 4 or 25%]

   Which do you have more chances of winning, a yo-yo or a book? [a book] How do you know? [The book section of the spinner is bigger than the yo-yo section; the book section of the spinner occupies 2/8 of the spinner while the yo-yo section occupies 1/8.]

4. Be sure to review with students the comparisons between eighths and quarters and the conversion to percents from fractions.

5. Try the spinner out with the class. Label the four corners of the room as book, ball, pencil, and yo-yo. Allow each student in the class a spin and have the student stand in the corner of the item they spin. When everyone has had a turn, compare the results with what was expected.

Enhancing English Language Learning in Elementary Classrooms
Study Guide Section 6: Math

6. If the results of your class were very different from what was expected based on probability, use the opportunity to discuss the nature of probabilities. Let the class spin again and see what happens a second time.

Carnival Prize Spinner

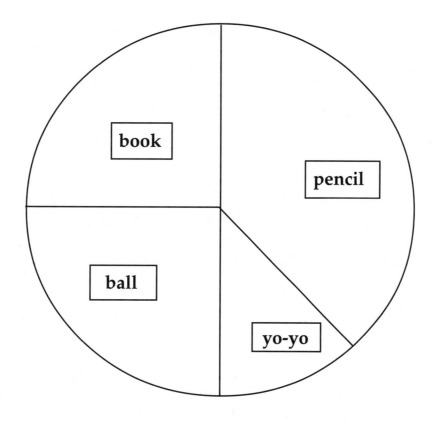

Spinning Probability: Group Activity

PREPARATION AND MATERIALS

Prepare sets of envelopes containing clue sets from the next page. Depending on the number of students in your class, you should make at least three envelopes of each set. Students will be trading envelopes with each other during the activity.

Make a copy of the student activity sheet for each student in the class.

PROCEDURES

1. Have the students pair. Give each pair an envelope containing one of the clue sets.

2. After reading and discussing the clues, each pair fills in the Student Activity Sheet by designing a spinner that reflects all the clues from that set. Remind the students to clearly label the parts of each spinner.

3. As pairs complete one set of clues, they trade it in for another set of clues until they have completed all five sets of clues.

4. When all groups have completed the spinners on the activity sheet, choose five pairs to draw spinners one through five (one spinner per pair) on the board or have them prepare an overhead of the spinner. Ask each pair in turn, one through five, to explain how they designed the spinner. All pairs check their spinners and any discrepancies are discussed at this time.

5. On the remaining blank spinner on the activity sheet, ask each student to design a spinner and a set of clues for homework.

6. Begin the next class by having students cut their clue sets from the bottom of the page and trade with class members. Have students compare and discuss the spinners they design from classmates' clues with the spinner they designed for homework. They should resolve any discrepancies during their discussions.

Spinning Probability: Student Activity Sheet

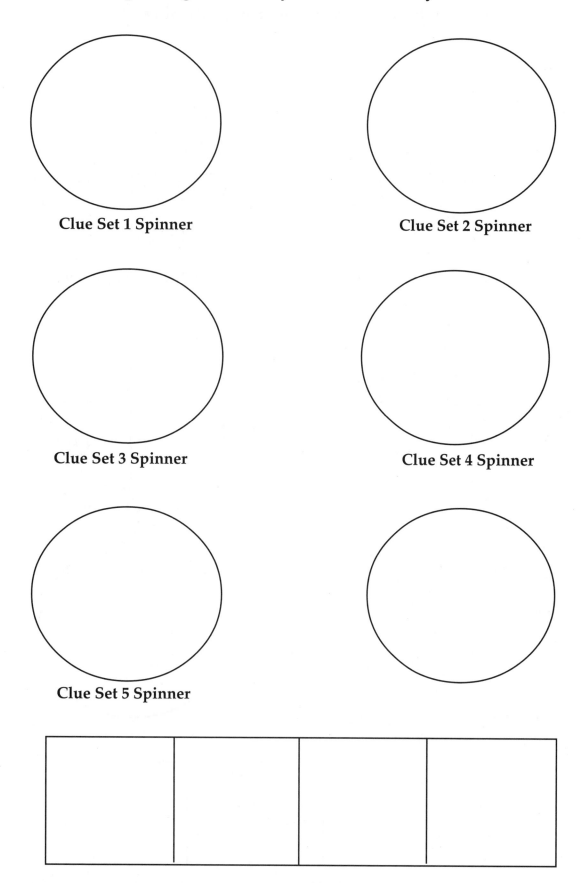

Clue Set 1 Spinner

Clue Set 2 Spinner

Clue Set 3 Spinner

Clue Set 4 Spinner

Clue Set 5 Spinner

Spinning Probability: Student Activity Sheet Key

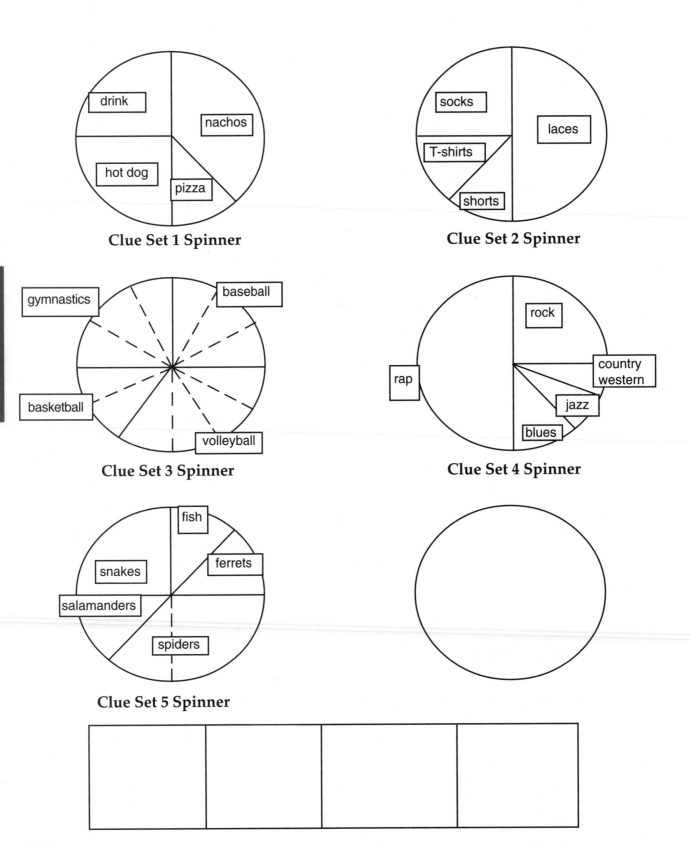

Clue Set 1 Spinner

drink
nachos
hot dog
pizza

Clue Set 2 Spinner

socks
laces
T-shirts
shorts

Clue Set 3 Spinner

gymnastics
baseball
basketball
volleyball

Clue Set 4 Spinner

rock
country western
rap
jazz
blues

Clue Set 5 Spinner

fish
ferrets
snakes
salamanders
spiders

SECTION 6

Spinning Probability: Clue Sets

Clue Set #1

> At the bowling alley, you can spin a spinner to win free food when you get a strike. You have the same chances to win a free drink as you do to win a hot dog.

> You will probably get cheese nachos 3/8 of the time.

> A free pizza comes up about 1/8 of the time.

> The chances of getting a hot dog are about 25%.

Clue Set #2

> The sports store has a prize spinner. You are likely to win a pair of socks about 1/4 of the time.

> You will probably win a pair of shoelaces about 50% of the time.

> The chances of winning running shorts are half the chances of winning a pair of socks.

> Your chances of winning a T-shirt are about 1/8.

Clue Set #3

A radio station is giving away tickets to Olympic events. You are likely to win tickets to see gymnastics in 1 out of every 4 spins.

In 100 spins, you are likely to win baseball tickets 25 times.

You will probably get basketball tickets about 1/6 of the time

You are twice as likely to win volleyball tickets as you are to win basketball tickets.

Clue Set #4

You can win a free CD at the local music store. The probability of winning a jazz CD is 1/16.

In 200 spins you are likely to get a rap CD 100 times and a rock CD 50 times.

You have the same chances of getting a country-western CD as you do to win a jazz CD.

You are twice as likely to win a rock CD as you are to win a blues CD.

Clue Set 5

At the pet store you can win a free pet by spinning. You are likely to get a snake about 100 times in 400 spins.

Snakes are twice as likely as salamanders to be spun.

Salamanders and fish have the same chances of being spun. You have the greatest chance of winning spiders.

You will probably spin things that begin with "f" about 1/4 of the time and things that begin with "s" about 3/4 of the time.

Ideas for Using Math Skills to Achieve Random Groups

The creation of random groups can provide the ELL student with yet another opportunity to purposefully interact with classmates. Try these ideas for creating random groups.

PUZZLES

Teachers can create small puzzles for students to put together to form groups. Use the front cover of old greeting cards (great around special holidays), computer drawings, holiday wall decorations, written directions for each group—whatever! You will need to make one puzzle for each group. (If you want 5 groups to be formed, you will need 5 DIFFERENT greeting card fronts, for example.) Cut up each picture into however many group members you want. If you have 25 students in the class, for example, you might cut up 5 cards into 5 pieces to achieve 5 groups of 5 people; or if you wanted groups of 3, you would cut up 8 cards into 3 pieces and a 9th card into 4 pieces to have 8 groups of 3 and 1 group of 4 (to pick up the odd number.)

When you determine how many puzzles you need and how many pieces each puzzle needs, shuffle all the puzzles together and put them in some kind of receptacle for the students to pick from. Let the students pick their puzzle pieces and work together to form their groups.

SORTING

For those of you who may be parents of young children and buried in small toys from fast-food meals, here is an opportunity to recycle those trinkets. For those of you who may not have this abundance of small objects to recycle, many fast-food restaurants will donate such items to your classroom upon your request.

Sort the items by categories which make sense to you and will be familiar to your students. Small cars, characters from specific movies, or dolls might be some of your categories. Decide how many groups you want. Decide how many members of each group you want. You will need a different category for each group (for example, toy cars) and the number of those objects to equal the number of members you want in that group.

Place all the objects into a receptacle for the students to choose from. Let the students pick their items and work together to identify the categories and form the groups.

CARDS

A regular deck of playing cards can give a wide variety of grouping challenges for your students to figure out together. Shuffle the cards and let students draw a card. Ask the students to work together to figure out what the grouping is without giving hints. Here are a variety of suggestions for how to make groups for a class of 25 students:

5 groups of 5 people:

(hearts)	Ace, 2, 3, 4, 5 and 9, 10, J, Q, K
(diamonds)	Ace, 2, 3, 4, 5
(spades)	Ace, 2, 3, 4, 5
(clubs)	Ace, 2, 3, 4, 5

5 groups of 4 people with one group of 5 people (6 groups):

Aces (all 4 suits)
2s   (all 4 suits)
3s   (all 4 suits)
4s   (all 4 suits)
(spades) 10, J, Q, K
(hearts) 9, 10, J, Q, K

7 groups of 3 people with one group of 4 people (8 groups):

(hearts)	3, 4, 5	AND	J,Q,K
(diamonds)	3, 4, 5	AND	J,Q,K
(spades)	3, 4, 5	AND	J,Q,K
(clubs)	3, 4, 5	AND	10, J,Q,K

SHAPES AND COLORS

Of course, you can have students draw from a bowl and choose a circle, or a square, or a triangle, or a rectangle to make groups…or you can add a higher level thinking twist:

On a random selection of circles, triangles, squares, and rectangles (NOT equaling the grouping you desire) use colors or draw symbols, which DO give the desired grouping (e.g., draw stripes, polka dots, happy faces, plaids, flowers). This time you will have to clue the class in just a bit. Tell them you are looking for 5 groups of 5 for example. When they only find 3 circles but 7 triangles in the bunch, they will have to keep investigating to achieve the groups you intended.

Problem Solving With the ELL in Mind

Problem solving is the ability to think, analyze situations, and apply appropriate skills to arrive at a solution. It is the ability to develop, execute, and evaluate a plan of action. Problems should relate TO THE REAL WORLD.

Problem solving skills CAN BE LEARNED. Concepts, strategies and processes can be taught. Problem-solving skills learned in the classroom can transfer to all areas of a student's life.

Problem-Solving Strategies:

— look for a pattern   — divide the tasks

— construct a table   — start with the known

— make an organized list   — look at familiar words or concepts

— guess and check   — use all resources

— draw a picture   — use reasonable estimation

— use objects or act it out   — "chunk" things that go together

— write an equation   — create a diagram

— simplify the problem

— change the point of view

— brainstorm

Problem Solving as a Process

The methods used to arrive at a solution and the thinking and analysis preceding the computation are more important than the solution itself.

FOUR STAGES OF SOLVING A PROBLEM:

1. Obtain a better understanding of the problem.

   -rephrase it
   -identify relevant information
   -determine if additional information is needed
   -estimate a reasonable answer
   -draw it
   -act it out

2. Devise an appropriate plan of attack.

   -look for similarities between this problem and others they have solved
   -draw a picture or diagram
   -break the problem into parts
   -simplify the problem
   -organize the information differently
   -look for a pattern
   -write a math sentence (a + b = ___)

3. Carry out the plan efficiently.

   -record all actions

4. Check the work.

   -double check calculations
   -make sure all answers are in proper form (feet instead of inches, for example)
   -determine if all the information given in the problem has been used
      (If not, why not?)
   -determine if this is the only possible answer to the problem
   -work the problem backwards

Teaching Problem Solving With the ELL in Mind

1. Model successful problem solving.

    -Discuss real-life problems that have arisen in your day. Explain how you solved the problems. Explain step by step. Discuss options you had. Ask students to suggest alternative solutions.

2. Suggest a variety of problem-solving strategies.

    -Create a list of strategies which have been used by your class. Add to the list as new strategies are learned or used. Refer to the list continually.

3. Provide many opportunities to solve different kinds of problems.

    -Create problems that require the use of concepts being learned in class. Allow students a variety of situations to solve the problems: sometimes individually, sometimes in groups, sometimes in pairs, etc.

4. Ask probing questions rather than correcting mistakes immediately.

    -Ask questions such as,
    "Why did you do it this way?"
    "Is this like another problem we have seen?"
    "What would happen if we tried another approach?"

Problem solving should start as early as pre-K.

Convince your students that problem solving is not a clear-cut procedure and that solutions are not found instantly.

Stress that process is more important than product.

Many problems have more than one solution or more than one way of being solved.

Practice, practice, practice!

Tips For Good Math Problems With the ELL in Mind

1. They are readily understandable to the students. (Use vocabulary and syntax familiar to the students.)

2. They do not involve new math concepts (ones the students have not been taught).

3. They are intrinsically motivating and intellectually stimulating.

4. They lend themselves to more than one method of solution.

5. They are somewhat open-ended so they can be generalized or extended to various situations.

6. They should motivate the student to experiment, search for additional information, use a variety of sources, discover patterns, and make judicious estimates.

7. **They require the student to THINK rather than perform only basic calculations.**

Enhancing English Language Learning in Elementary Classrooms

Study Guide

Section 7
Integrated Instruction

Integrated Instruction

Goal

To learn to integrate academic language development into content area lessons and to connect lessons to other learning and to students' lives and cultures.

Performance Objectives

- Evaluate a sample lesson for methods of integrating instruction.

- Enhance lessons by adding strategies that develop academic language.

- Develop a lesson/unit which integrates language and content.

- Reflect on one's own priorities for implementation to help ELLs achieve academic success.

ESL Standards for PreK-12 Students.

Full proficiency in English is critical for the long-term personal, social, and economic development of all students in the United States. In *ESL Standards for PreK-12 Students*, TESOL outlines a framework for considering and planning language education for ESOL students and for interpreting and making use of the ESL standards. The ESL standards describe the proficiencies in English that ESOL students need to acquire so they can attain the same high level standards in other content domains, including English language arts, as fully proficient English-speaking students. Thus, the ESL Standards for PreK-12 Students is the starting point for developing effective and equitable education for ESOL students.

Planning effective English language instruction for ESOL students cannot be done in isolation. It must be part of a comprehensive and challenging educational program that takes into account ESOL students' social, educational, and personal backgrounds as well as their existing skills and knowledge bases. It must understand and respond appropriately to the interrelationships between language, academic, and sociocultural development. The linguistic, cognitive, and sociocultural competencies that ESOL students bring to school are a solid base for building their future, in terms of educational and career success. Only if ESL instruction is part of a comprehensive, challenging, and enriching educational program, however, will the promising futures of ESOL learners be realized.

Goal 1: To use English to communicate in social settings

A primary goal of ESL instruction is to assist students in communicating effectively in English, both in an out of school. Such communication is vital if ESOL learners are to avoid the negative social and economic consequences of low proficiency in English and are to participate as informed participants in our democracy. ESOL learners also need to see that there are personal rewards to be gained from communicating effectively in English. This goal does not suggest, however, that students should lose their native language proficiency.

Standards for Goal 1

Students will:

1. use English to participate in social interaction

2. interact in, through, and with spoken and written English for personal expression and enjoyment

3. use learning strategies to extend their communicative competence

Goal 2: To use English to achieve academically in all content areas

In school settings, English competence is critical for success and expectations for

ESOL learners are high. They are expected to learn academic content through the English language and to compete academically with native-English-speaking peers. This process requires that learners use spoken and written English in their schoolwork.

Standards for Goal 2

Students will:

1. use English to interact in the classroom

2. use English to obtain, process, construct, and provide subject matter information in spoken and written form

3. use appropriate learning strategies to construct and apply academic knowledge

Goal 3: To use English in socially and culturally appropriate ways

ESOL students in U.S. schools come into contact with peers and adults who are different from them, linguistically and culturally. The diversity in U.S. schools mirrors the diversity in this country and around the world that young people will encounter as they move into the 21st century world of work. In order to work and live amid diversity, students need to be able to understand and appreciate people who are different and communicate effectively with them. Such communication includes the ability to interact in multiple social settings.

Standards for Goal 3

Students will:

1. use the appropriate language variety, register, and genre according to audience, purpose, and setting

2. use nonverbal communication appropriate to audience, purpose, and setting

3. use appropriate learning strategies to extend their sociolinguistic and sociocultural competence.

SECTION 7

Goals of This Section

Goals

To learn to integrate academic language development into content area lessons

To learn to connect lessons to other learning and to students' lives and cultures

Relationship of Section 7 to Sections 9 and 11

• Section 7–Integrated Instruction–Participants will develop an integrated unit (primarily science or social studies). In Outside Assignment #3, participants will prepare to share a portion of this unit in a poster session in Section 11.

• Section 9–Assessment–Participants will add a teacher-made assessment to the unit.

• Section 11–Putting It All Together–Participants will share part of their unit in a poster session activity. Selected participants will present to the group.

SECTION 7

Integrating Language and Content Instruction: Strategies and Techniques
by Deborah J. Short

Introduction

The number of limited English proficient (LEP) students in American schools for school year 1989-90 was estimated at approximately 1,927,828 which represented around 5.2 percent of all students in school (U.S. Department of Education, 1991). The previous school year (1988-89), the percentage of LEP students in U.S. schools was estimated at about 4.6 percent (U.S. Department of Education, 1991). The increase in LEP students has been dramatic in many areas of the country. This rapid growth implies that many teachers are finding an increasing number of students in their classrooms who have to master content matter in a language that is still in the process of being learned. Research indicates that the academic language utilized in content areas acts as a barrier to the success in school of many LEP students (Cummins, 1981). Postponing content instruction until these LEP students master English sufficiently to keep pace with their English-speaking peers often results in underachievement and eventual school leaving.

Current research in second language acquisition indicates that a critical element in effective English as a second language instruction is access to comprehensible input in English (Krashen & Biber, 1988). One way to provide comprehensible input directly to the LEP student is by teaching content in English using strategies and techniques that make the content comprehensible to the second language learner. Research confirms that students in classes where such strategies and techniques are employed acquire impressive amounts of English and learn content matter as well (Krashen & Biber, 1988). It has long been known that a second language can be effectively learned when it is the medium of instruction, not the object (Lambert & Tucker, 1972; Campbell, Gray, Rhodes & Snow, 1985).

The philosophical basis underlying language and content integration is that a child's whole education is a shared responsibility distributed among all teachers. The integration of language and content involves the incorporation of content material into language classes as well as the modification of language and materials in order to provide for comprehensible input to LEP students in content classes. The former is often referred to as content-based language instruction; the latter can be referred to as language-sensitive content instruction. An integrated approach bridges the gap that often separates the language and content classrooms. By utilizing an integrated approach, LEP students can begin academic studies earlier. Such an approach increases the understanding of subject matter by LEP students, which facilitates their academic success. At the same time, the LEP students are able to increase their proficiency levels in the English language.

An Integrated Language and Content Approach

The approach presented here focuses on three principal factors which apply equally to the language and the content teachers:
- the use of multiple media
- the enhancement of the students' thinking skills
- student-centered organization of instruction

Reprinted from *Integrating Language and Content Instruction: Strategies and Techniques* by Deborah J. Short. Published in 1991 by the National Clearinghouse for Bilingual Education.

In order to make English language input as comprehensible as possible, the teachers should present information through diverse media: realia, graphs, demonstrations, pre-reading, and pre-writing strategies. The focus of the instruction should be motivated by the content to be learned, which will help identify the language skills required to learn that content and the reasoning abilities needed to manipulate it (analyzing, synthesizing, and evaluating). Instruction should be student-centered where the teacher has the role of facilitator with the goal of increasing student-to-student interaction.

Strategies and Techniques

The following guidelines, strategies and techniques are for teachers who wish to use an integrated approach in their classes. Many of these are things that good teachers do naturally; however, it is worth enumerating them here so that their relationship to integrated instruction is explicit. The list is not exhaustive; rather it reflects activities teachers can incorporate as they begin to integrate language and content instruction. Teachers may find that adaptations of techniques they currently use will be appropriate to an integrated approach as well.

Several of the strategies and techniques described below are used in the model lesson plans that follow. These lesson plans describe language and content objectives, the thinking/study skills that may be addressed, the general theme and vocabulary, the necessary materials, the basic procedure, and extension activities for enrichment and other uses.

Preparing for the Integrated Approach

The following sequential steps are recommended during the planning of integrated instruction.

Observe classrooms

The language teacher should see what academic language and instructional methods and materials the content teacher is using, while the content teacher can see which strategies the language teacher uses with LEP students.

Collaborate with colleagues

Working together, language and content teachers should identify the language and/or academic difficulties and demands that particular subjects or courses may present for LEP students. Some examples of those demands are

- reading textbooks
- completing worksheets
- writing reports
- doing library research
- solving mathematical and scientific word problems
- using rhetorical styles in essays (e.g., cause and effect, compare and contrast, argue and persuade)

Examine the content materials

The teachers should identify specific problems LEP students may have with material in advance. Such problems do not result solely from the complexity of the passages, but from factors like the skills needed to complete accompanying exercises.

Select a theme
The teachers can develop several lessons around a theme. The theme should be addressed in the language and content classes. For example, an environmental theme, such as deforestation, might be the focus of ESL and science lessons. (The model lessons that follow designed around themes.)

Identify objectives of the unit
While developing the curriculum and syllabus for a course, teachers should keep in mind the specific objectives and adjust the material accordingly in order to eliminate extraneous detail that may confuse a LEP student.

Identify key terms and words
Key terms can be pulled out and introduced in advance. The teachers should reinforce the new vocabulary throughout the lesson. Of particular interest are words that can clue students in to what is expected of them, such as the terms *altogether, more,* and *less* in math word problems, and *contrast* in expository writing.

Look for appropriate text materials
The language teacher can choose content passages that illustrate the language structures or functions being taught. The content teacher can look for alternate versions of general textbooks that present the subject matter more clearly for LEP students or can adapt materials to suit the language proficiency level of the students.

Adapt written materials
If a lesson objective is to present new content information to LEP students, it is important to make materials more comprehensible to the LEP students. (How to do this is discussed below.)

Helping the LEP Student Adjust to the Classroom
LEP students are still learning English and the style of the American education system, so teachers should take this into consideration when presenting information.

Announce the lesson's objectives and activities
It is important to write the objectives on the board and review them orally before class begins. It is also helpful to place the lesson in the context of its broader theme and preview upcoming lessons.

Write legibly
Teachers need to remember that some students have low levels of literacy or are unaccustomed to the Roman alphabet.

Develop and maintain routines
Routines will help LEP students anticipate what will happen (e.g., types of assignments, ways of giving instructions) without relying solely on language clues.

List and review instructions step by step

Before students begin an activity, teachers should familiarize them with the entire list of instructions. Then, teachers should have students work on each step individually before moving on to the next step. This procedure is ideal for teaching students to solve math and science word problems.

Present information in varied ways
By using multiple media in the classroom, teachers reduce the reliance on language and place the information in a context that is more comprehensible to the students.

Provide frequent summations of the salient points of the lesson
 • try to use visual reviews with lists and charts
 • paraphrase the salient points where appropriate
 • have students provide oral summaries themselves

Adjusting Teaching Style
It is important to provide LEP students with ample opportunities for interaction and participation in the classroom. Teachers should not rely on a lecture approach. They should be more conscious of their own speech patterns and tolerant of their students' mistakes.

Develop a student-centered approach to teaching and learning
Teachers need to become facilitators and let students assume more responsibility for their learning. When activities are planned that actively involve students in each lesson, the students can better process the material presented and acquire the language as well.

Reduce and adjust teacher talk
Increasing the amount of student communication about the subject matter is important.
 • Allow students more time to speak.
 • Concentrate on talking about the subject material rather than about classroom discipline.
 • Be prepared to rephrase questions and information if the students do not understand the first time.

Increase the percentage of inferential and higher-order thinking questions asked
These questions encourage students' reasoning ability, such as hypothesizing, inferencing, analyzing, justifying, and predicting. The language used by the teacher or students need not be complex for thinking skills to be exercised. For example, to help students predict, a teacher might read the title of a story and ask, "What will this story tell us?" Teachers need to model critical thinking skills in a step-by-step approach to reasoning.

Recognize that students will make language mistakes
During the second language acquisition process, students make mistakes; this is natural in the process of learning a language. Make sure that the students have understood the information, but do not emphasize the grammatical aspect of their responses. When possible, though, model the correct grammar form.

Teaching Multilevel Classes
Frequently, teachers have classes with students of mixed abilities/proficiency levels. There are several strategies that can help when these situations arise.

Use cooperative learning

This strategy provides for diversity and individuality in learning styles and aids students in the socialization process. Pair and group activities promote student interaction and decrease the anxiety many students feel when they must perform alone for the teacher in front of the class. It is important for each student in the group to have a task that he or she may accomplish and thus contribute to the activity (e.g., by being recorder, final copy scribe, illustrator, materials collector, reporter). The ideal size for these groups ranges from two to five students. (See Cochran, 1989, for additional suggestions.) Special considerations should be given to students whose home culture may make them feel uncomfortable participating in cooperative learning activities. While all students should be invited to participate, the teacher should respect the wishes of any student who prefers not to participate.

Incorporate peer tutoring

The students learn and share among themselves with the teacher as a facilitator who checks on the students' understanding and progress. The tutors learn to explain and clarify concepts while the tutored students have the benefit of one-on-one interaction in a non-threatening manner. Some supplemental textbooks, such as *English Skills for Algebra* (Crandall, et. al., 1989), are specifically designed as peer instruction materials.

Incorporate process writing

Process writing, though initially implemented in language arts classes, is easily extended into content-area classes. As with process writing exercises, students begin with pre-writing activities such as viewing a film or sharing the reading of an article that sets the stage for the content area topic. The class may also review key concepts and vocabulary to incorporate into the writing. During the process the students learn about language–specific to the content topic selected–in a meaningful and motivating manner. Word processing programs are particularly useful with process writing and should be used if available. They facilitate the draft and edit stages of the process and also allow students to concentrate on their writing style and organization, not on their handwriting.

Design lessons for discovery learning

These activities allow students to discover new information on their own with guidance from the teacher. Teachers help organize the data and sometimes set out the procedures for students to follow. Students, individually or in groups, discover the results. Problem-solving activities (math) and open-ended experiments (science) are examples of discovery learning.

Use inquiry learning

In these activities, students investigate a topic of their own choosing and teachers act as facilitators. They identify a problem, hypothesize causes, design procedures or experiments, and conduct research to try to solve the problem. These activities work well in science and social studies classes.

Include information gap activities

These activities, which include jigsaws, problem solving, and simulations, are set up so each student (in a class, or more generally, in a group) has one or two pieces of information needed to solve the puzzle but not all the necessary information. Students must work together, sharing information while practicing their language, negotiating, and critical thinking skills.

Plan lessons around questionnaires/interviews

Designing questionnaires and interviewing respondents are excellent activities for heterogeneous groups. In the design phase, all students can contribute and evaluate questions for inclusion. In the interview phase, the number of people each student may be expected to interview can be adjusted to the student's ability. Also interviews may be conducted in students' first languages, though responses must be reported in English. A report and analysis of the interview responses may be conducted orally or in writing.

Motivating Students and Providing Background Knowledge

Many LEP students are at a disadvantage in content classes because they lack necessary background knowledge and/or experiential familiarity with the topic at hand. Teachers must plan activities in their instruction to provide some background schema for these students.

Motivate students with semantic webbing

Often used as a pre-writing activity, semantic webbing is also an excellent task for students before they read or discuss a new topic. This more sophisticated version of brainstorming allows students to organize their thoughts and categorize information. Students (with or without the teacher's assistance) may list items first and web later or they may web as they list, creating new strands as categories occur to them. The web is then used by the students as they write on the topic (in the example below, the War of 1812), using the categories to organize their thoughts into paragraph form.

In the following example, students start with the War of 1812 and add on more information about the historical event. (The numbers represent the order of students' ideas in building the web.)

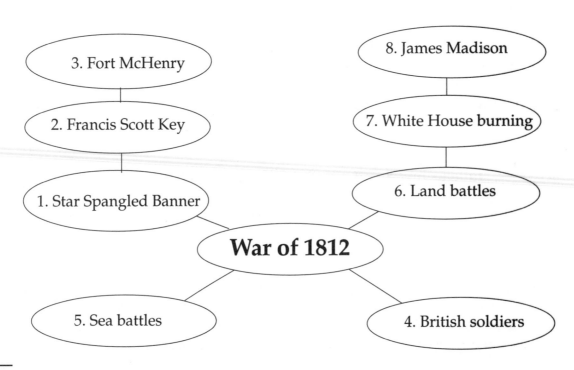

Use realia, illustrations, maps, photos
Although the use of realia and other visual materials is a common activity for language classes, it is less frequently found in content classes. These items provide a quick, often non-language-dependent means of introducing students to the lesson topic.

Organize students into small groups and then share with whole class
The teacher may announce the lesson topic for the day and ask small groups of students to list what they already know about it. After a few minutes, the teacher has the groups share their ideas with the class as a whole.

Include "theme" listening activities
Sometimes it is helpful to get students "in the mood" for a topic. The stage may be set by asking students just to listen to a song, a poem, or even a short story and having a brief discussion about it afterward.

Include discussion of student experience
While introducing new topics in class, encourage students to share knowledge they may already have about the topic, along with any relevant real-life experiences they may have had.

Begin units with the K-W-L technique
Using a standard form (see sample below), teachers distribute the "Know-Want-Learned" sheet to students individually at the start of each unit. Students complete the first two categories at this point. The "learned" category is completed at the close of the unit.

UNIT THEME: *Food Groups*

What I know about *Food Groups:*

What I want to learn about *Food Groups:*

What I learned about *Food Groups:*

Adapting Traditional ESL Techniques to the Content Classrooms
Language teachers providing content-based instruction and content teachers teaching LEP students can modify the following ESL techniques for their lessons.

Bring realia into the lessons
Teachers should use visual displays (e.g., graphs, charts, photos), objects, and authentic materials, like newspaper and magazine clippings, in the lessons and assignments. These help provide nonverbal information and also help match various learning styles.

Do demonstrations
When teachers use actions, they can show the meaning of new words (especially verbs), explain a science experiment, model language functions in the context of a dialogue, etc.

Use filmstrips, videotapes, and audiocassettes with books
Borrowing films and other audiovisual materials from school/district media centers can help improve a content lesson. It is useful to preview the audiovisual materials before

showing them to the class, both for possible language difficulties and misleading cultural information.

Have the students do hands-on activities
Content teachers should plan for students to manipulate new material through hands-on activities, such as role plays and simulations, TPR (total physical response), laboratory experiments, drawing pictures and story sequences, and writing their own math word problems.

Design lessons with music and jazz chant activities
Language teachers frequently use music and chants in their classes. These activities are motivating for students and also help teach English pronunciation and intonation patterns. Songs and chants on subject area topics would work well, too. Although some high school students may be reticent to sing aloud in class, all students should be able to do listening activities with music and chants.

Schedule sustained silent reading (SSR) sessions
As educators try to promote more student reading both in and out of school, many teachers (often reading, language arts, and ESL) have incorporated sustained silent reading in their classes. SSR adapts easily to content classes and is particularly effective in middle schools. Once a week, for example, students choose a book or magazine and read silently for 20-30 minutes. The teacher reads, too. Teachers with LEP students can stock their classrooms with magazines, picture books, reference books, and trade books on topics they are studying. There need not be any discussion about the reading selections, but some teachers may ask students to fill out reading logs (described below).

Meeting the Students' Cognitive Academic Needs
In many instances, LEP students need coaching and practice to improve their cognitive processing and production of content material. In order to do so, it is important for teachers to build upon the skills and knowledge students have already mastered. Each lesson should include critical thinking and/or study skills. Some of these skills may have been initially developed in the students' first language and will transfer to English.

Examine the topic through the students' listening and speaking skills first; then expand the topic through reading and writing activities.
Since the students' oral language skills usually develop more rapidly than their written skills, teachers can check the students' comprehension orally and clarify any trouble spots before introducing any reading or writing activities.

Be conscious of different learning styles
Teachers can help meet the different learning styles of their students by varying the presentation and reinforcement of information.
- Alternate activities to address the visual, aural, tactile, and kinesthetic modes of learning.
- Find out if your students prefer to learn from listening to theory or from applying information through hands-on activities.
- When reteaching information, choose a different mode of instruction. (For more information, see Hainer, et al., 1990.)

Incorporate thinking skill activities
When planning each lesson, teachers must create opportunities to focus on thinking skills. Thinking skills can be developed through teacher-student questioning or through scheduled activities like problem solving and decision making.
- Predicting, categorizing, and inferencing are easily addressed in the warm-up and motivation phases of a lesson.
- Observing, reporting, and classifying, which can be done orally, in writing, or pictorially, fit nicely into the presentation and application phases.
- Sequencing, summarizing, and justifying are skills that suit lesson reviews.

Teach study skills
LEP students frequently need assistance in learning how to study. This is especially true of students in middle schools. By teaching them study skills, teachers will give the students an important tool that they can use throughout their academic careers. Show students how to develop and use graphic organizers:
- **outlines** for summarizing, for making predictions
- **timelines** for organizing and sequencing events chronologically, for comparing events in different settings (e.g., states, countries)
- **flow charts** for showing progression and influences on an outcome, for showing cause and effect
- **mapping** for examining movement and spatial relations
- **graphs and charts** for organizing and comparing data
- **Venn diagrams** for comparing and contrasting

The following is a sample Venn diagram to use to examine Christopher Columbus and Neil Armstrong. Where the two circles intersect, students write some similarities. Where the circles do not intersect, students write some differences. (Some students may only write a few words; others, several sentences.) This structure can become the draft for an essay comparing and contrasting the two explorers.

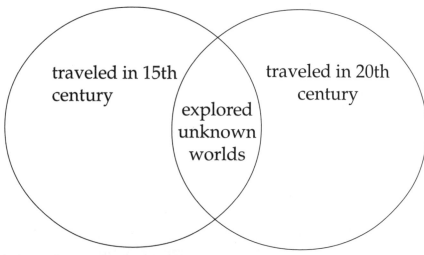

Christopher Columbus   Neil Armstrong

(Venn diagram: Christopher Columbus circle — "traveled in 15th century"; Neil Armstrong circle — "traveled in 20th century"; intersection — "explored unknown worlds")

Develop the students' ability to use texts and other written materials

Since the acquisition of details within a particular content topic is not the primary objective of the language course, teachers have more time to develop the students' skills in analyzing:

- **text as a whole**–teachers demonstrate how to use (a) the parts of a book (table of contents, index) to find information and (b) headings, subheadings, and illustrations in chapters to organize and enhance the information.
- **passages**–teachers help students learn to draw inferences, synthesize information, make judgements, and provide justifications.

However, because these skills are demanded of the students once they are mainstreamed, content teachers need to incorporate activities to review student knowledge in their areas, too.

Plan activities to train the students in attacking academic tasks, such as research projects, problem solving, and essay writing

Carefully planned academic activities help students make the transition from language class to mainstream content class. Teachers may plan a library project, for example, and walk the students through it step by step, preferably with peer tutors. They may also use process writing methods to help students write essays and research reports.

Present models for writing assignments

Assignments required by mainstream content classes, like research papers and laboratory reports, are of particular interest to LEP students and their teachers. It is beneficial to discuss the model clearly so that the students know how each section is structured and why each section is important. Students should then be given practice using the model before doing a required assignment with it.

Checking Student Comprehension of the Content

Use strip stories, sentence strips

Teachers write a summary of a lesson or reading passage or write out the steps for solving a math problem or for doing a science experiment on individual strips-either one sentence per strip or several sentences. These strips are distributed, out of sequence, to the students, in groups or as a whole class. The students then organize the strips into the proper sequence.

Sample strips for math:

$$2 \ 1/2 + 3 \ 1/4 =$$

$$5/2 + 13/4 =$$

$$10/4 + 13/4 =$$

$$23/4 =$$

$$5 \ 3/4 =$$

Set up dialogue journals

Many school systems are adopting "writing across the curriculum" approaches to encourage and improve student writing. Often teachers will use journal writing in their classes. Dialogue journals go one step further by having teachers respond to student writing in positive and supportive ways. Dialogue journals are not vehicles for editing student work; they are opportunities for students to express themselves. (For further discussion, see Peyton & Reed, 1990.)

Teachers decide how often they want students to write (e.g., daily, twice a week) and how often they will read and comment on the journals. Some teachers will respond to every piece of writing; others will respond once a week or less. The teacher comments may vary in length and depth also. Also, teachers may ask less proficient students to start with illustrations in their journals and slowly move into writing. In this way all students in a heterogeneous class can participate.

Some teachers choose to let writing be entirely student-derived; others provide the topics, at least some of the time. Some teachers use dialogue journals for lesson closure or motivation by having students summarize what they learned in the lesson (that day or the day before).

Although dialogue journals are not designed for correcting student work, they can guide teacher instruction. Teachers who see consistent problems in student writing or in student comprehension of the lesson topics can develop new lessons to address those issues.

Plan activities using drama and role play
Another language teaching technique that works well in the content classroom is using drama. Teachers can ask groups of students to act out an event or a topic studied, from the sprouting of a plant to a mock legislative debate in the state government. Teachers may assign roles impromptu or may have groups research and write dialogues before performing. Mime also works well with students from beginning to advanced levels of English proficiency.

Have students complete reading logs
These logs can be used in any content class to reflect reading done from a textbook, a supplemental reader, a trade book or magazine, and newspaper articles. Three categories may be set up on a standard form : What I understood, What I didn't understand, and what I learned.

Reading title: _____	
What I understood:	What I didn't understand:
What I learned:	

Check comprehension with cloze exercises
Cloze exercises, popular for assessing reading comprehension, may also be applied to different subject areas. For many clozes, teachers write a summary or take an excerpt (of a reading passage or lesson or class activity) and then delete every *x*th word. Students then "fill in the blank" with teachers deciding if they will score by an exact word or an acceptable word method.

The following is an example of a cloze passage derived from a passage in a civics textbook:

The First Amendment says we have_____of religion, speech, the press, and _____. We can follow any religion, say_____, write our thoughts, and meet in _____.

Have students do story summaries
As the graphic below shows, this activity has both a written and pictorial component. Students summarize a lesson, reading, or experience (individually or in groups) by drawing illustrations and describing them. A format may look like this:

SECTION 7

Illustration	

	Illustration

Encourage students to write headlines
Students can practice their summarizing skills and, as they get more proficient, their descriptive language skills, by writing news headlines for lessons and topics discussed in class. For example, teachers may ask students to write a headline describing the results of a science experiment or to create a title of an imaginary book review of a book they had read.

Let students perform experiments
Teachers may plan performance-based activities to determine student comprehension of the subject matter. A traditional example is the lab practical for science classes. This idea can be easily adapted to math classes, especially those that use manipulatives.

Incorporate the LEA (Language Experience Approach) method
This method has grown out of the movement to teach adults literacy skills, namely to read and write. After students have an experience (e.g., going on a field trip), they dictate to the teacher a summary of what happened. (Teachers usually record on the board exactly what the students say.) Students then work together to organize the written ideas and if desired make corrections. Teachers may copy the dictation to use another day for review, motivation, or even a lesson on editing.

In a class with mixed proficiency levels of students, this activity can work well in small groups. The most proficient student in the group can be the scribe while the others contribute, organize, and edit their work.

Have students write character diaries
Frequently in social studies and from time to time in other subjects, the lives of important individuals in the field are studied. Students may read biographies and trade books or watch films and videos and then write a character diary, chronicling a week or two in the life of a particular individual. Students place special emphasis on the setting of the diary as well as the path toward accomplishment that the individual underwent during the week(s).

Developing Lesson Plans

In integrated lessons teachers and students work toward content and language objectives. When developing lesson plans for integrated instruction, it is important to identify both types of objectives and plan activities accordingly. It is often useful to specify critical thinking or study skills to target as well. A teacher's or school district's preferred lesson format can then be used to develop the lesson.

The lesson format presented below includes four phases: (1) warm up or motivation; (2) presentation of new material, in whole group or small group work; (3) practice and application of new material; and (4) review or informal assessment to check student understanding. Most lessons also contain extension activities to reinforce or extend the concepts covered. A series of lessons thematically linked into units provides for sustained student interest as well as the opportunity to build systematically on prior activities.

The model lesson plans in this section deliberately offer an extensive range of techniques and strategies. They demonstrate the possibilities available to teachers for making integrated language and content more comprehensible. It is important to note that teachers may not have time to incorporate all these suggestions into their lesson plans every day but should try to vary the activities they plan.

Certain procedures are more critical than others. These are

1. selecting principal vocabulary terms to teach as a pre-activity

2. providing the opportunity for students to discuss the information and material orally, preferably before any written work is assigned

3. designing class activities for student-to-student interaction

4. deciding to use real literature or adapted materials

The following model lesson outline may be used for integrated language and content lessons. While all lessons should include some language and some content objectives, an individual lesson need not address all the subcategories within. Some lessons may reach content objectives from different subject areas, such as math (use division) and science (calculate average rainfall). Some may have literature; some may not. Some may focus on reading skills without listening practice. Following the model are two sample lessons illustrating the use of this outline and some of the strategies discussed earlier.

Lesson Plan Format: Integrated Instruction
THEME
LESSON TOPIC
OBJECTIVES
> **Language Skills**
>> **Speaking/Listening**
>> **Reading/Writing**
>> **Structures**
>
> **Content Skills**
> **Thinking/Study skills**
> **Key Vocabulary**

LITERATURE
MATERIALS
MOTIVATION
PRESENTATION
PRACTICE/APPLICATION
REVIEW/EVALUATION
EXTENSION

References

Campbell, R., Gray, T., Rhodes, N., and Snow, M. (1985). Foreign language learning in the elementary schools: A comparison of three language programs. *The Modern Language Journal.* Vol 69, Issue 1, pp. 44-54.

Cochran, C. (1989). *Strategies for Involving LEP Students in the All-English-Medium Classroom: A Cooperative Learning Approach.* Washington, DC.: National Clearinghouse for Bilingual Education.

Crandall, J. , Dale, T., Rhodes, N., and Spanos, G. (1989). *English Skills for Algebra.* Englewood Cliffs, NJ: Center for Applied Linguistics/Prentice Hall Regents.

Cummins, J. (1981). The role of primary language development in promoting success for language minority students. In California State Department of Education (Ed.), *Schooling and Language Minority Students: A Theoretical Framework.* Los Angeles, CA: California State University; Evaluation, Dissemination, and Assessment Center.

Hainer, E., Fagan, B., Bratt, T., Baker, L., and Arnold, N. (1990). *Integrating Language Styles and Skills in the ESL Classroom: An Approach to Lesson Planning.* Washington DC: National Clearinghouse for Bilingual Education.

Krashen, S., and Biber, D. (1988). *On Course: Bilingual Education's Success in California.* Sacramento, CA: California Association for Bilingual Education.

Lambert, W. and Tucker, G.R. (1972). *Bilingual Education of Children.* Rowley, MA: Newbury House.

United States Department of Education. (1991). *The Condition of Bilingual Education in the Nation: A Report to the Congress and the President.* Washington DC: Office of the Secretary, U.S. Department of Education.

Sample Lesson 1

This model lesson can be used with upper elementary and middle school students. It may take two to three days.

KEY THEME: Agriculture–Important food crops (for American social studies when discussing Native Americans, Pilgrims, or current agricultural resources; for world social studies when discussing any corn-producing country's agricultural system, differences between agricultural and industrial economies, or current events regarding international trade)

TOPIC:	Corn
OBJECTIVES:	
Content:	Recognize different uses of corn (in the US/around the world) Locate corn producing areas on a (US/world map)
American studies:	Recognize the role corn plays in American history
World studies:	Recognize corn as an important import/export crop
Language:	
Listening/Speaking:	Listen to a poem
Reading/Writing:	Read a poem Complete a comparison chart
Thinking Skills:	Interpret a poem Compare the uses of corn in two countries Solve a problem Use reference materials
Key Vocabulary:	Corn, maize, kernel, stalk, sheath, husk, crop, fodder, grind, cornmeal, import, export, trade
LITERATURE:	"Song of the Cornfield," poem by Gabriela Mistral (Chilean)
MATERIALS:	An ear of corn in husk, individual corn kernels, maps (US/world), black line masters of poem, outline (US states/world) map, outline chart

Note: In some countries (e.g., France, Germany) corn is not used by humans as food; it is only fodder. In other countries (e.g. Mexico, Guatemala), it is a major food staple.

Motivation: Have two students volunteer to close their eyes; give each a kernel of corn and ask them to identify it. Show class the kernels and an ear of corn with the husk to introduce vocabulary, and ask students to share their native languages' name for corn.

Teacher uses realia so students identify corn tactilely. Their interest in the topic is enhanced when they share their native language names for corn.

Presentation: In small groups, ask students to list any experiences they have had with corn–growing, eating, grinding, cooking. Share these lists with the whole class, and look for comparisons in students' experiences.

Students interact and discuss prior experiences with corn.

Read the poem "Song of the Cornfield" to the class and ask students to discuss the images it creates for them and if the poem applies to their experiences with corn. Distribute copies of the poem to small groups, and ask them to complete the worksheet.

As a class, share group responses and discuss the steps of corn production from planting kernels to finding corn in markets/groceries, in cornmeal, or in fodder.

The literature models language in the content context. Students interpret the poem by describing images. Students of different ability levels are able to work in groups to complete tasks.

Practice/Application: Distribute the chart to small groups and explain that students will examine corn in two states/countries. As a class, brainstorm additional categories to compare on the chart (e.g., if the country makes corn products–meal, oil, etc.). Then, in small groups, have students choose their two states/countries to examine and complete the chart, using reference materials and textbooks.

Teacher uses a chart to help students organize and compare the information. The chart format allows students to use words and phrases, applying key vocabulary.

Using their group chart, have students write a few sentences in their journals comparing the role of corn in the two states/countries.

Students do individual journal writing.

Review: Display the outline map (US or world) on an overhead projector. As a class, develop a key for the map, and have groups share their information to plot areas of corn agriculture, industry, etc. Then, using arrows to show trade, have students indicate sources of corn for areas that do not grow it.

Teacher checks class comprehension as a whole with group's input. Students also review some map skills.

Home tasks:

1. Interview parents and neighbors about their experiences with corn, growing, eating, using as fodder, etc.
2. Collect recipes from your culture that use corn.

Extensions:

1. Have students bring in news articles or shopping advertisements that relate to corn.
2. Make a display of corn products (drawings, magazine cutouts, or real objects) such as oil, cornmeal, cornstarch, popcorn, etc.
3. Make popcorn in class; compare a popcorn kernel to a "regular" kernel, discuss role of heat in the changes of state in the kernel.
4. Have students illustrate the poem in the lesson.
5. Prepare a class recipe book of corn favorites.
6. Have students bring in corn dishes to share.

These tasks and extensions extend and apply the information students learned and shared in class. The activities are varied to meet the academic needs and learning styles of the students. They also involve parents and others outside the classroom.

7. (American studies) Read *Corn is Maize* by Aliki. (World Studies) Make a bar graph to show top four or five corn-producing countries.

Long-term projects:

These projects are designed to promote students' creativity while practicing the language and help develop some problem-solving skills.

1. Write a short story about the life of a kernel, and draw cartoon illustrations to accompany it.

2. Research the production and distribution of corn that is grown in one country and exported to another. Design a sequence flow chart.

3. Imagine there is a severe drought in a country which produces corn and uses it for food. This country is very poor and cannot buy corn from another country. The leader asks you to investigate several options (there are three or four) for this country and make a recommendation.

Song of the Cornfield©

by Gabriela Mistral

The ears of corn
Look like little girls:
Ten weeks in the stalks
Tightly held they sway.

They have little golden fuzz
Like that of new-born babes
and motherly leaves
Shield them from dew.

And within the sheath
Like little children hidden,
With two thousand golden teeth
They laugh and laugh without reason.

Reprinted by permission of : JOAN DAVES AGENCY. Copyright.

Read this poem together and discuss it in small groups:
1. Where is the corn the poet is describing?
2. What does the poet compare corn to?
3. Does the poet like or dislike corn? What words or phrases in the poem justify your response?
4. What role does corn play in your culture?
5. What do you think will happen to the corn described in this poem?

Note: A nice addition would be to use the original Spanish version too.

Sample worksheet

COMPARING THE ROLE OF CORN		
Role of corn	(state/country name)	(state/country name)
name for corn		
source: produced or imported		
uses: food fodder		

Enhancing English Language Learning in **Elementary Classrooms**
Study Guide Section 7: **Integrated Instruction**

Sample Lesson 2

This model lesson plan was created for ESOL students, but may be adapted for mainstream grades 6-12. If presented in full detail, the lesson may require one to two weeks.

KEY THEME: Environmental Pollution

TOPIC:	Littering (Solid Waste)
OBJECTIVES:	
Content:	Recognize environmental problems
	Identify litter and patterns of littering
	Identify human influences on the environment
Language:	
Listening/Speaking:	Recite/listen to a dialogue with meaningful content
	Discuss environmental issues as a whole class and in small groups
	Conduct interviews and report orally
Reading/Writing:	Design a questionnaire, write questions
	Complete a list or chart
	Write in a journal
Structure:	Question Formation
Thinking Skills:	Analyze problems Generate solutions Infer reasons for human actions
Key Vocabulary:	Litter, garbage, dump, mess, environment, trash, cause, solution, solid waste, pollution, survey

MATERIALS: Teacher-made dialogue, poster, items of trash (empty soda cans, paper wrappers, broken glass, etc.)

Motivation: *(Before lesson is presented)*

Two weeks before introducing this topic, hang a scenic poster on the wall. Some students may comment on the lovely view or ask vocabulary questions about objects in the scene. Every other day, attach an item that might be considered trash (candy wrappers, an empty box, an aluminum can) to the poster, thus creating a trash collage. The students may be curious, but do not reveal the purpose.

This activity whets the students' interest and visually represents some background information about the topic.

(To introduce the lesson)

Turn to the "Trash Collage" and ask students what they think it represents. Write student ideas on the board. Finally, through guided questioning, if necessary, lead the students to recognize that the lovely place is being ruined by litter.

Changing the focus, turn from the poster scene to the local environment, and add some additional vocabulary to the list. Then ask some of the more advanced students to explain why this happens and write comments on the board. Some students may venture consequences of the littering problem.

All students can participate. Teacher helps them make speech-print connections by writing their comments on the board.

Presentation: Ask two of the more advanced students to volunteer to come to the front of the class and role play the following dialogue:

LITTERING AT SCHOOL

Student 1: Don't throw that on the ground.

Student 2: Why not? What's the big deal?

This dialogue introduces, in an interactive way, some key vocabulary and causes associated with littering.

Student 1: Our school looks like a garbage dump.

Student 2: So what? Tell one of the younger kids to clean it up.

Student 1: But you littered.

Student 2: Everyone does it. Teachers do it too.

Student 1: You're impossible. Do you know what our school will look like if everyone continues to litter?

On the board, write the headings: PROBLEMS, CAUSES, SOLUTIONS, in chart form. Categorize and expand the vocabulary list with student input. Show students a written form of the dialogue.

Having begun with concrete examples (poster, dialogue), students can now expand and organize their information.

In order to check on comprehension and practice writing questions, have the students take dictation. Dictate the following questions:

This activity incorporates some language practice for the students.

> Where are they?
> Who is talking?
> What happened?
> Why is one student upset?
> Does this happen at our school?

Have pairs compare their work and ask volunteers to write their dictations on the board. Encourage students to peer edit. Discuss relevant grammar points (e.g., question words, verb-noun positions).

Ask students to think of additional questions about the dialogue. Write the student-dictated questions on the board. Work as a class to edit errors.

If desired, add questions, such as "Why is there a problem?" (cause) or "What can you do?" (solution).

This paired activity allows for oral language practice in the context of the lesson topic.

Application 1: Have pairs role play the dialogue "Littering at School" and discuss the vocabulary and issues together. Then have pairs ask each other the class-generated questions (more advanced students should answer first).

Students work individually at first, then with peers.

Review: After this structured conversation, ask students to write ten questions and answers about the topic (littering). Before they hand it in, encourage students to peer edit.

This task applies the topic directly to their lives.

Home task: For homework, have students write in their journal about the trash they see as they go to and from school for several days. As this task continues expand the vocabulary list under PROBLEMS and put it on a poster or chart to hang in the room. Make two other posters, one with CAUSES, and the other with SOLUTIONS.

This group work offers all students a chance to participate.

Application 2: In small groups, have students discuss the causes of littering, then share ideas with the class. Write them on the CAUSES poster. Then ask groups to consider solutions. Share their suggestions and write on the SOLUTIONS poster.

This activity reinforces the language structure objective.

Next have small groups design a questionnaire to interview classmates, teachers, neighbors, family, and friends. The

SECTION 7

questionnaire should be limited to five questions. If needed, help groups plan their questions, but do not provide them with a full list. Possibilities include:

> Does litter bother you?
> Do you litter?
> What do people throw away as litter?
> Why do people litter?
> Who is responsible for solving this problem?
> What can be done about this problem?

Home task: Have students conduct a survey for three days, each interviewing 10 people. (If they interview non-English speakers, they may ask questions in the native language but should write responses in English.)

This task encourages interaction with non-classmates on the topic and may provide clarification practice, as students explain their task to others.

Follow-up and Extension: Have students share this information in their groups. Have recorders in the group organize the results of the survey and a representative of the group reports to the whole class. Help the whole class find ways of organizing and presenting the results of the survey. (Some students may list the results on posters, others may do a chart and quantify the responses. Some may prepare an oral report or a debate between individuals who litter and those who don't. Other students may create a role play or drama. Some may design a visual display or collage, highlighting *before* and *after* scenes.)

Each group contributes to the whole class. Optional presentations allow each group to choose the one best suited to their learning styles and academic skills.

Have students write a composition. Display the papers and, if appropriate, encourage some students to submit their work for publication in a school/class newspaper.

Long-term Projects: Expand this introduction to individual generation of and influence on solid waste pollution to heighten the awareness of students to other sources of solid waste (industrial, agricultural, municipal) and methods of disposal. Design additional lessons to help students research sources of solid waste in their communities and learn about local disposal methods, such as dumping, burying, burning, recycling, etc. Students may want to form action groups to decrease solid waste pollution in their towns.

These projects further students' problem-solving and study skill development.

Lesson Plan Checklist: Integrated Instruction
Sample Lesson 1

Directions: Read Sample Lesson 1 (Corn), pp. 173-176 at the end of the Deborah Short article. Working with a partner or small group, make notes below on how the lesson implements each of the five characteristics listed. You will recall that the first three characteristics are The Three Principles presented earlier in this course.

1. How does the lesson *increase comprehensibility* for English language learning students?

2. How does the lesson *increase interaction* among students, including ELLs?

3. How does the lesson *increase thinking and study skills* among students, including ELLs?

4. How does the lesson explicitly *develop academic language* for all students?

5. How does the lesson *make connections* to other learning and to students' lives and cultures?

Developing Academic Language and Literacy Skills

Four "Levels of Attention"

1. <u>Comprehensive Strategies</u>—These are strategies that teach a process or an approach to doing an integrated task such as reading a chapter or writing an essay. They include:

   • Directed Reading-Thinking Approach: preview, predict, read, review, summarize.

   • The Writing Process (or Writer's Workshop): brainstorming, organizing, drafting, reviewing/getting feedback, revising, editing/proofreading, and publishing.

   • Teacher Read Alouds for Information: The teacher reads aloud from an informational source that the students can understand, but cannot read independently (e.g., reference materials, newspapers, textbooks); in the early grades, students are exposed to academic skills and language, in later grades, to more complex ideas and language.

2. <u>Focused Strategies</u>—These are strategies that focus on a more specific objective, such as reading for information or understanding cause and effect, or on a more specific language function, such as following directions or explaining a process.

   • Graphic Organizers teach relationships and key words and ideas, but don't stop there; have students put the ideas on the graphic organizer into academic language in a few sentences or in an oral or written summary (teacher may Write Aloud or use the Language Experience Approach for very young students); use story maps and outlines to show how different types of text are organized.

   • Think Alouds by teachers and students show how to understand a text or to solve a problem and how to use problem-solving language.

   • Extended Discourse (longer chunks of language), both oral and written, causes students to fully describe and explain their ideas using academic language; teachers may stimulate extended discourse by asking higher-order thinking questions and follow-up questions, and by increasing "wait time ."

   • Think-Pair-Share and Numbered Heads Together provide students thinking time and peer language models.

3. <u>Language Structures</u>—The teacher calls attention to specific language structures (e.g., forming questions, using suffixes) and the meaning they convey, and creates an opportunity for students to use these structures correctly and in the context of the lesson.

   • Focus on one or two language structures in each text or lesson— identify the structure and how it "encodes" meaning; e.g., in a text, ask students to find sentences that compare one thing to another, identify the most common sentence pattern(s), list other ways to make comparisons, provide practice with frame sentences, dictation, sentence writing, editing, or summarizing the lesson; in assessment, require use of the structure to express understanding of the ideas of the chapter. Other examples of language structures are "if" statements, question forms, cause-effect, subject-verb agreement, suffixes, parts of speech. Remember that the structures should "grow out of" the content lesson.

- Graphic Organizers can also be used to teach specific language structures such as cause and effect, compare and contrast, sequencing, etc.; be sure to have students use the language in an authentic task such as summarizing the lesson in their own words.

4. <u>Academic Vocabulary</u>—The vocabulary that all students are learning at the same time is not generally the main hurdle for ELLs; teachers must realize that a great deal of the vocabulary that other students are assumed to know may also be new to ELLs.

- Identify and teach both "technical" and "non-technical" content-related vocabulary in each lesson; e.g., all students may be learning "tide" and "currents," but ELLs also need to learn "waves" and "motion" and "affect."

- Identify words that have multiple meanings in different content areas; e.g., power, radical, force.

- Use vocabulary strategies such as introducing lessons with semantic webs to identify vocabulary that students know and to introduce new vocabulary; introducing lessons with demonstrations which include vocabulary; vocabulary games (categorizing, guessing); personal word banks or dictionaries for students.

"Tips" for Developing Academic Language and Literacy Skills

1. Choose the academic language and literacy skills to be taught based on the content and the activities in the lesson. This provides natural context and motivation to learn.

2. Make the most of every activity by thinking "What academic language or skill can this activity teach the students?" Have students use the new language to express their understanding of the lesson's content.

3. Don't focus primarily on grammar as grammar, but rather how to use English to do classroom activities and assignments and to talk about what is being learned. For example, think about the language that students need to participate in cooperative learning activities: they need to accept or reject a role, ask questions about their task, state their ideas, agree/disagree with others politely, etc. This kind of language can be taught through class discussion, dialogs, role play, and frame sentences. The class can develop a rubric to evaluate cooperative group process and language.

4. Call attention to the language you are modeling and how students can use the model in their work.

5. Limit most corrections to activities that are focusing on language per se (e.g., role plays or sample sentences) or to written student work that uses academic language that has been taught.

6. Have students read and write in every content area.

Academic Language Functions (grades 4-6)

	Science	Math	Social Studies
LISTENING			
1. Understanding explanations.	●	●	●
2. Listening for specific information.	○	●	○
3. Understanding explanations without concrete referents.	○	○	
4. Following directions for experiments.	●		
5. Understanding oral word problems.		○	
SPEAKING			
1. Answering questions	●	●	●
2. Asking for clarification.	●	●	●
3. Participating in discussions.	●		○
4. Explaining and demonstrating a process.	○		
5. Presenting oral reports.			○
6. Explaining how an answer was derived.		○	
READING			
1. Understanding specialized vocabulary.	○	○	○
2. Understanding information/explanations in textbooks.	○	○	○
3. Finding information from graphs, charts, and maps.	○		○
4. Following directions for experiments.	○		
5. Finding information in reference materials.	○		○
6. Reading at varied rates (skimming and scanning).			○
7. Reading mathematical notations and equations.		○	
8. Understanding written word problems.		●	
WRITING			
1. Writing answers to questions.	●		●
2. Noting observations.	○		
3. Describing experiments.	○		
4. Writing reports.	○		○
5. Labeling maps, graphs, and charts.			○
6. Writing verbal input numerically.		○	

Key: ○ Some emphasis
● More emphasis

Summarized from Chamot, A.U. & O' Malley, J.M. (1986). *A Cognitive Academic Language Learning Approach: An ESL Content-Based Curriculum*. National Clearinghouse for Bilingual Education. (ED 338 108).

SECTION 7

Teaching Thinking Skills

QUESTIONING FOR QUALITY THINKING

Knowledge - Identification and recall of information
    Who, what, when, where, how_____?
    Describe_____.

Comprehension - Organization and selection of facts and ideas
    Retell_____in your own words.
    What is the main idea of_____?

Application - Use of facts, rules, principles
    How is _____an example of _____?
    How is _____related to _____?
    Why is _____significant?

Analysis - Separation of a whole into component parts
    What are the parts or features of _____?
    Classify_____ according to_____.
    Outline/diagram/web_____.
    How does ____compare/contrast with_____?
    What evidence can you list for_____?

Synthesis - Combination of ideas to form a new whole
    What would you predict/infer from_____?
    What ideas can you add to_____?
    How would you create/design a new_____?
    What might happen if you combined_____
    with_____?
    What solutions would you suggest for____?

Evaluation - Development of opinions, judgement, or decisions
    Do you agree_____?
    What do you think about_____?
    What is the most important_____?
    Prioritize_____.
    How would you decide about_____?
    What criteria would you use to assess_____?

STRATEGIES TO EXTEND STUDENT THINKING

*Remember "wait time I and II"
    Provide at least three seconds of thinking time after a question and after a response

*Utilize "think-pair-share"
    Allow individual thinking time, discussion with a partner, then open up for discussion

*Ask "follow-ups"
    Why? Do you agree? Can you elaborate? Tell me more. Can you give an example?

*Withhold judgment.
    Respond to student answers in a non-evaluative fashion

*Survey the class
    "Could you please summarize John's point?"

*Allow for student calling
    "Richard, will you please call on someone else to respond?"

*Ask students to "unpack" their thinking
    "Describe how you arrived at your answer." ("think aloud")

*Call on students randomly
    Not just those with raised hands

*Student questioning
    Let students develop their own questions

*Cue students' responses
    "There is not a single correct answer for this question. I want you to consider alternatives."

Reprinted with permission from: *Cueing Bookmark*, Language Development and Early Learning Branch, Division of Instruction, Maryland State Department of Education, no date.

Video Observation Matrix

Directions: First, identify strategies used by the teacher in the video. Then, suggest additional strategies for each column. Make notes on the matrix.

Video Clip	Develop Academic Language	Make Connections
#1.		
#2.		
#3.		

SECTION 7

Integrated Instruction: Personal Priorities

Directions: The purpose of this activity is to develop a list that will remind you of strategies and techniques that you learned in this course and that you choose to incorporate into your teaching. (a) First, think back on the strategies and techniques that were covered in this section and in earlier sections of this course and list two or three of your priorities under the appropriate item below. Then, skim the article titled Integrating Language and Content Instruction and note a few additional strategies. (This article is a good resource to use for fresh ideas throughout your teaching.) (b) Second, share the ideas generated within your small group. (c) Finally, circle a few ideas that will be your first priorities to implement.

1. Increase Comprehensibility

-
-
-

2. Increase Interaction

-
-
-

3. Increase Thinking/Study Skills

-
-
-

4. Develop Academic Language and Literacy

-
-
-

5. Make Connections

-
-
-

Developing an Integrated Lesson

Directions: Work in small groups of two or three and develop a lesson or unit that integrates language and content and, in particular, develops academic language and literacy skills in a science or social studies topic area. You may, of course, integrate other content areas such as math, art, or literature. The lesson/unit should extend over multiple days or weeks. Use the sample lessons at the end of the Deborah Short article as a model. When you are finished, check that you have incorporated the five criteria on the following checklist.

THEME:

LESSON TOPIC:

OBJECTIVES:
- **Content**

- **Language**
  Speaking/Listening
  Reading/Writing
  Structures

- **Thinking/Study skills**

- **Key Vocabulary**

LITERATURE:

MATERIALS:

(Continued, next page)

MOTIVATION/PREPARATION:

PRESENTATION:

PRACTICE/APPLICATION:

REVIEW/EVALUATION:

EXTENSION:

Adapted with permission from Short, D. (1991). *How to Integrate Language and Content Instruction: A Training Manual.* Washington DC: Center for Applied Linguistics.

Lesson Plan Checklist: Personal Lesson

<u>Directions:</u> Review the lesson that you have developed with your partner or small group and make notes below on how the lesson implements each of the five characteristics listed.

1. How does the lesson *increase comprehensibility* for English language learning students?

2. How does the lesson *increase interaction* among students, including ELLs?

3. How does the lesson *increase thinking and study skills* among students, including ELLs?

4. How does the lesson explicitly *develop academic language* for all students?

5. How does the lesson *make connections* to other learning and to students' lives and cultures?

Reflection: Personal Lesson

Directions: As soon as possible, teach your personal, integrated lesson to your students, then complete the reflection items below.

1. Overall, how did the lesson work for your students?

2. What part of the lesson worked particularly well?

3. Did any part of the lesson work less well? Why?

4. How did you assess student learning of the academic language and literacy skills taught in the lesson? How well did the students learn these skills?

5. What will you do differently next time you teach this lesson?

6. What did you learn from this lesson that you can apply to other lessons?

Outside Assignment #3

Directions:

The purpose of this assignment is to prepare a display for a "Poster Session" that will be conducted in Section 11. Your display will be based on your Personal Lesson developed above.

Poster Sessions are frequently held at conferences. Presenters prepare a display that shows selected aspects of their work on a bulletin board; sometimes the display is supplemented with samples of materials or handouts. The presenters also stand near the display to answer viewers' questions and to provide further information, but the display should be self-explanatory.

Your display should contain the following:

1. The topic of the lesson.

2. A visual overview of the main lesson activities.

3. At least one example of how the lesson developed academic language and literacy skills.

4. At least one example of how the lesson made connections for the students.

5. In Section 9, Assessment, we will add an example of a teacher-made assessment.

In Section 11, your display will be viewed by others and some displays will be selected for a short presentation to the class.

Enhancing English Language Learning in Elementary Classrooms

Study Guide

Section 8
Reading to Learn

Section 8
Reading to Learn

Goal

To develop strategies which help ELLs increase learning when reading in the content areas

Performance Objectives

- Use three guiding principles to enhance the ELL's learning when reading in the content areas.

Comparing Lessons

Traditional Delivery of Lesson	Lesson Illustrated in Example
Based on students using a textbook.	
Presents new vocabulary in text using written explanations occasionally accompanied by an illustration.	
Presents new content in text using written explanations occasionally accompanied by an illustration.	
Individuals work alone to read text, answer questions, and define vocabulary in writing.	
Teacher leads discussion, reviewing written answers to questions; one individual is asked to answer one question.	

Parts of a Flower Lesson
Grade 4 Science

<u>Objective</u>: Students will be able to identify the names of the basic parts of a flower.

<u>Materials</u>:

Large wall chart illustrating a flower with the parts labeled
Brown paper bags (lunch size) enough for each student
Cut flowers (chrysanthemum family works best; look for donations from local florists)
        enough for two per student
One potted flower plant
Black string or yarn
Large construction paper
Glue
Scissors
Markers

<u>Preparation</u>:

Pull a flower apart and drop its pieces in a brown paper lunch bag. Include a few black strings. Roll the top of the bag down so its contents are not visible. Repeat this until there is one bag for each student in the class.

Place the bags in a place where they can easily be seen by the students as they enter the classroom.

On the remaining flowers, thread an embroidery needle with several black strings. Pierce the bottom of each flower stem and pull the strings through to simulate roots.

Post the wall chart of the flower in the classroom where it can easily be seen by all students.

<u>Procedures</u>:

Provide each student with a flower from the large bunch. Hold the potted plant.

The teacher uses TPR (total physical response) technique to lead the class:

> <u>Teacher</u>: This is a flower. Look at your flower. Feel your flower.
> (Students look and feel.)

> <u>Teacher</u>: This is the stem. (Teacher indicates stems.) Show me the stem
> of your flower. (Students show teacher their stems.) Feel the stem. Tell
> me how the stem feels. (Students provide adjectives that describe the
> stem.)

> Teacher: This is the leaf. Show me your leaf. Feel the leaf. Two of them are leaves. See, one leaf; two leaves. Tell me how the leaf feels. (Students provide adjectives.)

> Teacher: Show me the stem. (Students show; teacher then indicates her stem.) Show me the leaf. (Students show.) Show me the leaves. (Students show.)

> Teacher: This is the petal of the flower. Touch your petals. Tell me what color the petals are. (Students answer.)

> Teacher: Show me the leaves. (Students show.) Show me the stem. (Students show.) Show me the petals. (Students show.)

Teacher repeats this process until all the parts of the flower have been discussed. When she comes to the roots, she pulls up the potted flower she has to reveal the roots. She shows that the black strings the students have on the bottom of their flowers represent the roots.

Teacher moves to the wall chart of the flower. Teacher renames the parts of the flower one by one by indicating the parts on the real flower, then pointing to the drawing, then pointing to the written word labeling the flower part.

Teacher provides each student with a large piece of construction paper, glue and markers.

Teacher gives each student a brown paper bag.

Teacher models by opening a bag and pouring its contents onto a piece of construction paper.

> Teacher: Look! Here are the parts of our flowers. But we need to put these flowers back together. It's like a puzzle. Put your flower together on your paper. (Teacher demonstrates.) Then use the glue to stick the pieces to the paper. (Teacher demonstrates.) After that, write the names of the parts of the flower on your paper. (Teacher demonstrates.)

Students work in small groups or pairs to complete the task.

Teacher then directs students to the science textbook. Students work in small groups or pairs and read the section of the text that presents the parts of the flower.

In the next step of the lesson, students will learn the functions and purposes of the parts of the flower.

Parts of a Flower

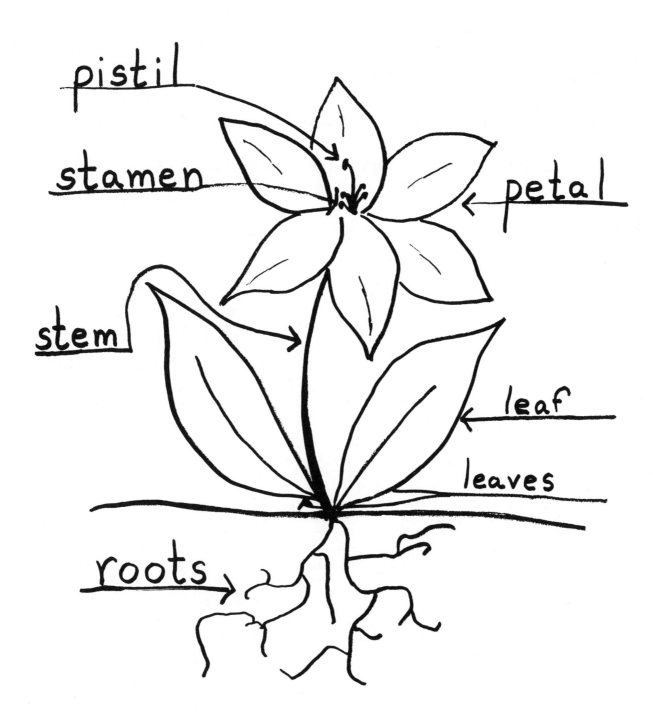

pistil

stamen

petal

stem

leaf

leaves

roots

SECTION 8

Increase Comprehensibility

How did the lesson –

move from prior knowledge to new knowledge?

move from concrete to abstract?

move from oral language to written language to text?

move from more context support to less context support?

Tips For Selecting Groups or Students to Share

Groups can be designated by colors, numbers, letters, shapes, animal figures, the variety is possibly endless. Certainly the theme of the group designations can be tailored to fit the instructional content. For younger children who have yet to learn to read, designating groups by colors uses a visual clue while practicing their colors. Varying how groups are designated during the school year helps keep cooperative activities familiar, but new and interesting.

Within the groups, individuals should receive a designation as well. It's easiest to give them numbers or letters, but creative teachers find ways to integrate content into the groupings as well.

Once each group has a designation and each individual has a designation, the teacher has a wide variety of ways to choose participants:

1. Put the designations in a receptacle (a hat, a bowl, a bucket, a plastic pumpkin, a holiday bag, etc.). You will need two separate ones: the first for the group designations and the second for the individual designations. Draw from the receptacle to choose participants.

2. Create a spinner and spin for participants.

3. Create an overhead grid with the numbers or colors covering the entire grid. Spin an object on the overhead (a coin, top, die). Where the object lands designates the participant.

4. Write the designations on ping-pong balls. Place the balls in a brown paper bag with a small hole cut in the bottom. Shake the bag and let one ball fall out of the hole. The group (or individual) whose designation is written on the ball participates.

Cooperative Writing Activity
Question Spinners or Dice

Question spinners can be purchased at teacher supply stores or can be teacher made. They can be used on the overhead projector when prepared on laminate film or can be made on tag board for individual student use.

To make a question spinner, draw two circles side by side on a piece of heavy paper or overhead laminate film. Draw lines to divide each circle pie style into six pieces. Poke a hole in the center of each circle and affix a spinner arrow which can be purchased in the teacher supply store. If no spinner arrows are available, place a thumb tack with the point up and glue onto the paper or overhead. Use a large paperclip as the spinner by looping the end of the paperclip onto the upthrust tack. Hammer down the upthrust tack a bit for safety, but leave enough so the paperclip can spin freely.

Write one of the following words in each of the six divisions of the pie circle on the left side of the overhead. (Write a different word in each of the six divisions.) What? Who? Which? Where/When? Why? How?

Write one of the following words in each of the six divisions of the pie circle on the right side of the overhead. Is? Can? Would? Will? Might? Did?

Question dice can be made by making paper cubes. For each pair of dice, use two different colors.

On the six sides of the first cube, write these words. (Write a different word on each of the six sides.) What? Who? Which? Where/When? Why? How?

On the six sides of the second cube, write these words. Is? Can? Would? Will? Might? Did?

The activity is a cooperative writing activity. Students will work in fours. Each group of four needs one pen or pencil, one piece of paper and one set of spinners or dice. Have each member of each group number off 1, 2, 3, & 4.

Person number 1 begins with the paper and pencil. Person number 3 begins by spinning the spinners (or tossing the dice). The group talks together to use the words that come up to make a question about the lesson. When the group decides on the question, person number 1 writes the question on the piece of paper.

The paper is passed to person number 2. Person number 2 must read the question aloud to the group and proof the question, making any written corrections necessary.

The spinners (or dice) are passed to person number 4.

Person number 4 spins (or tosses), the group decides on a question, person number 2 writes it down, and the roles continue to rotate until the teacher calls time.

At that point the spinners (or dice) are set aside. Now the groups must reread the questions they have written and write answers.

Starting with the person who is next in line for a turn (for example, person number 3), the person rereads the first question written. The group discusses an answer. When the group agrees on an answer, person number 3 writes a sentence that answers the question. The paper is then passed to person number 4. That person must proof the sentence written. Then that person reads the next question on the paper. The group discusses, and the process continues until all questions are answered in writing.

The teacher collects the paper.

As an alternative, students can exchange papers after the questions are written. The groups then read and answer the questions written by another group.

Cooperative Writing Activity
Why?

This writing activity can be used after most any lesson. It is a cooperative activity designed to foster positive interaction using higher-level thinking skills.

Teacher preparation for the activity

1. The teacher writes simple, thought-provoking questions about the content. The questions should begin with the word "why" for this activity. The questions should cause thinking, inference, supposition, imagining, and discussion on the part of the students as opposed to simple recall of information from the song.

2. The teacher prepares the questions on overhead. It is better to use overhead rather than the board so questions can be displayed one by one. That way the cooperative groups will concentrate on each question one by one, and the teacher can monitor the time spent on each question. Questions need to be clearly written or typed. Consider putting each question on a separate overhead for greater emphasis.

Procedures for the activity

1. Students work in groups of four during this activity. Each group has overheads to write on and one overhead marker for the group.

2. Assign each member of the group a number: 1, 2, 3, or 4.

3. Display the first question on the overhead. Tell the class to read it aloud in chorus.

4. The group discusses an answer to the question. The group needs to come to a consensus on what their group's answer will be for the question. No one writes during the discussion. The teacher should allow 1 to 3 minutes for discussion and consensus. Alert the groups when 1 minute is remaining.

5. Discussions stop. The overhead sheet is passed to person #1. With coaching from the other members of the group, that person writes an answer for the group onto the overhead. When it is written, the overhead is passed to person #2, who initials to signal agreement with the answer. Then it is passed to person #3, then #4, who do the same.

6. The teacher chooses a group to bring their answer to the overhead. The group reads the answer in chorus.

7. The teacher leads a debriefing of the answer written for **content and analysis of thinking**. Penmanship, spelling, and other errors that do not prohibit the understanding of the intended message are overlooked, since the purpose of the activity is to stimulate

thinking and a desire to communicate ideas through a written message.

8. The teacher congratulates the groups on their successful cooperation and displays the next question. The process continues.

Sample "WHY" questions for the song "Sweet Betsy from Pike"

(This song and these questions would nicely complement a unit studying the pioneers.)

Why do you think that pioneers like Ike and Betsy were so willing to endure such major hardships in order to move west?

Why did Ike and Betsy take the cow?

Why do you think Ike was willing to turn around and return home?

Why do you think Betsy was so determined to continue west?

Why did the pioneers travel in groups rather than alone?

Why would crossing a river be a dangerous thing for Ike and Betsy to do?

Why would climbing and crossing mountain ranges be a difficult thing for the pioneers to do?

Why would moving a family west in the days of the pioneers be so much more difficult than moving a family west today?

Sweet Betsy From Pike

Oh, do you remember sweet Betsy from Pike

Who crossed the wide prairies with her husband Ike

With two yoke of oxen and one spotted hog,

A tall shanghai rooster, an old yellow dog?

(Chorus)
Sing too ra li oo ra li oo ra li ay
Sing too ra li oo ra li oo ra li ay

The alkali desert was burning and bare

And Ike cried in fear, "We are lost, I declare!

My dear old Pike County, I'll go back to you."

Said Betsy, "You'll go by yourself if you do."

(Chorus)
Sing too ra li oo ra li oo ra li ay
Sing too ra li oo ra li oo ra li ay

They swam the wide rivers and crossed the tall peaks.

They camped on the prairie for weeks upon weeks.

They fought with the Indians with musket and ball.

They reached California in spite of it all.

(Chorus)
Sing too ra li oo ra li oo ra li ay
Sing too ra li oo ra li oo ra li ay

Using Graphic Organizers

Graphic organizers can be used to enhance reading comprehension and stimulate writing. The visual nature of a graphic organizer allows all students an option for understanding the message in text in addition to simply reading it. In the technique presented here, any graphic organizer that accurately reflects the relationship it is depicting from the song can be chosen and used. It is the sequence of instruction that is important in this technique. Choosing a few good graphic organizers to use repeatedly in the classroom rather than presenting a different one each time will allow students to become comfortable with their use and further aid in comprehension. It also cuts down on presentation time for a new activity when the graphic organizer is recycled from previous lessons.

Follow these steps when using a graphic organizer with a song as a stimulus to writing:

1. Choose a graphic organizer that is appropriate for the song. The graphic organizer must visually and accurately reflect the relationship it is depicting.

2. Present schema activities which develop vocabulary and background knowledge for the song. Visuals are especially helpful to students with limited language and/or reading ability.

3. Provide students with a copy of the written words to the song. (You may choose to use an overhead display at first and give out individual copies in later activities. This way in the next step, you can point to the words as they are sung to encourage everyone to follow along.)

4. Play the song as the students follow along.

5. Provide discussion activities to develop the meaning from the song. Replay the song and encourage students to sing along, to say the words along with the song rather than sing, or at least to follow the words as they are sung.

6. Display the graphic organizer. The goal of the teacher is to allow students to become progressively independent in their use of graphic organizers. The teacher should start by showing students graphic organizers that have been completed, then selecting the graphics but having students fill them in, then guiding the class in selecting graphics, and finally having students work in groups to determine their own graphics. It takes time and practice for students to learn to use them well.

7. Have the students work in pairs. Use a pair share activity (one student talks while the other listens and gives feedback; then the second student talks while the first student listens and gives feedback; and so on until time is up) to have the students generate language using the graphic organizer as a guide.

8. Have the students write from the graphic organizers. Students can be asked to use the

graphic organizer to write a list of complete sentences or to organize an essay. They can make individual points in random order or sequence events. They can summarize the song, retell the events, or simply organize the information in a way that is easier for them to understand.

9. Have the students peer edit their writing.

10. Have the students share their writing (Author's Chair, Pair Share, Inside/Outside Circle, for example).

11. Replay and sing the song often. Songs students have learned can be played while students are arriving in the morning, cleaning up after activities, as transitions between lessons. There are many, many opportunities during the school day to have students sing along with a song they have learned. (Work time is not a good time to play these songs, as students trying to concentrate on an academic task may be distracted by a song they want to sing. Work time is a good time to play soft instrumental music.)

Language and Literature Activities
to use with CAUSE AND EFFECT graphic organizer

Use a graphic organizer which shows cause and effect of events in the song. A sample is included at the end of this section. Follow the steps outlined for using graphic organizers to improve reading comprehension and stimulate writing. The following activities can be adapted for use with a variety of songs. They can also be adapted for use in content subjects.

Rudolph the Red Nosed Reindeer

When the graphic organizer is supplied, have the first two "cause" blanks filled in. Leave the next two empty. Display the graphic organizer on the overhead. Have students work in pairs for this activity.

1. Read the first cause. Ask students to turn to their pair and (quietly) discuss the cause and determine what the effect was.

2. Choose a pair to report what they determined was the effect. Write the effect on the graphic organizer. (Students should fill in their copy, too.)

3. Ask if any pairs came up with a different effect for the same cause. Discuss other possibilities if necessary.

4. Repeat the process for the second cause.

5. Now point to the next cause blank which is empty. Ask students to turn to their pair and discuss another event from the song that caused something else to happen. Have them fill in the cause and the effect on their graphic organizer.

6. Choose several pairs to share their ideas and write them on the overhead copy.

For the writing activity, have students use their graphic organizers to write sentences. Point out words that show cause/effect relationships. For example:

> Rudolph's nose was red, so the other reindeer called him names.

(Point out that when you use "so," the first phrase is the *cause* and the second is the *effect*.)

> Santa was worried about the trip because it was so foggy.

(Point out that when you use "because," the first phrase is the *effect* and the second is the *cause*.)

English has many ways to express cause and effect, and depending on the connecting word, the order of cause and effect in the sentence varies. Showing some examples of connecting words and pointing out their use may help:

The "cause" is the first part of the sentence when you use connecting words like these:

>   so, consequently, therefore, as a result

The "effect" is the first part of the sentence when you use connecting words like these:

>   because, due to the fact that, due the reason that

The Cause & Effect graphic organizer is a great way to explore the construction of these sentences and their meanings.

SECTION 8

Cause - Effect Chart

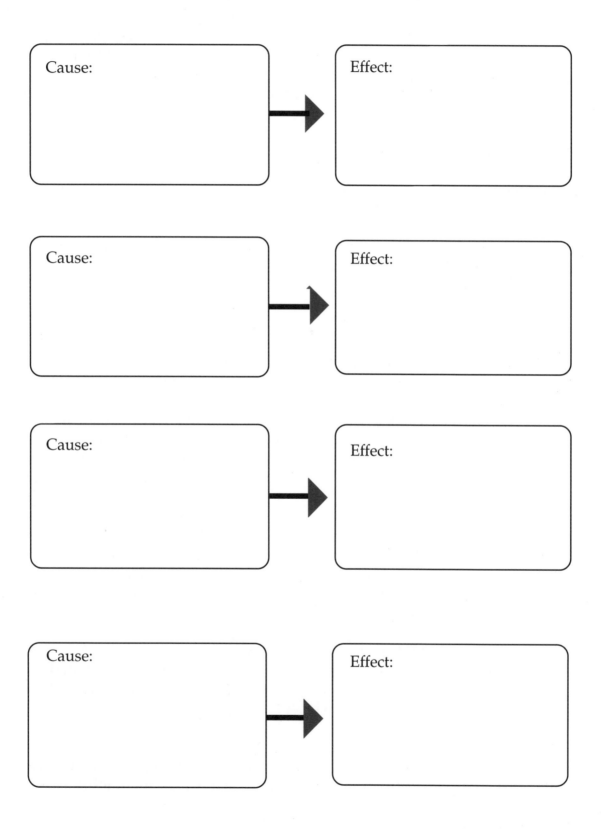

SECTION 8

Language and Literacy Activities to use with NARRATIVE ESSAY graphic organizer

Songs are a great way to introduce students to the structure of a narrative essay. Repeated use of the same graphic organizer with a variety of songs during the school year will reinforce the structure you are working with here. How to use the graphic organizer will depend on the grade level of the students. A completed and a blank sample graphic organizer for narrative essays are included.

Rudolph the Red Nosed Reindeer

A sample graphic organizer has been completed at the end of this section for the song "Rudolph the Red Nosed Reindeer."

**Note that when this example is used as a reading activity, it starts with number 3. When it is used as a writing activity, it starts with number 1.

Here are some suggestions for using it:

Grade 1: Fill in and point out only main sections on the graphic (problem; first, second, and third events; climax; and solution). You may discuss details and feelings, but use the basic shell as an introduction at this grade.
Remember, writing starts as reading. Provide the students with an introduction to narrative writing by pointing out as often as possible during the school year the narrative structure many stories and songs follow. Ask students to begin writing stories on their own following this basic structure after several songs and/or stories have been shared with students using it.

Grade 2: Provide students with a completed copy of the graphic organizer. Discuss each sequential event on it (start with number 3 since this is a reading activity). Point out the basic structure first; then point out the details for each event. Discuss the "feeling" included along with the two details.
Remember, writing starts as reading. Use this graphic organizer as often as possible during the school year to point out the structure that many stories and songs follow. Ask students to complete the main sections on it (problem; first, second, third events; climax; and solution) on their own using a variety of songs and/or stories often. Encourage students to use the main sections of the graphic organizer when planning stories they write.

Grades 3 and up: Provide students with a completed copy of the graphic organizer the first few times it is used. Discuss each sequential event on it (start with number 3 since this is a reading activity). Point out the basic structure first; then point out the details for each event. Discuss the "feeling" included along with the two details.

Provide students with a partially completed page the next few times the graph organizer is used and ask them to fill in the blank parts. Providing the details and asking them to provide the event is a good place to start. Then switch.

Finally, after they have used the graphic organizer several times, have them fill it out themselves using a song or story.

Encourage students to use the graphic organizer when planning the writing of their own stories.

Example: Rudolph the Red-Nosed Reindeer

NARRATIVE GRAPHIC ORGANIZER

7. CLIMAX: It was very foggy on Christmas Eve. Santa couldn't see well enough to fly his sleigh.

6. WHAT HAPPENED THEN? The other reindeer didn't let Rudolph play.

DETAIL 1 They didn't invite Rudolph.

DETAIL 2 They found ways to exclude him.

FEELING Rudolph felt left out.

8. SOLUTION Santa asked Rudolph for help.

DETAIL 1 His nose was bright.

DETAIL 2 Santa needed the light.

FEELING Rudolph felt proud.

5. WHAT HAPPENED NEXT? The other reindeer laughed at Rudolph.

DETAIL 1 They laughed right in front of him.

DETAIL 2 They called Rudolph names.

FEELING Rudolph was unhappy.

9. ENDING: Rudolph's red nose was a benefit and very special.

(ENDING SHOULD RETURN TO PROMPT)

4. WHAT HAPPENED FIRST? Rudolph was born with a red nose.

DETAIL 1 His nose was a shiny red.

DETAIL 2 His nose glowed brightly.

FEELING He felt embarassed because he was the only reindeer with a red nose.

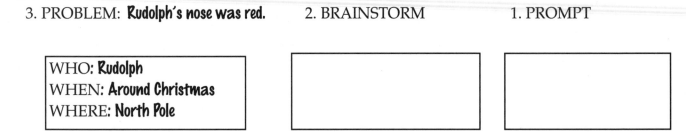

3. PROBLEM: Rudolph's nose was red.

WHO: Rudolph
WHEN: Around Christmas
WHERE: North Pole

2. BRAINSTORM

1. PROMPT

Enhancing English Language Learning in Elementary Classrooms
Study Guide Section 8: Reading to Learn

SECTION 8

Narrative Graphic Organizer

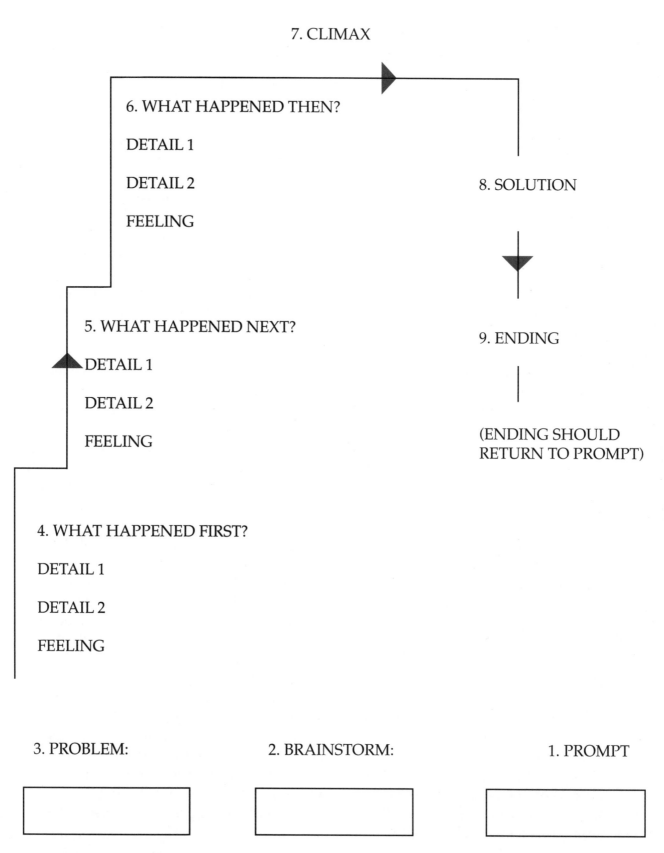

7. CLIMAX

6. WHAT HAPPENED THEN?

DETAIL 1

DETAIL 2

FEELING

8. SOLUTION

5. WHAT HAPPENED NEXT?

DETAIL 1

DETAIL 2

FEELING

9. ENDING

(ENDING SHOULD
RETURN TO PROMPT)

4. WHAT HAPPENED FIRST?

DETAIL 1

DETAIL 2

FEELING

3. PROBLEM:

2. BRAINSTORM:

1. PROMPT

Content Reading Instruction in the Primary Grades: Perceptions and Strategies

by Mary W. Olson and Thomas C. Gee
The Reading Teacher, December 1991.

Schools provide young readers in the primary grades with instruction in numerous content subjects. Even in the first grade when most children are just beginning to read, they are given content textbooks with the expectation that they will learn some of the content by reading. In fact, many schools commonly ask and expect beginning readers to read and learn from science, health, and social studies textbooks–an expectation that continues throughout their schooling.

Young children need to develop proficiency with simple expository texts in order to keep pace with the ever increasing number of subject area textbooks they will experience now and as they progress through school. Although primary–age children are certainly building knowledge about the world through daily experiences, they often have difficulty when confronted with information in content textbooks. For example, children may be learning about life, earth, and physical science in and out of school through discovery, experimentation, and observation. Learning novel or additional science information through expository text, however, may be particularly onerous for some children (Alvermann & Boothby, 1982; Olson, 1985).

A number of factors account for young children's difficulties with expository text. Limited background knowledge to link with new information hampers comprehension. Texts written to inform rather than to entertain may lower motivation for some children. Unfamiliar text organizational structures are difficult to follow. Writing that lacks logical connectives and transition words requires increased cognitive effort. An inability to recognize many words in print hinders comprehension, particularly for young readers. If teachers consider the cognitive burden such texts make on young children, it becomes obvious they need much guidance and many experiences reading expository text in order to deal successfully with content books.

A number of practices for helping secondary students read content materials have been offered in content reading textbooks authored by such writers as Criscoe and Gee (1984), Readence, Bean, and Baldwin (1989), and Vacca and Vacca (1986). Suggestions are given to help students develop background knowledge, understand unfamiliar text organizational patterns, learn new vocabulary associated with the content, and overcome other challenges associated with content materials. Many of the practices have been validated as effective through empirical research. Alvermann and Moore's (1991) and Alvermann and Swafford's (1989) reviews, for example, found that activating background knowledge before reading increased children's awareness of information they already had and helped them link new information to their existing framework of knowledge.

Informed opinion and empirical research aimed at developing content reading skills have been aimed mostly at upper elementary and secondary readers. Very little work has been focused on beginning readers. This article, therefore, has two purposes: (a) to share commonly recommended practices primary teachers find helpful in developing their children's content reading skills, and (b) to suggest specific strategies that represent the general practices these teachers find useful.

Enhancing English Language Learning in Elementary Classrooms
Study Guide Section 8: Reading to Learn

A survey

We asked 47 primary-grade classroom teachers–14 first-grade teachers, 15 second-grade teachers, and 18 third-grade teachers from school districts in southwest Texas, central North Carolina, and central Florida–to respond to a survey. The survey asked, "How helpful have you found these 17 'recommended' practices to be in helping your students to learn to read expository texts?"

The 17 general practices (see Table) we included in the survey were selected because they are representative of the advice content reading textbook authors give, are grounded in empirical research, or represent long-standing practice. For example, reviews of secondary school reading have found research supporting the use of study guides, questions, graphic overviews, summarizing, outlining, previewing vocabulary, and imagery (Alvermann & Moore, 1991; Alvermann & Swafford, 1989). Activating prior knowledge (Anderson & Pearson, 1984) and retelling (Gambrall, Pfeiffer, & Wilson, 1985) are also supported by research. Using a glossary, SQ3R, cloze passages, audio or computer materials, and reading aloud to students are additional practices advocated by content textbook authors (e.g., Criscoe & Gee, 1984; Readence, Bean & Baldwin, 1989). Using manipulatives, narratives on content topics, and role playing are common classroom practices we have observed.

Teachers' response to the survey

The participating elementary schools had adopted content textbooks in primary classrooms and expected their teachers to use them. The districts' reading/language arts coordinators administered the survey to the primary teachers during faculty meetings. The teachers were asked to indicate whether content textbooks were easier or harder than stories for their students; to list factors they believed made content materials difficult for students; and to rate 17 general practices as to their usefulness in helping primary children comprehend content textbooks. We tallied the results and computed percentages for the responses.

Results of this survey indicated that primary teachers recognize that the expository texts that typically occur in their content textbooks are more difficult for children to read than stories: 70% of the teachers found content texts more difficult than stories; 27.4% found the texts about the same level of difficulty; and 2.6% thought content textbooks were easier for children to read than stories.

Earlier we cited five reasons for young children's difficulties with expository texts. The teacher's responses reflected these same problems: 36 of the 47 (77%) teachers believed that difficulty with new concepts was a major factor that caused children to find expository texts difficult; 10 (21%) teachers also thought children were not interested in expository texts; 11 (23%) of the teachers said that text characteristics such as sentence length, page format, inadequate presentation of topic and lack of aids on how to read expository texts presented the greatest problems; 32 (69 %) teachers responded that primary grade children could not read the texts because they did not know the words.

Of special interest to us were the teachers' ratings of 17 general teaching practices as to their helpfulness to children reading content material (see Table). The six highest rated practices, which the teachers identified as offering "outstanding help," were previewing concepts and vocabulary (77%), using concrete manipulatives to develop concepts (73%), requiring retellings (71%), developing summaries (56%), visualizing information (49%), and brainstorming (45%). In fact, when the "outstanding help" and "very good help" ratings were collapsed, these first six strategies were identified by 85% of the teachers. The teachers thought the following practices provided little or no help: (a) providing partial outlines; (b) searching for the who, what, when, where, how, and why of passages; (c) using a study guide; (d) turning chapter titles and headings into questions to answer as they read; or (e) providing a graphic overview prior to reading.

Strategies for primary children

The six practices noted previously that were rated as providing "outstanding" or "very good" help by at least 85% of the teachers guided our selection of content reading strategies to recommend to primary teachers. We were also guided in our selections by empirically-or theoretically-validated strategies that reflect these practices. Having research or theoretical support along with teacher consensus argues for their use in primary classrooms.

Table
Content reading strategies for primary students

1 = Provides outstanding help   2 = Provides very good support
3 = Provides some help   4 = Provides little or no help

(Percent of responses)

	1	2	3	4
1. Preview vocabulary/concepts	77%	19%	4%	0%
2. Manipulations (maps, pictures, etc.)	73%	21%	6%	0%
3. Retelling	71%	23%	4%	2%
4. Individual or class summary	56%	25%	17%	2%
5. Visualization	49%	38%	11%	2%
6. Brainstorming	45%	40%	13%	2%
7. Narratives on same content topic	40%	45%	9%	6%
8. Audio or computer materials	36%	52%	6%	6%
9. Act/role play	30%	28%	36%	6%
10. Graphic overview	30%	36%	13%	21%
11. SQ3R	28%	21%	30%	21%
12. Glossary use	28%	23%	32%	17%
13. Study Guide	23%	37%	17%	23%
14. Partial outline	17%	13%	28%	42%
15. Read aloud; students follow along	17%	30%	47%	6%
16. Cloze passages	11%	23%	51%	15%
17. Who, what, when, where, how, why	11%	43%	25%	21%

$n = 47$

The instructional strategies described next may reflect more than one of the general practices rated effective by teachers. In fact, the strategy we chose to illustrate each practice may accommodate several recommended practices. For example, semantic mapping includes opportunities for children to brainstorm about a topic as well as preview vocabulary and concepts. As we discuss each strategy we will link it to the appropriate general practices.

Semantic mapping

Children learn new words and concepts effectively when they can relate them to words or notions they already understand. Semantic mapping (see Figure 1) can be an effective strategy emphasizing brainstorming and previewing vocabulary and concept development by graphically displaying words in categories, showing how they are related to one another (Johnson, 1984). It is important to remember that the active participation of the children and the ensuing discussion are critical components of semantic mapping. The following steps allow the creation of a semantic map:

1. After reviewing the passage, the teacher selects a word that represents the major theme or subject of the section or chapter.
2. The teacher writes the subject word on the chalkboard or on a large chart.
3. The children brainstorm as many words as they can that are related to the selected word. This can be done in small groups or as a whole class activity. If small groups are used, one child in each group records the group's efforts. As the children think of words, they should help the recorder group the words into categories. If this step is a whole class activity, the teacher is the recorder.
4. The children in small groups share their lists with the whole class as the teacher writes them on the chalkboard or chart using broad categories. At any point, the teacher may add additional words that will be necessary to understand the passage.
5. The teacher simultaneously leads a discussion as words are entered on the semantic map, discussing aspects of the theme word.
6. After the map is completed and the textbook is read, new information may be added to the map. New information could be in different colored print to highlight what was learned from reading the textbook. The discussion and questions the tacher asks as the map is completed are the heart of the strategy. Because of the differences among children's experiences, some disagreements may occur; however , the teacher simply changes or eliminates words as necessary.

Figure 1
Sample semantic map
for a science selection on hawks

K-W-L: What I know, What I want to learn, What I learned

Another strategy that helps children combine new information with prior knowledge to build concepts and vocabulary is K-W-L (Ogle, 1986). K-W-L includes opportunities for children to brainstorm, to preview vocabulary and concepts, and to retell what they read. The strategy also creates purposes for reading the assigned text. Ogle (1989) argues that using K-W-L allows teachers to model the procedures children should use when reading content texts. With teacher support, we believe K-W-L can be used in the primary grades.

The teacher first has children divide a paper into three columns, or the teacher

SECTION 8

draws three columns on the board (see Figure 2). Then the teacher asks the children to brainstorm what they already know about the main topic of the reading selection, recording that information in the first column. As the teacher records the children's contributions, he or she helps them organize the information before they read the assigned text.

Figure 2
K-W-L worksheet for a science selection on toads

K What we know	W What we want to find out	L What we learned and still need to learn
Toads (1). small animal (1.) gray (1.) has a long tongue (3.) jumps (3.) spits poison (2.) eats bugs (2.) eats spiders Categories (1.) description (2.) food (3.) what toads do	Are toads the same as frogs? If not, how are they different? Where do toads live in the winter? In the summer? What do toads eat? How do toads protect themselves? How far can they jump?	

Next, the teacher points out gaps or disagreements in the recorded information which the teacher and children transform into purposes for reading. The children may also formulate their own questions, writing them in column two. After reading, children retell and review what they learned from the test, return to any purpose questions, identify questions that were not addressed, and record new information in column three.

Concrete manipulatives and experiences

Most children in the primary grades learn best when concrete experiences are part of the learning activity (Bruner, 1966; Piaget, 1926). The primary teachers in our survey strongly supported the use of concrete manipulatives to reinforce learning–including concrete examples, hands-on experiences, and simulated models. Using manipulatives provides for vocabulary and concept development and enhances visualizations.

The teachers noted they used films and educational games to make content reading about any subject easier for their students. They used discovery techniques and experiments in science, maps and scaled models in social studies, manipulatives in math class, and concrete models in health class. More specifically, teachers can create terrariums and aquariums to understand earth science concepts, or they might cover a lighted candle to discover that fire needs oxygen. Teachers may build topographical maps to illustrate geographical terms; set up a store for children to become fluent in monetary terms and concepts; or take field trips to transform social studies concepts and words into meaningful experiences.

It is important to provide concrete experiences *with discussions* so children have a better chance of understanding concepts in content texts. Subject area teacher manuals or district curriculum materials usually have descriptions of concrete manipulatives and experiences. We suggest those activities and accompanying discussions precede reading the textbook because they build or augment conceptual background necessary for full text comprehension.

Expository paragraph frames

When children retell what they have read, comprehension is improved. Expository paragraph frames provide children practice retelling. Helping children develop a schemata for expository paragraph structures enhances their retellings (Taylor, 1982; Taylor & Samuels, 1983). Teachers can use expository paragraph frames "to review and reinforce specific content and to familiarize students with the different ways in which authors organize material in order to inform" (Cudd & Roberts, 1989, p.392).

Ideas in content textbooks can be organized in several ways. Piccolo (1987) identifies five basic expository text structures; *descriptive patterns* (a topic is introduced followed by its attributes); *sequence patterns* (a topic is introduced and followed by details that need to be presented in order); cause/effect patterns (an action and its effects are revealed); *comparison / contrast patterns* (two or more things are compared and contrasted); and *problem/solution* (a problem is introduced and followed by a solution). The following steps illustrate how to use expository paragraph frames.

First the teacher uses the textbook selection to be read to create a paragraph frame for the review (see examples in Figure 3.) Next the teacher has the children read the selection, after

Figure 3
Sample expository paragraph frames

Sequence frame (Based on a passage about how cloth is made.)
I learned many interesting things about how cloth is made.
First I learned that _____
_____
Next, I learned that, _____
_____
Third, I learned that _____
_____
Finally, I learned that _____
_____
As you can see, it is interesting to learn how cloth is made.

Contrast frame (Based on a passage comparing oceans and lakes.)
Oceans and lakes are different in several ways. They are different in size. Oceans are
_____ than lakes. Their water is different too. Ocean water is
_____ while lake water is _____ . Different
kinds of fish live in oceans and lakes. _____ and _____ fish
live only in ocean water while _____ and _____ fish
live only in lakes. It is interesting to learn how oceans and lakes are different.

which each child retells the selection to a partner. The teacher then presents the paragraph frame, asks students to fill in missing information, and invites them to again recall information that is missing from the frame. As they supply the missing information, they are developing a well-structured expository paragraph that restates the information in the text they have read. Figure 3 presents a sequence frame for a passage about cloth is made and a contrast frame based on a passage contrasting oceans and lakes.

Group summarizing

Teachers reported that developing class summaries helped children review and remember information–a sound practice which requires readers to understand and condense information (Brown, Day, & Jones, 1983). A modified version of Farris's (1988) strategy for research writing can be used to prepare summaries. For example, prior to reading about armadillos, the class might decide to read for descriptions of armadillos, information about armadillos' food and homes, and interesting facts about armadillos. The teacher then has the children divide the chalkboard into four parts and label the sections "Description," "Food," "Home," and "Interesting Facts." The sections on the chalkboard provide the children with a purpose for reading. After the children read the text, the teacher asks the class to volunteer information for each of the categories on the chalkboard, recording the information in sentence form (see Figure 4). As the information is recorded, the teacher encourages discussion. The teacher then helps the students develop class summaries from

---

Figure 4
Sample organizational format for group summarizing activity

Description	*Food*
Nine-banded armadillos are about 2 feet long and weigh about 15 pounds.	Armadillos eat insects, earthworms, spiders, and land snails by licking them up.
They have strong claws for digging and a shell of hard bony plates for protection.	
Home	*Interesting facts*
Armadillos live in a tunnel hole filled with leaves to keep them warm.	Armadillos protect themselves by digging a hole or curling up into a ball. They have four babies at a time that are all males or females.

---

the recorded information. Summarizing is a sophisticated skill; therefore, this strategy will probably require a great deal of support and modeling by the teacher.

Visual imagery

Creating mental images of text content is recommended for improving comprehension (Gambrell, Kapinus, & Wilson, 1987). Primary teachers in our survey also believe helping children make visual images in their minds enhances comprehension. Mental images can be created during or after the reading of a text.

Teacher modeling of the process of creating mental images helps children acquire this ability. To do this, describe the content of a text, talking about any associations that come to mind as you read it aloud. Alternately, you can read the text aloud and describe the imagery process after reading the passage. Children can be encouraged to form their own mental pictures along with the teacher, sharing their thoughts as they visualize the information. Children can then read a passage themselves and imagine the contents of the selection. Verbalizing the process to a partner helps children focus on the content of the text.

Here's an example of this process. In an account of how wool was used to make cloth in past years, a teacher might first discuss what the text was about. The teacher then asks the children to read the step-by-step account of the process: Shearing the sheep; washing, carding, and spinning the wool into yarn; and weaving the yarn to make cloth. The teacher next reads the passage aloud, thinking aloud about images that come to mind– images of wool being processed in the home, the slowness of the process, the lack of power tools to do the work, and the pride a family took in producing cloth to deep themselves warm. The children are also invited to participate in this imaging. The visual images generated in this process can help children link their prior experiences to the new ideas, thus building richer schemata for the topic. Richer schemata will, in turn, provide the foundation for greater understanding the next time the same or related content is read.

Summary

Because the amount and diversity of expository text reading increases significantly for children as they grow older, we believe it is important to provide sound and effective instruction for young children when they read content textbooks. In fact, to learn how to learn from content books requires many experiences with those texts. The skills and habits children acquire with primary level content texts will help them as the number and diversity of texts increase in later grades.

Results of our survey revealed that primary grade readers have problems similar to those older readers have in reading content materials, specifically problems in understanding vocabulary, concepts, and text organization. Teachers in our sample identified six areas of general instructional practices as effective in helping their students read content passages. Specific teaching strategies were described that reflect the general practices teachers believe are helpful to primary children and have a research or sound theoretical base.

Mary W. Olson is Professor and Associate Dean of the School of Education at the University of North Carolina at Greensboro. Thomas C. Gee is Professor of Education at the University of Houston at Clear Lake. Both have researched and written about content reading strategies.

SECTION 8

References

Alvermann, D.E., & Boothby, P.R. (1982). Text differences: Children's perceptions at the transition stage in reading. *The Reading Teacher*, 36, 298-302.

Alvermann, D.E. & Moore, D.W. (1991). Secondary school reading. In R. Barr (Ed.), *Handbook of reading research* (2nd ed.) (pp. 951-983).

Alvermann, D.E. & Swafford, J. (1989). Do content area strategies have a research base? *Journal of Reading*, 32, 388-394.

Anderson, R.C. & Pearson, P.D. (1984). A schematheoretic view of basic processes in reading. In P.D. Pearson (Ed.), *Handbook of reading research* (pp. 255-292). New York: Longman.

Brown, A.L., Day, J.D., & Jones, R. (1983). Learning to learn: On training students to learn from texts. *Educational Researcher*, 10, 14-24.

Bruner, J.S. (1966). *Toward a theory of instruction*. Cambridge, MA: Belknap Press of Harvard University.

Criscoe, B.L., & Gee, T.C. (1984). *Content reading: a diagnostic/prescriptive approach*. Englewood Cliffs, NJ: Prentice Hall.

Cudd, E.T., & Roberts, L. (1989). Using writing to enhance content learning in the primary grades. *The Reading Teacher*, 42, 392-405.

Farris, P. (1988). Developing research and writing skills in elementary and middle school students. *Florida Reading Quarterly*, 25(2), 6-9.

Gambrell, L., Kapinus, B.A., & Wilson, R.M. (1987). Using mental imagery and summarization to achieve independence in comprehension. *Journal of Reading*, 30, 638-642.

Gambrell, L., Pfeiffer, W., & Wilson, R. (1985). The effects of retelling upon reading comprehension and recall of text information. *Journal of Educational Research*, 78, 216-220.

Johnson, D.D. (1984). *Teaching reading vocabulary* (2nd ed.). New York: Holt, Rinehart and Winston.

Ogle, D.M. (1986). K-W-L: A teaching model that develops active reading of expository text. *The Reading Teacher*, 39, 564-570.

Ogle, D.M. (1989). The know, want to know, learned strategy. In K.D. Muth(Ed.), *Children's comprehension of text* (pp. 205-223). Newark, DE: International Reading Association.

Olson, M.W. (1985). Text type and reader ability: The effects of paraphrase and text-based inference questions. *Journal of Reading Behavior*, 17, 199-215.

Piaget, J. (1926). *The language and thought of the child*. London: Routledge & Kegan Paul Ltd.

Piccolo, J. (1987). Expository text structure: Teaching and learning strategies. *The Reading Teacher*, 40, 838-847.

Readence, J.E., Bean, T.W., & Baldwin, R.S. (1989). *Content area reading: An integrated approach* (3rd. ed.). Dubuque, IA: Kendall/Hunt.

Taylor, B.M., & Samuels, S.J. (1983). Children's use of text structure in the recall of expository material. *American Educational Journal*, 20, 517-528.

Vacca, R.T. & Vacca, J.L (1996). *Content area reading* (2nd, ed.). Boston, MA: Little, Brown.

Enhancing English Language Learning in Elementary Classrooms

Study Guide

Section 9
Assessment

Assessment

Goal

To learn to adapt traditional assessments and design alternative assessments to allow ELL
students opportunities to demonstrate their knowledge in the content areas.

Performance Objectives

• Compare and contrast classroom and standardized assessments.

• Identify and reduce language and cultural bias on classroom tests.

• Develop a practical alternative assessment for content material.

• Develop a rubric for evaluating student work.

• Develop personal guidelines for grading ESOL students in mainstream classrooms.

SECTION 9

Directions: Work in small groups to fill in the cells below. You will have 10 minutes.

Classroom vs. Standardized Assessments: Worksheet

	Classroom Assessments	Standardized Assessments
Examples:		
Purposes:		
Pros:		
Cons:		

SECTION 9

Testing English Language Learners

Standardized and Classroom Tests:

- Read the instructions out loud. Explain in the native language if necessary.

- Check students after a few minutes of test-taking to make sure they understood the instructions and are on track.

- Allow bilingual dictionaries which give direct translations (with minimal definitions).

- Teach test-taking skills and practice on sample items throughout instruction.

Classroom Assessments:

- Teach to the assessment; let students know in advance how achievement will be measured.

- Align instructional methods and assessment methods.

- Check comprehension frequently throughout instruction.

- Supplement tests with other measures of content understanding such as observation, participation, talking to students, alternative assignments like projects.

- Review tests "through the eyes of an ELL": look for difficult language and cultural bias; provide support such as word banks.

- Read tests to beginning ELLs.

- Allow more time for ELLs or give the test in sections.

Corn Lesson Assessment

Directions: Review the activities that will be assessed and work with a partner to complete items 1 and 2.

Objectives: Compare the uses of corn in two countries.
Use reference materials.

Activity:
(a) Distribute the chart to small groups and explain that students will examine corn in two states/countries. As a class, brainstorm additional categories to compare on the chart (e.g., if the country makes corn products–meal, oil, etc.) Then, in small groups, have students choose their two states/countries to examine and complete the chart, using reference materials and textbooks.
(b) Using their group chart, have students write a few sentences in their journals comparing the role of corn in the two states/countries.

Sample worksheet: Comparing the Role of Corn

Role of corn	(state/country name)	(state/country name)
name for corn		
source: produced or imported		
uses: food fodder		

1. List the most important criteria to assess these activities:
   a. Complete the chart using reference materials and textbooks.

   b. Using the group chart, write a few sentences comparing the role of corn in the two states/countries.

2. How will you make the assessment a learning experience?

3. How will you support beginning ELLs in this task?

Corn Lesson Rubric

Directions: Review your criteria for the Corn Lesson and revise them if necessary. Then, develop a four-level rubric and a form to record student achievement of the criteria. Sketch the form (incorporating the criteria for each level) below.

SECTION 9

Developing a Rubric

1. Identify Desired Results

- What should students *know* and *be able to do* at the end of the lesson/unit?

- Desired results are Essential Learnings from the unit. Teachers should plan units to teach essential learnings identified in state and national standards.

2. Determine Acceptable Evidence

a. What *performance* (task) will the students do?

- The performance should be designed to demonstrate that the student knows and is able to do the *essential learnings* of the unit (not just do nifty things).

- The performance should *integrate* and *apply* learning from the unit in a real life (or approximately real life) task (e.g., present a position to an authentic audience, gather and report data, design and conduct an experiment, solve a real life math problem).

b. What are the *criteria* for assessing the performance?

- The criteria should reflect the *most important* factors required to demonstrate achievement of the desired results.

    (1) What are the most important criteria?

    (2) What should the completed project look like? Is this a factor?

    (3) What will the student be expected to do to accomplish this task? Think step by step here. Should the process be a factor in the rubric?

- Weight the criteria if necessary.

- Determine levels of achievement of the criteria.

- Develop a form to record student achievement of the criteria.

- Make the rubric clear to the students when the assignment is given.

- Check with the students at intervals during their work to make sure they are on target.

- When possible, give students a chance to revise their "final draft" work so that it better meets the criteria of the rubric. (For example, hold a conference with a student before he turns his work in and jointly evaluate it using the rubric, then give the student an opportunity to improve his work before turning it in for the official assessment.)

- Involve students in developing rubrics when possible.

3. Plan Learning Experiences and Instruction to Lead to This Performance

Informal Assessment Techniques for Young Students or Beginning English Language Learners

Use pictures to assess vocabulary

Have students draw the concept

Ask students to point to the correct answer

Ask the student to paraphrase concepts

Allow students to explain orally

Allow oral reports instead of written ones

Have students develop a drama or role play

Allow students to record concepts on a graphic organizer or in a list instead of in an essay

Provide a word bank for beginning ELLs

Have students create a poster or display to demonstrate their understanding

Use a project for assessment

Use pair and group reports

Use Numbered Heads Together, Think-Pair-Share, and other cooperative techniques

Review student journals and notes

Maintain Reading Journals or Logs. At intervals, record three books at the student's reading level and attach a photocopy of a page from each book.

Allow the use of a bilingual dictionary

Other:

Practical Alternative Assessments for the Content Areas

1. Learning Logs and Journals

Each student keeps a journal which summarizes his learning in the class in his own words. A good way to start journals is for each student to write a one sentence summary of what he has learned at the end of each class period (or unit). The summaries in the journal create a personal record of learning over time. Teachers may need to teach students to write good summary statements and may wish to discuss sample summary statements occasionally to help students edit and improve their own.

Teachers can vary the contents of the students' learning journals by varying the prompts or sentence starters. Good sentence starters (for the students to complete) include:

> I learned ...
> I had reinforced ...
> I was reminded of ...
> I want to learn more about ...
> I think ...
> This topic made me wonder about ...
> What I really enjoyed was ...
> I didn't like ...

Journals can also be used for content-based dialogue between students and teachers. Themes or topics are selected from the curriculum and the student can ask questions, provide reflections on information learned, integrate concepts, synthesize material and more. The teacher responds to the student in writing and asks questions that will elicit more information. These journals provide an opportunity for students to combine their personal reflections with the information learned. The teacher can use these student contributions to assess the students' overall comprehension of content.

In learning journals or logs, teachers should focus on the meaning of the student communication and its indication of content understanding, not the mechanics of writing.

2. Role Play

Students role play characters from literature, social studies, or other relevant content areas. This provides an opportunity for the teacher to assess students' mastery of specific content, and an opportunity for students to use different skills, talents, and varieties of language in an interactive and meaningful context. Role plays need not simply enact known events, but can create responses to hypothetical situations that are consistent with known facts, such as a conversation between King George and Thomas Jefferson.

3. Student Self-Ratings

Students rate their own performance using either a teacher-developed checklist or one they compose cooperatively based on curricular objectives. This provides an indication for the teacher of how the student assesses his own abilities. In addition to rating their performance or knowledge, student self-ratings can address learning styles and preferences. For example, ask students:

> Which activities helped you learn best? Why?
> Do you prefer to work in groups or alone? Why?
> How do you feel about your ability to learn in this class? Why?
> What can I, the teacher, do to help you learn better?
> What can you, the student, do to learn better?

4. Venn Diagrams and Other Graphic Organizers

Students compare two concepts—ideas, books, or other concepts in any content area—using a Venn diagram format (two overlapping circles). This type of assessment provides the student with an opportunity to utilize higher-order thinking skills individually or in pairs. The graphic organizer focuses student attention on ideas and reduces concern with language (e.g., putting the ideas into complete sentences). Matrices, webs, and timelines can be used for assessment as well.

5. Projects and Other Performance Assessments

To assess learning goals that transcend mere recall, educators are turning to performance assessments such as projects, exhibitions, investigations, and portfolios (see below). Today's teachers don't want to just dispense knowledge; besides teaching about history, literature, math, and science, teachers also want to give students opportunities to be historians, literary critics, mathematicians, and scientists. Performance assessment tasks call on students to write, debate, create products, conduct experiments, and so on. Using such performance assessments sends a new message to students: that teachers value in-depth understanding, the ability to apply knowledge in new situations, and high-quality work.

For example, Larry Lewin, a middle school teacher in Eugene, Oregon, asked himself: "How should a present-day teacher assess his students' understanding of 1492?" Lewin wanted to assess his students' understanding of the relationships among Columbus, the Spanish, and the Native American Tainos, but he didn't want to give a traditional short-answer test, which would "put a ceiling" on how much learning his students could demonstrate. So Lewin asked his students to write a persuasive letter to the monarchs Ferdinand and Isabella of Spain. In their letters, students were expected to define the encounter between Europeans and Native Americans by a key word of their choice—discovery, visit, invasion—and then argue why that word fit. Students had to call upon their newly acquired knowledge of history to defend their points of view. When finished, the letters were assessed against criteria that the class had helped generate.

The letter-writing task revealed more about the students' learning than a traditional test would have, Lewin says, because it required students to *do* something with their knowledge—not just regurgitate it. For the same reason, the task was "definitely more inherently motivating," he believes. "Kids are more motivated to write to dead monarchs than to take a test" (ASCD).

Examples of other performance assessments are: a teacher teaching/evaluating research methods asked her students to research how their town got its name; she evaluated their choice and appropriate use of multiple research methods to obtain the answer. A math teacher asked students to read and critique the use of statistical methods in news articles on current events such as the Florida net ban and its effects on fish and people. A social studies teacher asked her class to prepare an exhibit on their family histories and roots as a project to accompany a unit on immigration.

6. Portfolios

A portfolio is a purposeful and systematic collection of student work to reflect growth and the achievement of curriculum objectives over time. The portfolio itself may be bound like a book, in a folder or binder, in a box, or on audio- or videotape.

Usually, the teacher is responsible for choosing the *purpose* of the portfolio and the contents (categories of work to be included); setting the timetable for the work; and determining who evaluates the portfolio. Usually, the student selects the individual items to be included; explains *why* each item is included (e.g., this is my best essay; this one shows that I learned ...); updates the table of contents; sets personal goals for learning, and assesses his personal goals. Teachers and students jointly develop criteria for assessment and determine how the portfolios will be shared with others.

Portfolios need not be restricted to language arts. For example, in a math class, a portfolio might include: a way I used math in real life, an article I read that used statistics, the hardest problem I learned to solve this month, etc.

References:

Association for Supervision and Curriculum Development (ASCD). On the cutting edge of assessment: Testing what students can do with knowledge. *Education Update*. Volume 38, Number 4, June 1996.

Empowering ESOL Teachers: An Overview. Menu of alternative assessment instruments. Section IX.3, Handout 7, 1996 Revised Edition.

Outside Assignment #4 and Worksheet

Directions: Outside Assignment #4 requires you and your partner(s) who developed the integrated lesson in Section 7 to design an assessment for that lesson and to visually present this assessment in your Poster Session in Section 11. Use the worksheet below to guide you in this process. Your presentation in the Poster Session must describe the following:

    1. the task(s) students will do

    2. the rubric (or criteria) the teacher will use to assess student performance, and

    3. how beginning ELLs will be supported.

Content Area Topic: _____

1. What do you want the students to know and be able to do at the end of the unit?

2. What task (performance) will students do to demonstrate their learnings?

3. What are the criteria for excellent performance? (List at least three.)

4. How will you provide students ongoing support and ongoing feedback during this work? What additional support can you provide to ELLs?

5. Does the activity require students to use new knowledge and skills (not just do nifty things)? What new knowledge and skills?

6. How are students made aware of what they have learned, how they have learned it, and how they can use this learning in the future?

Issues in Grading Limited English Proficient Students

When I begin a session working with teachers on grading and assessment issues, I often put this quote on the overhead and ask the teachers what it means to them in the context of assessment: "You don't fatten your lambs by weighing them." (Vermont farmer)

To me, this quote is a reminder that measuring and assigning scores to student work often does not, in itself, add to student learning. Sometimes, in fact, this weighing process discourages students from learning because it does not adequately use their strengths or recognize what they have accomplished.

Some grading and assessment issues apply to all students, but teachers of Limited English Proficient (LEP) students are faced with additional issues as well.

Below are some issues teachers face concerning grading LEP students:

- The LEP student's limited English affects the student's ability to communicate his or her content knowledge.
- The LEP student works hard, but the student's achievement falls short in comparison to others in the class because of the LEP student's limited proficiency in English.
- The teacher worries that recognizing the LEP student's effort and progress will be setting two standards of achievement: LEP and non-LEP.
- The teacher and the LEP student have different expectations and interpretations of the grade.

There is no easy answer to these issues. The following suggestions are offered to help teachers develop a grading and assessment plan:

1. Focus on the LEP student's *meaning*, instead of language errors such as grammar mistakes or awkward phrasing. Ask yourself: Did the student understand the question? Did he/she answer the question? How well did the student develop his or her thoughts?

2. Grade a combination of process and product for all students. Thomas Guskey, a well-known educator, illustrates with a hypothetical gym class situation. Imagine assessing two students: One is a brilliant athlete; the other has poor movement skills but always tries his or her hardest and is unfailingly a good sport. Using only product criteria, such as how high the student can jump and how fast the student can run, would not recognize the second student for the things that student does well and which are equally legitimate and relevant criteria for the class.

3. Early in the school year, explain to students what and how you grade. Show examples of good work. Use scoring rubrics with clear criteria. Involve students in developing criteria for evaluating assignments. Teach students to evaluate their own work.

4. Have grades reflect a variety of performances (some less dependent on fluent language skills) such as participation, projects, portfolios, and oral explanations.

5. Adapt tests and test administration. For example, allow more time for LEP students, or read the test to them. Teach test-taking skills and strategies. Since grading on a curve is often unfair to beginning ELL learners, use criterion-referenced tests.

6. Teach students how to evaluate their own work. Have students conduct self-evaluations. Talk to students after grading if you think their expectations were different from the grade they received.

7. Grade beginning ELL students as "satisfactory/unsatisfactory" or "at/above/below expectations" until the end of the year. Then assign a letter grade for the year.

8. Put a note on the report card or transcript to identify the student as an English Language Learner. Write comments to clarify how the student was graded.

In addition to developing a grading plan, also occasionally perform a "self-check" of your methods of assessing students. The following questions could be used:

Do I test what and how I teach? For example, if I'm teaching complex thinking and thematic units, am I assessing student knowledge of relationships and interdependence, or am I assessing knowledge of isolated facts? If my teaching requires students to apply and use new knowledge, does my assessment involve application of knowledge or does it only require recall or recognition of information?

Do I use a variety of assessments, including alternative assessments? Alternative assessments may reflect better what and how a teacher teaches. Projects, for example, often require integration and use of skills and knowledge in a way that approximate performances required in real life. Portfolios show student growth over time and include student self-evaluation and reflection.

When I use more traditional tests, such as multiple choice or short answer, do I review the tests to make sure that language and cultural bias has been minimized, and do I teach test-taking strategies to all my students?

Teachers who think through the grading issues that are most relevant to their classes; who develop guidelines that work for them and that they can clearly and consistently explain to students, parents and others; and who self-check their assessments periodically, will surely fatten their lambs while weighing them.

Judy Jameson, Center for Applied Linguistics

This publication was developed under a contract with the U.S. Department of Education and Educational Testing Service. The opinions represent the professional judgment of the writers and do not necessarily reflect the positions or policies of the USDOE, ETS or the State Departments of Education in the region.

SECTION 9

Enhancing Language Learning in Elementary Classrooms

Study Guide

Section 10
Family/Parent Involvement

Family/Parent Involvement

Goal

To foster and encourage effective parent involvement for the parents of ELL students.

Performance Objectives

- Define the categories of parent involvement.

- Identify what elements of effective parent involvement look like.

- Identify strategies to foster and encourage effective parent involvement.

- Conduct a successful interview with the parent of an ELL student.

SECTION 10

Working with Families

Families and teachers both are preparing children for the future. Both have the goal of nurturing and educating children. And yet, despite this common goal, families and schools often encounter difficulties collaborating in children's education.

Laurie Olsen and her co-authors of *The Unfinished Journey: Restructuring Schools in a Diverse Society* found that family involvement, especially for language minority families, is one of the most critical features of restructuring schools, but also one of the most difficult to implement. In their two and one half year investigation of school restructuring, they visited 32 California schools, all with language minority students. They found many types of family involvement, which they categorized into three paradigms. In planning family involvement, schools should consider how to implement components from each of these three paradigms.

First paradigm: Schools involve families in supporting the education of their children.

In this paradigm, schools encourage parents and other family members to provide home support for the schools' educational program. However, providing this support may be difficult for families who are recent immigrants and who are still learning English themselves. Schools may assist these families in a variety of ways. They may set up native language orientation for families about the U.S. school system or they may create literacy, ESL, and parent education classes for adults. Family involvement specialists may facilitate family attendance at orientation nights and parent/teacher conferences. Teachers may create family learning projects for families and students to finish together at home after the activities are introduced to students in the classroom. Topics in family learning projects could include using the newspaper index, using the comics to learn, or comparing TV shows for similarities or differences.

In *A Magical Encounter* Alma Flor Ada describes a family literacy program called "Parents, Children and Books" in which parents collaborate in creating books to share with their children. In a series of meetings, facilitators read illustrated children's books with parents in small groups; parents then share the books with their families at home, reading or retelling the story based on the illustrations. After experiencing dramatic readings of illustrated stories, parents participate in creating books based on their own experiences, dictating text in their native language to a facilitator on topics such as "From yesterday to tomorrow" (a collection of riddles, sayings and rhymes), or "When my life changed..."(a sharing of oral histories). The facilitator types the texts into books, which are returned to parents for sharing with their families. Through this program, parents learn how to read or discuss books with their children, promoting "their children's cognitive and language development, while at the same time, creating a home atmosphere that is conducive to the sharing of experiences and feelings."

Second paradigm: Schools involve families as advocates for school programs.

In this paradigm, families support schools by helping to solve problems brought on by budget cuts or by advocating innovations created by the schools. Family members may volunteer in the school or raise funds for field trips or textbooks. Family members and teachers may band together as advocates on important issues. In one school, parents and teachers formed the Partnership School Committee to petition the school board to expand the school's immersion program from a strand within the school to a schoolwide program. "Immersion parents shaped the outcome....The board finally approved immersion. It was a wonderful victory." In this paradigm, schools and families join forces in support of educational programs that schools might not be able to carry out by themselves. As a result of this collaboration, family members learn how to advocate effectively for educational innovations.

Third paradigm: Families have a right to democratic participation in the functioning of the school.

In this paradigm families are deeply involved in decision-making in their children's schools as the most important advocates for their children and their children's education. In this role, families help to ensure that education is culturally and linguistically appropriate.

This paradigm is the most critical for the wellbeing and education of language minority students. Furthermore, in some states family participation in school decision-making is mandated by law. In many cases, however, this paradigm may be the most difficult to implement and the one most likely to lead to conflict. How and in what areas will family members participate in decision-making? In classroom visits? On committees making curriculum decisions? Because this paradigm brings families into non-traditional areas of influence in the school, teachers and administrators, as well as family members, may need to learn new roles and ways to communicate.

Differing cultural and language expectations can also be barriers to this type of family involvement. For example, teachers might introduce math concepts through the use of manipulatives, whereas some parents might view these activities as "play" rather than education. In some households parents might expect children to accept the opinions of their elders, whereas teachers might expect children to voice and defend their own opinions in class.

By creating lines of communication among families, teachers, and other school personnel, schools can begin to mediate differences. One teacher links families and schools through "parent interactive journals," which she writes with the families of her first graders. Once a week, each student takes home a journal in which the teacher has written a short note in English or in the family's native language. Any family member may respond in writing, over the telephone, or in a meeting with the teacher. These journals and exchanges become interactive records of families' lives, experiences, and expectations of the schooling process.

Implementing the three paradigms:

All three of these paradigms are critical for students and their families. There must be family academic support for student learning, financial and advocate support for schools buffeted by budget cuts, and meaningful collaboration between families and schools. In addition, families have a vital role to play in informing schools about the culture, values, and languages of their children. Thus, it is important to create ways for families to participate meaningfully in educational decision-making.

Dr. Maria Derrick-Mescua, Center for Applied Linguistics

This publication was developed under a contract with the U.S. Department of Education and Educational Testing Service. The opinions represent the professional judgment of the writers and do not necessarily reflect the positions or policies of the USDOE, ETS or the State Departments of Education in the region.

Reprinted with the permission of Educational Testing Service from Derrick-Mescua, M. (1999). *Working with families.* From Theory to Practice, No. 10, Region XIV Comprehensive Center at ETS: Tampa, FL.

SECTION 10

Fostering Home-School Cooperation: Involving Language Minority Families as Partners in Education

by Emma Violand-Sanchez, Christine P. Hutton, Herbert W. Ware

Introduction

Now, as perhaps never before, the need to strengthen the bond of cooperation between home and school is being felt nationwide. Schools face the challenge of preparing an increasingly diverse generation of young people for a society in which literacy is a must, an understanding of technology and its many applications is required, and the ability to solve problems and find answers to questions not yet posed is essential. Families, for their part, must prepare their children for a future in which they can expect to move and change jobs or careers many times. As they become adults, today's youth must be able to make not only the decisions that affect their own lives, but also the critical choices about how this country will conduct its affairs, what roles the United States will assume in the international arena, and how we will survive in a changing world of competing interests and limited resources.

Clearly the challenges of education are ones which neither schools not families can meet alone; they must support each other. When families and schools cooperate, the children reap the benefits–they learn more, they enjoy school and the learning process, and they experience a consistent sense of commitment and support from the important adults in their lives (Epstein, 1986).

This monograph has been designed to provide useful information about parent involvement in general, and practical strategies for developing partnerships with language minority parents in particular. A framework is presented for fostering cooperation between home and school, given the special factors that should be considered as non-native English speaking families become more familiar with their new communities. The authors would like to share the experiences and approaches of the Arlington (Virginia) Public Schools, at both the district and school levels, and describe the ongoing efforts to develop and nurture cooperative links between schools and the families they serve.

The Importance of Parent Involvement

A growing body of research documents the multiple benefits that occur when parents are actively involved in their children's education. Comer (1984) discusses the emotional support that children need in order to learn, indicating that such an environment of support is optimally created when families and school personnel cooperate. Rich, et al. (1979) point to the improvements in student attendance and behavior and in parent–teacher relations that happen as a result of parental involvement. Bennett (1986) cites the benefits to parents themselves as they gain greater confidence and expertise in helping their children succeed academically. And, as mentioned above, students are the ultimate beneficiaries when their families collaborate closely with the schools (Simich-Dudgeon, 1986).

Reprinted from Violand-Sanchez, E., et al. (1991). *Fostering Home-School Cooperation: Involving Language Minority Families as Partners in Education* (Program Information Guide No. 6). National Clearinghouse for Bilingual Education.

In this document, the terms "parent involvement" and "family involvement" are used interchangeably in order to give recognition to the fact that students may and often do have a variety of adults who can provide the types of support and interaction described below. For many language minority students, the adults in the household may include members of the extended family who assume an active role in the child's upbringing.

Categories of Involvement

Epstein has been one of the principal researchers on the important topic of parental involvement and its effects on student achievement, parental attitudes, and education practices. In her work (1986), she identified five categories of parent involvement in the education of their children:

1. Providing for children's basic needs

By seeing that children are fed, clothed, have enough sleep, and enjoy a secure, loving environment, parents contribute to the well-being a child needs to focus attention on learning both at home and at school. One school-related example is ensuring that children have necessary school supplies and a place to study at home.

2. Communicating with school staff

All schools seek to communicate with parents in one form or another during the school year. The ability of parents to understand such communication depends on a variety of factors, including their literacy level and their proficiency in the language (usually English) used to send the information home. When schools are able to provide written communications in a language the parents can understand and make available a person at the school with whom they can communicate personally, cooperation between schools and language minority parents is greatly facilitated.

3. Volunteering or providing assistance at their child's school

This kind of involvement was traditionally expected, particularly of mothers. However, in Epstein's study, such involvement rarely includes more than a few parents in any school. More than 70 percent of the parents surveyed had never participated by assisting staff at the school. As more and more parents work outside of the home during the school day, this traditional form of parent involvement has become increasingly less frequent.

4. Supporting and participating in learning activities with their children at home

Epstein looked, in particular, at parental activity which related to the children's work in class. Epstein discovered the following:
- More than 85 percent of parents spend at least 15 minutes helping their child at home when asked to do so by the teacher; most said they would spend more time if they were told what to do and how to help.
- Elementary students whose teachers emphasize parent involvement gain more in reading an math achievement than students in other classrooms where the teachers do not emphasize similar involvement; students whose teachers stress parent involvement have more positive attitudes toward school, and more regular homework habits.

5. Participating in governance and advocacy activities

"Governance" and "advocacy" refer to the avenues by which parents and the community can influence decision making in a school system. Epstein distinguishes the two in the following way: governance activities occur under the auspices of the school system, e.g., school-appointed advisory committees; advocacy activities are organized and conducted independent of the school system: one example would be a citizens' group formed to lobby the school board on changes in the curriculum. Each type of participation requires a certain level of understanding of the school's programs and confidence on the part of parents. Each also requires a willingness and commitment on the part of educators to include families in the decision-making process in meaningful ways.

In summary, there appears to be a positive relationship between parent involvement in education and the progress that students make in academics and in their attitudes toward learning. Parent involvement takes many forms and can occur at home, in the school, and in the community. School personnel have an obligation to reach out to all families so that all students may benefit. Because modern communities are increasingly diverse in their social, cultural, and linguistic composition, new flexibility and approaches for reaching out are needed to ensure that no one is excluded.

Fostering Home-School Cooperation

Changing Demographics

The notion of home-school cooperation cannot remain static while characteristics of the home are changing. Nationally, we are becoming an increasingly heterogenous society. The 1990 census shows a dramatic increase in the numbers of individuals with linguistic, ethnic, and racial minority backgrounds during the last ten years in every geographic region of the country. More than a third of the nation's population increase since 1980 is the result of immigration. During the past decade, Asian and Pacific Islanders more than doubled (from 3,500,439 to 7,273,662) while the number of Hispanics rose by 53 percent (from 14,608,672 to 22,354,059) (Vobejda, 1991).

An example of this change is Arlington County, Virginia, where our experience is based. The changes in demographics have been dramatic and, in all likelihood, may preview the changes that will occur throughout the United States during the final decade of the century. The Asian population in Arlington peaked in the mid-1980s but showed a net increase of 74.3 percent from 1980 to 1990. The number of Hispanics in the county rose by 160 percent; Hispanic youth now comprise the largest minority group in the Arlington Public Schools. During the last 15 years, the system's student population has evolved from being a predominantly middle class, white, monolingual English-speaking one to a student body with a diverse multicultural, multilingual composition.

At the local level, two other factors–family composition and family economic conditions–have also changed over the last ten years. Today, there are many more single parent families served by the school district. Further, the nature of the family constellation has changed, with more school children residing with extended family members than before. On the economic level, it appears that many parents, especially single parents, are facing severe financial limitations and, increasingly, finding it necessary to have two or three jobs.

Overall, the changes in cultural and linguistic heritage, family structure, and economic conditions witnessed on the local school level are reflective of broader national trends. These changes, in turn, have profound implications regarding a school's expectations for home-school cooperation and will require dynamic innovations by educators to ensure that our rapidly changing school age population receives a rewarding and effective education.

Changing Attitudes about Parent Involvement

Have you ever heard any of the following comments about parent involvement in your school community?

- "Parents should be able to take time during the day to come to school to talk with staff."
- "Decisions about education practices and curriculum should be left to professional educators who know what's best for students."
- "Working and/or single parents don't have time to become involved in their children's education."
- "Non-English speaking parents can't really participate in school activities or in helping their children learn."

In the context of the communities and families served by the public schools today, such comments indicate unrealistic attitudes. Schools seeking parental participation and input need to recognize parents as the primary educators of their children and be both flexible and innovative in reaching out to the diverse community. For example, such practices as evening or early morning conferences, bilingual communication, childcare during meetings, parent education classes, personal contact with families, and learning activities for families to use at home are effective strategies which enable families to become involved in their children's education. In the case of families who may be recent arrivals to this country, or not yet fluent or literate in English, or unfamiliar with the culture of U.S. public schools, these innovative strategies become doubly important.

Experience has shown that language minority families (the term which will be used to apply to all three categories of individuals mentioned previously) do care deeply about their children's schooling. What is required is for educators to act as partners in education with these and other families, recognizing the important contributions that all families can make to the schools and to their children's success.

A Framework for Involving Language Minority Families in the Schools

Arlington's approach to fostering home-school cooperation with its language minority families is to recognize and encourage all five types of involvement identified by Epstein. At the same time, the school system recognizes that the vast majority of its language minority families are still in the process of adjusting to the mainstream culture and language of the United States. While more and more of Arlington's non-native English speaking students are born in the United States, nearly all of their families have come here as immigrants or refugees. Thus it has been appropriate to take into consideration the stages of adjustment used to describe the newcomer's experience in coming to terms with the language and culture of the new home country. These stages are described in Figure 1. It has

Figure 1: Stages of Adjustment for Newcomers

ACCULTURATION

Parent feels comfortable in the "new" cultural setting. Encourage participation in all activities, provide opportunities for leadership and mentoring of other parents, and acquaint them with options for participation in the wider school community.

ARRIVAL/SURVIVAL

Parents require orientation and information on the school community, how to enroll their children, what is required. Information given in the native language is particularly helpful. Time for participation may be quite limited, but interest level may be high.

COPING

As parents begin to become familiar with a new cultural system and their role in it, encourage their participation in school activities, provide specific well-defined tasks and responsibilities, and encourage them to reach out to others who need support and assistance.

CULTURE SHOCK

During this emotionally stressful time, parents' energies are drained and their enthusiasm for things "American" may be minimal. Parental support groups, personal contacts from school personnel, and minimizing demands on their time while keeping lines of communication open can be of great benefit.

likewise been useful to recognize that these different stages of adjustment may elicit different responses from parents with respect to their willingness and/or availability to be actively involved in their children's education. For example, all newcomers to the school system need basic information about school requirements, routines, schedules, and the like. For language minority newcomers, such information may need to be given in the home language and in a setting where there can be personal, face-to-face clarification. Similarly, as families become more settled in the community and feel more familiar with how the school system operates, they may be more willing to participate in governance and advocacy activities. It should not be assumed that only parents who are in the final stage of adjustment will take part in school decision making. The purpose of considering the cultural and language adjustment process is to be able to offer a network of support strategies that will enable families to take advantage of the various opportunities to participate.

Implementing a Participation Model

How can a local school system encourage the participation of parents who are newly arrived and/or whose English proficiency is limited? Experience has shown that success is possible because such parents do care about their children's education and want to be involved in their local schools. When a school system provides caring, sensitive, and enlightened avenues for these parents they become active partners in education.

Factors that Affect Parental Involvement

In designing appropriate support systems for parents in general, the experiences and resources of language minority parents should be acknowledged and respected. After all, these factors will have a strong influence on their initial and later involvement. Although every family entering the school system is unique, sone generalizations can be helpful. Differences in levels of involvement may be influenced by the factors described below:

1. Length of residence in the United States
Newcomers to this country will most likely need considerable orientation and support in order to understand what their child's school expects in the way of participation and involvement. Native language communication, cultural orientation sessions, and support of others who have been newcomers can be extremely helpful to newly arrived families during what may be a stressful period of adjustment.

2. English language proficiency
Parents whose English proficiency is limited may find it difficult or intimidating to communicate with school staff or to help in school activities without bilingual support from someone in the school community. These parents can, of course, participate successfully, and can help their child at home, so care must be taken to see that they receive information and that their efforts are welcomed and encouraged.

3. Availability of support groups and bilingual staff
Native language parent groups and bilingual school personnel can make a crucial differ-

SECTION 10

ence in fostering involvement among parents. Bilingual community liaisons can also translate the information provided to parents. These services not only ensure that information is understood, they also demonstrate to parents that the school wants to involve them actively in the life of the school and their children's academic development.

4. Prior experiences

Language minority families differ widely in the extent to which they are familiar and comfortable with the concept of parental involvement in schools. Some newcomers may have been actively involved in their children's education in the home country, while others may come from cultures where the parents' role in education is understood in very different terms. Parents whose families have resided in this country for generations may feel unwelcome or uncomfortable in their child's school and may need encouragement and support in their efforts to participate. Others, as indicated in Epstein's study (1986), may need only some specific suggestions on how to "help" in order to participate more actively in education at home and at school.

Family Involvement Model–District-Wide

Successful implementation of programs and strategies to involve language minority families requires both a district-level response and school-based initiatives. Both components of one school district's model are described more fully below. Figure 2 illustrates the district-wide response; Figure 3 details the initiatives of one school within the system.

Intake Center

For newly arrived and/or non-native English speaking families, an Intake Center can be an effective first point of contact with the school system. An Intake Center can provide multilingual assistance in registration, placement, testing, and information services. It can also provide translation and interpretation services for parent/teacher conferences and other school activities. Throughout the year, Intake Center staff can interpret at individual school orientation meetings. At the beginning of the school year, a district-wide orientation meeting for all parents new to the district can be organized by Intake Center staff; at the end of the year, a special workshop in which parents can be informed about summer school offerings, summer recreational options and summer youth employment opportunities will also be helpful to families. An Intake Center can help to bridge the communication gap between English-speaking school staff and parents who may not yet be fluent in the language.

Bilingual Staff

Bilingual (community resource) assistants can be a valuable link between the schools and language minority families. They can ease both students' and parents' transition into active school involvement. Bilingual staff can help families feel welcome in the school from the start and can encourage their participation in school activities. In Arlington, bilingual assistants develop and implement activities that address the particular needs of each school and serve as links to district-wide information and programs.

Figure 2: Model for Involving Language Minority Families

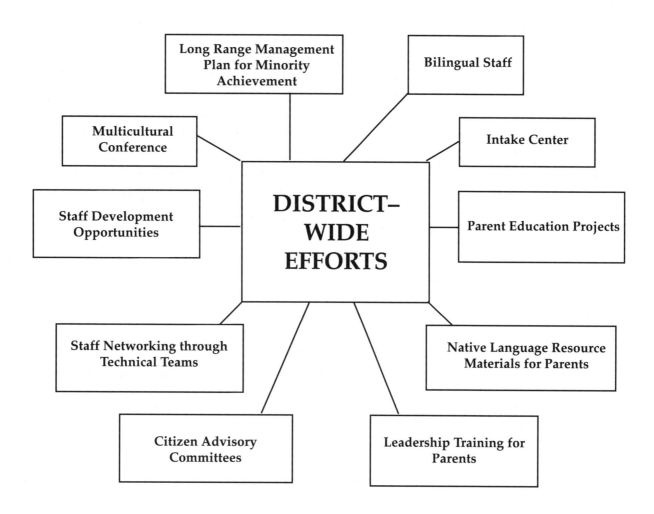

Orientation for Parents

When language minority families first enter the school, they may be in need of basic information in their native language in order to understand school policies and community resources. Because these parents vary in their experiences and skills, ongoing orientation workshops for parents on topics such as homework, school attendance and classroom discipline should be offered. An orientation handbook translated into several languages is also extremely helpful. The handbook should contain information on school and community resources of interest to parents.

Back-to-School Night and Parent/Teacher Conferences

Two important activities that can take place in the schools are Back-to-School Night and Parent/Teacher conferences. In Arlington County, Back-to-School Night is held yearly in September, and Parent/Teacher Conferences are held twice a year. Both events provide opportunities for parents and teachers to meet and to share important information about the school and/or student progress. Priority is given to providing interpreters at Back-to-School Night and at Parent/Teacher Conferences so that all teachers and parents can benefit from the exchange.

In Arlington County, the Intake Center provides paid interpreters for conferences between parents and teachers. These interpreters contact parents before conferences and help put them at ease by conveying the purpose for the meeting. They arrange to meet parents at the school and escort them to the conference. Because these conferences are so important, care must be taken to schedule them for the convenience of both working and non-working parents. Alternative times for conferences, such as early morning or evenings, should explored to enable parents to participate. Letting parents know that their participation is important and providing a welcoming, reassuring environment helps create the conditions needed for substantive communication between home and school.

Figure 3: Barrett Elementary School

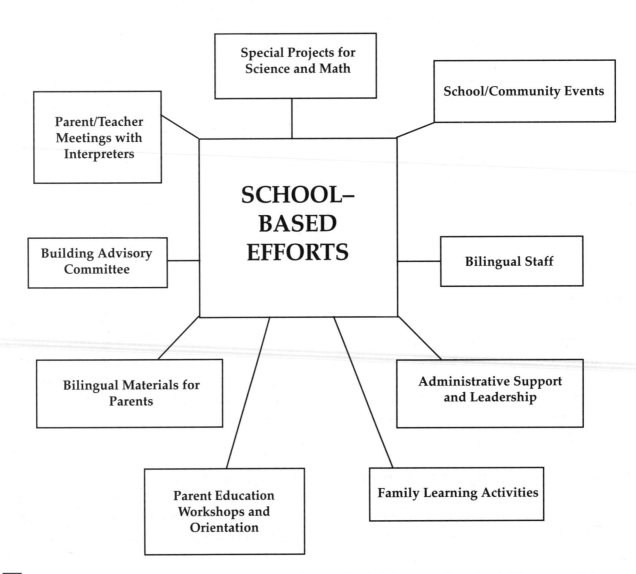

Parent Education Workshops

In addition to orientation sessions for parents and parent/teacher conferencing, parents have shown an interest in attending school-sponsored workshops which help them improve their parenting skills and enable them to work more confidently with their children on school-related tasks. A sample workshop on the topic of reading appears in the Appendix.

Language minority parents may respond more positively to those workshops conducted in their native languages or with native language interpretation provided. The provision of onsite childcare also increases attendance.

Multilingual Family Learning Activities

Multilingual family learning activities for home use provide another avenue for parents to support the school curriculum and help their children learn. Such activities are extensions of the classroom curriculum. In Arlington, staff provide an orientation for parents on the use of the family learning activities, introduce the activities to students in the classroom, then send them home on a regular basis. Parents and students complete response sheets, sometimes including a product based on the activities, and return them to the teacher. In our experience, response from parents has been outstanding, especially when there is a continuous monitoring of completed and returned activities and when participants receive recognition for completing the activities.

Native Language Parent Groups

When there are concentrations of minority languages in a given school or community, native language groups can be an excellent way to bring parents into the schools. The group becomes a vital source of information and a means of establishing a network of friends within the community. Through the group, parents can develop the leadership skills needed for participation in other governance and advocacy activities. Parents need to be involved in making the decisions that affect their children's education.

In Arlington, several language-specific parent associations have been formed in recent years. These parent groups not only reach out to newly-arrived parents but also provide a link to organizations like the Parent-Teacher Association (PTA) and other district-wide organizations.

Citizen Advisory Committees

Another way to enhance parent participation is by establishing a network of citizens' advisory committees which can make recommendations to the school board on a variety of issues. In Arlington County, those citizens' advisory committees meet monthly. One of these committees advises the board on how to improve services for language minority students and parents; others advise administrative staff on individual curricular subject areas. The school board has made concerted efforts to recruit language minority participation on each of its advisory committees.

District Support for Staff

Fostering home-school cooperation requires that school personnel receive support in their efforts to reach out to families, communicate effectively, and work in partnership with parents. This can be accomplished through–

Staff development on topics such as:
- understanding cultural differences and diverse learning styles;
- planning and conducting effective parent meetings;
- utilizing cultural heritage to support instruction; and
- working with family learning activities.

Staff development should be offered on an ongoing basis to enable staff to identify and employ successful strategies with their students' families.

Development of resource materials on topics such as:
- cultural background of minority language groups represented in the student population;
- working with language minority parents; and
- working effectively with interpreters.

Offering stipends and recertification credits:
- for conducting workshops and developing materials after school hours.

Offering opportunities to network with colleagues:
- to share concerns, questions, success stories, and the challenges encountered in the process of working with parents to enhance the academic achievement of students. School districts should seek to provide such opportunities both formally and informally. For example, monthly administrative staff monitoring meetings, which include discussion of issues related to involving language minority parents, can be implemented. A district-wide committee on parent involvement might be established to enable teachers, aides, and resource assistants to come together on a regular basis to share experiences and resources. In Arlington County, a committee was formed to explore avenues for providing leadership opportunities for Spanish-speaking parents.

District–Wide Multicultural Conference

For the past ten years, Arlington Public Schools has sponsored an annual conference to address issues of importance to language minority parents and to celebrate the County's rich cultural heritage. Initially, the Multicultural Conference consisted primarily of informative workshops for parents conducted in several languages. In recent years, it has emphasized the importance of the County's cultural diversity and has sought to involve more staff, students, and families in both the study and celebration of the contributions made by all ethnic groups represented in Arlington. In 1990, more than 800 parents, students, and teachers participated in this festive event, which is seen as a major cooperative effort of the community, families, and the schools.

Developing a Long Range Plan

Ideally, planning should be long range and should precede program implementation; realistically, the reverse is often true. In the Arlington Public Schools, the success experienced in relatively small-scale family involvement initiatives has led to the development of comprehensive, district-wide, long-range plans to involve language minority families. The plan calls for the identification of strategies and mechanisms to address achievement and participation of all minorities, including coordination with other program areas, staff development, and parent and community involvement. The plan has the support of the superintendent and the school board.

District-level initiatives establish the broad framework for outreach to parents and community. How the framework described above is translated into action at the school level with a particular group of parents and teachers varies from school to school. The following is a case study of one elementary school that has made intensive efforts to foster home-school cooperation with its language minority families.

Barrett Elementary School: Empowering Parents

Kate Waller Barrett Elementary School is one of eighteen K-5 elementary schools in Arlington County. Of its 315 pupils, 82 percent are language and racial minority students. Sixty percent of Barrett's pupils are Hispanic. Nearly half (46.7 percent) of the students at Barrett are identified as limited English proficient (LEP); county-wide, 16 percent of all students are designated as LEP.

The Role of the Principal in Parent Involvement

Given Barrett's student population, staff have found it both unreasonable and ineffective to expect the more traditional form of home-school cooperation with "parents-in-the-school" involved as volunteers in highly successful fund drives. New expectations focus on a broader meaning of cooperation, requiring that much of the initiative be taken by the school. The principal assumes a new role as a facilitator, seeking to open the school to a variety of groups for multiple purposes. He provides leadership and encouragement to both staff and parents to work together to improve the environment of the school, to establish a sense of community among a diverse group of families, and to support a climate of high academic expectation for all students.

When Barrett's current principal assumed that role in 1982, he made parent involvement a high priority on his personal agenda. His goals included the following:

- hiring staff who are bilingual and who view working with parents as a high priority;
- sending written communications home in two languages and providing interpreters for parents at school events;
- acquainting parents with the resources that are available to ease their transition into their new community; and
- encouraging the integration of language minority families into existing PTA activities and programs.

Working toward these goals has required a willingness on the part of the principal to tolerate possible grievances from applicants who are not bilingual. It has meant dealing with some individuals' initial impatience with bilingual interpretation at meetings where both monolingual English-speaking parents and language minority parents were present. It has necessitated ongoing encouragement of staff and parents when they become discouraged about the extra time and effort it takes to reach out to a diverse community. And, finally, it has required the flexibility to schedule many events during non-school hours, to provide childcare so that families can attend school functions, and to find translators so that no one feels excluded from the life of the school.

School-Based Efforts

Several policies and programs for fostering home-school cooperation make up the model that has been implemented at Barrett. They are illustrated in Figure 3. Each is described briefly below in relation to the five broad categories of parent involvement outlined previously.

1. *Helping parents meet their children's basic education needs*

The parents at Barrett School are very much concerned about their children's well-being and education. However, because many of them are newcomers to the United States, they sometimes have limited understanding of, or experience with, school expectations and methods of instruction in this country. Sometimes the newcomers follow cultural parenting norms that differ significantly from those that school personnel may expect, and the changes of lifestyles resulting from immigration can produce both confusion and stress. For these reasons, Barrett has initiated activities designed to educate parents about cultural expectations, the school program and curriculum, their new community, and parenting.

Orientation to Barrett School

Three sessions are held each year to introduce all parents to the curriculum and special program options at the school. These orientations are conducted in English and Spanish.

Back-to-School Night is held in September of each year. Parents attend presentations by their children's teachers, which address curricular objectives, behavioral expectations, grading and homework policies, the nature of the student's day, and projects to be expected in the course of the school year.

An Evening for Kindergarten Parents is held in October or November of each year, During the meeting, kindergarten teachers and reading teachers illustrate for parents the developmental steps for children learning to read and write.

An Evening on the Gifted and Talented Program is also held in the fall. Typically, this meeting addresses the school district's criteria and procedures for identifying students as gifted or talented. Parents learn how students are served and see the units used at each grade level.

Parent Education Workshops

The school's bilingual community resource assistant coordinates a series of bi-weekly parent education meetings for newly arrived parents of children in grades K-12. These workshops address topics such as school expectations, child development, effective discipline, and basic concepts taught in school. Childcare is provided at these meetings; often, there are as many children attending as adults.

The last evening in this series includes an awards ceremony where parents are recognized with certificates for their frequency of participation. A potluck supper completes the evening.

Parenting Workshops

The counselor at the school sought and obtained a special grant from a local organization to help parents deal with the stress of immigration and the problems resulting from that stress. The counselor initiated bi-weekly parenting sessions on a variety of topics, including understanding children's feelings, assertive behaviors, and family communication patterns; preventing substance and drug abuse; and understanding developmental differences in childhood.

2. *Improving communication between home and school*

Bilingual Staff

As mentioned earlier, the principal has made it a priority to hire bilingual staff whenever vacancies occur. (Currently, 13 of Barrett's 41 staff members are bilingual.) The bilingual community resource assistant is a key person because she works with students, teachers, and parents, serving as a vital link between home and school.

Bilingual Materials

Communications from the school are sent home in both English and Spanish. The PTA newsletter is translated as well. Bilingual staff regularly call parents to ensure that information has been received and understood.

3. *Bringing parents into the school as participants*

Although volunteering at school during the day is not an option for many of Barrett's working parents, a number of activities are held outside of regular school hours that are of interest to the diverse elements of the community. These activities are often sponsored by the school's PTA and include evening meetings, a book fair, an international potluck, the Sock Hop, and the annual Spring Fair.

Typically, evening meetings feature some aspect of student work, such as music performance, art displays, drama performances, a science fair, or a colonial fair. These generally require no more parental effort than that required to attend and enjoy and, in doing so, demonstrate support for what their child is doing.

4. *Helping parents support their children's learning in the home*

Barrett School has two special projects designed to involve parents in working directly with their children on curricular objectives at home. The first is the Family Learning Project, which involves children and parents in a series of special learning activities. The second is Project Discovery, which focuses on science and mathematics for all families and has two parent support components.

The Family Learning Project

The goals of the ten-week Family Learning Project are to have parents and children learn together, at home, through the use of family learning activities. Such activities increase the likelihood of student success in school. The project begins and ends with a meeting for parents. The first meeting is devoted to orienting parents to the project and includes demonstrations of how the activities are done. In 1990, the activities for upper grade students included the following:

SECTION 10

- using the newspaper index
- understanding parts of the newspaper
- using the comics to learn
- buy it
- making a study schedule
- recording your study time
- what TV is best to watch?
- which TV shows are alike?

At the end of the ten-week project, there is a potluck supper and awards ceremony. Certificates and silver dollars are presented to families who have completed all eight lessons. Families who complete at least five activities receive certificates of accomplishment. Each child's picture is taken with his/her family as part of the ceremony. Approximately $500 to $800 is required to support the Family Learning Project.

Project Discovery

This project, begun in 1990-1991 as part of a larger district initiative, addresses learning in science and mathematics. One important component of the project is a series of monthly evening workshops taught by The Project Discovery Teacher in the school's science-mathematics laboratory, during which parents learn about science, mathematics, and resources available for each. In addition, there are two "festival" evenings. The first is devoted to patterns, the second to plant and animal life during which the school is converted into a "swamp."

5. *Involving parents in governance and advocacy activities*

In Virginia, each school is required to have its own parent advisory committee. Barrett's parent advisory committee is charged with reviewing the school's annual plan and assessing student academic progress, as well as other aspects of the school or district educational program. It typically consists of two representatives from the PTA Executive Committee and four other parents. To encourage language minority participation, the principal contacts parents directly if they do not respond to an invitation in the PTA newsletter.

On other occasions, such as the self-study process for regional accreditation, other committees are needed to effectively examine school programs. At Barrett, the self-study and the design of Project Discovery required substantial parent involvement. The principal directly nominated or appointed representatives from the different language groups to committees or sought nominations from knowledgeable staff members.

The PTA has organized groups of parents to provide input to the school board when important issues arise. For example, a representative group appeared before the school board to contest consideration of changing the Barrett school boundaries, an action that would have reassigned their children to other schools. Parents addressed the board in both English and Spanish, with interpretation provided.

Evidence of Success

What evidence do we have that these efforts to involve parents are successful? Do we know that parents value them? There are several indirect measures that serve as indicators of success at Barrett:

- Parent representatives to the Advisory committee attend at least five of the six meetings held annually;

- International Night is typically attended by more than 150 parents and their children;

- Parent Education evenings are regularly attended by 18 to 30 parents;

- Between 30 and 40 parents attend the orientation or awards evenings for the Home Learning Project, and even more families participate in the project's activities;

- Back-to-School Night hosts between 150 and 180 parents each year;

- Attendance at the Kindergarten Evening ranges from 12 to 20 parents;

- The Gifted and Talented Program evening draws from 4 to 15 parents;

- Project Discovery workshops attract from 12 to 30 parents;

- Project Discovery Festival evenings draw more than 150 parents and their children;

- Student attendance at school is consistently above 95 percent; and

- Parent participation in Parent Teacher Conferences averages more than 80 percent.

On various standardized measures, Barrett students perform on a par with other Virginia students even though the majority of Barrett's students are non-native speakers. Each fall, Arlington fifth-grade students take the Degrees of Reading Power test in order to identify students who may need additional assistance to meet the literacy level required to graduate from high school. Of Barrett's 29 fifth graders, 11 are native English speakers and 18 are language minorities. Twelve of the students scored high enough on the Reading Power test to be able to predict their ability to pass the literacy test when it is administered in high school. Seven of the 12 were non-native English speaking students.

Can such results be directly linked to parent involvement? Perhaps not, but what Barrett staff do know for certain is that staff and parents cooperate as partners to ensure student success in school. Communication is two-way; parents feel comfortable and welcome at the school; staff work directly with parents to encourage student learning at home; pupil attendance is consistently high; and parent participation at the school and county level is evident. Research studies conducted in other locales strongly suggest that such collaboration yields positive gains in student achievement.

Conclusion

Fostering home–school cooperation in today's world requires time, effort, and an investment of both human and financial resources. It calls for a re-examination of the assumptions that have traditionally defined parent involvement in the school. If cooperation is to be realized, there must be a commitment to opening opportunities for participation to all families, regardless of the parent's language background, level of education, or familiarity with school procedures and policies. School staff need administrative support, time, and access to resources if they are to work cooperatively with their students' families. The end result, of course, is that students benefit, and all who are involved reap profound rewards.

The activities suggested above are only a few that have been tried and found to be successful. There are more activities that might be initiated that can develop closer home-school relationships.

References

Bennett, W, J. (1986). *First lessons: A report on elementary education in America.* Washington, D.C.: Department of Education.

Comer, J.P. (1984, May). Home–school relationships as they affect the academic success of children. *Education and Urban Society*, 16(3), 323-337.

Epstein, J.L. (1986, June). Parent involvement: Implications for limited-English-proficient parents. In C. Simich-Dudgeon (Ed.), *Issues of parent involvement*. Proceedings of symposium held at Trinity College, Washington, D.C.

Rich, D., Van Dien, J., & Mallox, B. (1979). Families as educators of their own children. In R. Brandt (Ed.), *Partners: Parents and schools*. Alexandria, VA: Association for Supervision and Curriculum Development.

Simich-Dudgeon, C. (1986). *Parent involvement and the education of limited-English-proficient students.* ERIC Digest. Washington, D.C.: Center for Applied Linguistics.

Vobejda, B. (1991, March, 11). Asian, Hispanic numbers in U.S. soared in 1980s, census reveals. *The Washington Post*, pp. 1,14.

Figure 4: Parent Workshop
Reading: A Shared Experience

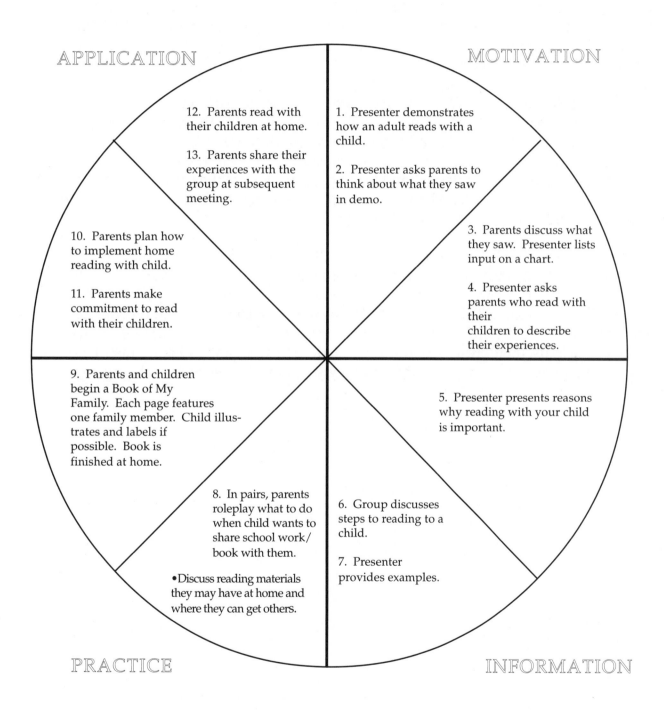

APPLICATION

MOTIVATION

12. Parents read with their children at home.

13. Parents share their experiences with the group at subsequent meeting.

1. Presenter demonstrates how an adult reads with a child.

2. Presenter asks parents to think about what they saw in demo.

10. Parents plan how to implement home reading with child.

11. Parents make commitment to read with their children.

3. Parents discuss what they saw. Presenter lists input on a chart.

4. Presenter asks parents who read with their children to describe their experiences.

9. Parents and children begin a Book of My Family. Each page features one family member. Child illustrates and labels if possible. Book is finished at home.

5. Presenter presents reasons why reading with your child is important.

8. In pairs, parents roleplay what to do when child wants to share school work/book with them.

•Discuss reading materials they may have at home and where they can get others.

6. Group discusses steps to reading to a child.

7. Presenter provides examples.

PRACTICE

INFORMATION

FOCUS:
To help parents understand why it's important to read with their children.
To help parents identify what to read with their children.
To help parents understand how to read with their children

Etta Johnson, ESOL/HILT
Arlington Public Schools, 1988

SECTION 10

About the Authors

Emma Violand-Sanchez is Curriculum Supervisor for ESOL (English for Speakers of Other Languages) and HILT (High Intensity Language Training) programs; she also directs a federally-funded Family-School Partnership Project for Arlington Public Schools. A nationally known Hispanic community leader and educator, Dr. Violand-Sanchez has served as a frequent consultant to school districts around the country and abroad. Her 1988 doctoral dissertation on learning and cognitive styles won national recognition from the National Association for Bilingual Education.

Christine P. Sutton is an ESOL/HILT elementary teacher for Arlington Public Schools and serves as the Project Specialist of the district's Family-School Partnership Project. As an educator she has also worked as a Training Specialist for the Georgetown University Title VII Multifunctional Resource Center, been a consultant to several school districts in the area of instruction and program design, and made presentations at the national conferences of both TESOL (Teachers of English to Speakers of Other Languages) and NAVAE (National Association of Vietnamese American Educators).

Herbert W. Ware has been principal of Kate Waller Barrett Elementary School in Arlington, Virginia since 1982. He has held a variety of other administrative positions in the district including those of Deputy Associate Superintendent for Instruction, Supervisor of Mathematics, and Director of Testing. In 1990, Dr. Ware gave a joint presentation with Dr. Violand-Sanchez at the annual convention of the National Association of Elementary School Principals; their presentation was entitled, "The Challenge: Quality Instruction and Parental Involvement for a Culturally and Linguistically Diverse Student Population."

Interview Preparation

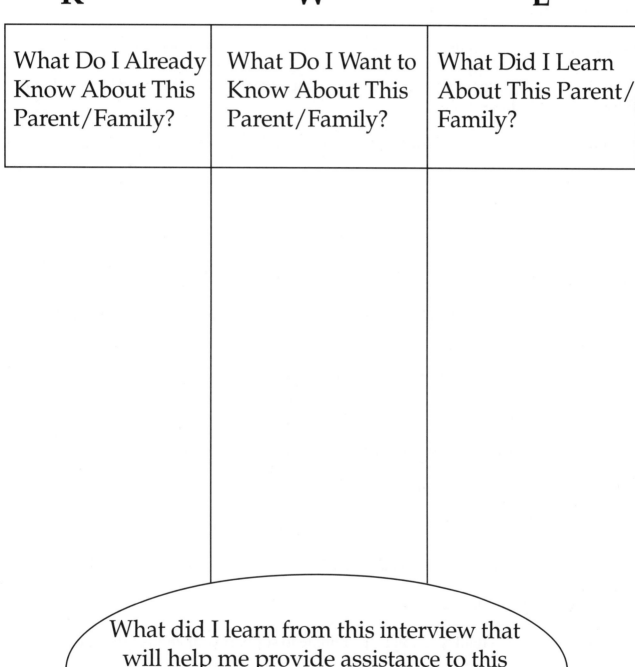

K	W	L
What Do I Already Know About This Parent/Family?	What Do I Want to Know About This Parent/Family?	What Did I Learn About This Parent/Family?

What did I learn from this interview that will help me provide assistance to this parent and family to increase their meaningful participation in their child's education?

Questions To Ask In Parent Interview

The following list of suggestions for a parent interview is intended as a guide rather than a checklist. Choose from these suggestions when preparing for an interview with a student's parent or guardian. The questions appear in no particular order.

What is the child called at home?

Who are the members of the child's family? Who among these lives with the child?

Who should receive communications from the school that concern the child? How should those communications be made?

Who will respond to communications from the school? How will those communications be made?

What would you like me to know about your child?

What do you see as an area of strength for your child?

What do you see as an area in need of improvement for your child?

What are the child's responsibilities at home? Does the child have chores or any obligation to work to help the family?

What do you hope your child will get out of school this year?

What is your child's typical morning routine?

What is your child's typical routine after school and into the evening?

What is your child's typical routine on a weekend?

Where does your child do homework? When does your child do homework?

What do you see as the purpose of education?

How do you define "success"?

In what ways do you think you can help at home to support your child's education?

In what ways do you think parents can help at school to support the education of their children?

What roles do you see parents having at the school site to support the education of their children?

Enhancing Language Learning in Elementary Classrooms

Study Guide

Section 11
Putting It All Together

Putting It All Together

Goal

To share participants' learning and plan to continue learning to improve instruction for ELL students.

Performance Objectives

• Share units integrating language and content.

• Assess schools as learning communities.

• Review one's own journal entries and reflect on their applications to the classroom.

Poster Session Display Components

Your Poster Session display shows selected aspects of your work for Outside Assignments #3 and #4. The display should include:

1. The topic of the integrated lesson/unit you developed in Section 7.

2. A visual overview of the main lesson activities.

3. At least one example of how the lesson develops academic language and literacy skills.

4. At least one example of how the lesson makes connections for the students.

5. The assessment for the lesson including the task (performance) students will do, the rubric (or criteria) to assess the performance, and modifications (or support) for beginning English language learners.

Praise-Question-Polish (PQP)

Directions: After reviewing all the Poster Session displays, go to your assigned display and review it thoroughly using the five components listed on the previous page. Then, complete the PQP format below (*on a separate paper*) for your assigned display. Be prepared to give the PQP form to the participants who made the display at the end of this activity.

What is PQP and how is it used?

Praise-Question-Polish (PQP) is a structure for evaluating one's own learning and for giving feedback to another person. Following a lesson, display, or presentation, three types of comments are provided:

- Praise or positive comments,
- Questions or ideas that are not clear or further information that is needed, and
- Polish or suggested changes to improve understanding.

We will use PQP to provide feedback to participants about their Poster Session displays, but it can be used in the classroom to structure peer feedback on student writing, oral reports, projects, and portfolios, or to give the teacher feedback on a lesson or presentation.

Name of display _____

Praise: _____

_____

_____

Question: _____

_____

_____

Polish: _____

_____

_____

Your name: _____

Creating a Learning Community at Your School

> What is a Learning Community?
>
> A learning community exists when a group of people commit themselves to continual learning and to supporting others in continual learning. It involves everyone in highly visible learning experiences. You learn from each other, with each other, and for each other. You share the knowledge that is gained, the excitement and challenge that comes with learning difficult material, and the benefits your learning produces.
>
> A strong learning community provides you with the kinds of learning experiences you want to provide for your students. It models for students lifelong learning and the production of useful knowledge. It provides a sense of efficacy and self-confidence for you and your fellow teachers as you face increasing challenges. A learning community improves your professional life and that of your fellow teachers and produces higher student achievement. A learning community legitimizes change and makes it an accepted part of life at your school.

Directions for Activity:

Step 1
Review the description of a learning community (above) and the list of activities that are characteristic of learning communities (next page). Check the activities (in the left column) that take place *consistently* at your school. This will provide an analysis of the extent to which a learning community already exists at your school.

Step 2
Look carefully at the list of benefits associated with these activities and determine if any additional benefits have been generated by the "learning activities" taking place in your school. If so, add them to the list.

Step 3
Examine the list of activities you did *not* check in Step 1 and identify those you feel could be instituted at your school. Think about the potential costs and benefits of the activities you selected and determine which activities you will initiate at your school.

Step 4
Identify the first steps of an action plan for initiating those activities at your school.

Reprinted with permission from Collins, David. (1997). *Achieving Your Vision of Professional Development.* Tallahassee, FL: Southeastern Vision for Education (SERVE), pp.. 31-32.

How is My School Like a Learning Community?

Learning Community Activities	Direct Benefits
using shared planning to develop units, lessons, and activities	divides the labor: saves time because no one has to do it all; increases quantity and quality of ideas
learning from one another by watching each other teach	provides concrete examples of effective practices; expands the observer's repertoire of skills; stimulates analytical thinking about teaching
collectively studying student work to identify weaknesses and plan new ways to teach to those weaknesses	increases quantity and quality of insights into student performance; focuses efforts on "the bottom line"– student learning; increases professionalism and self-esteem of learning community members
sharing articles and other professional resources for ideas and insights; conducting book studies of books on teaching and learning	expands pool of ideas and resources available to members of the learning community
talking with one another about what and how you teach and the results your teaching produces	decreases feelings of isolation; increases experimentation and analysis of teaching practices; increases confidence of teachers; provides teachers with greater access to a range of teaching styles, models, and philosophies
providing moral support, comradeship, and encouragement	enables teachers to stick with new practices through the rough early stages of learning to use new skills; decreases burnout and stress; increases team member's willingness to try new methods and to share ideas and concerns with other members of the learning community
jointly exploring a problem, including data collection and analysis; conducting action research	improves quality of insights and solutions; increases professionalism
attending training together and helping each other implement the content of the training	helps learning community members get more out of training; enables them to go to one another with questions or to get clarification about what was presented during training
participating in continual quality improvement activities	creates more efficient use of time; takes advantage of particular talents or interests of learning community members
using collective decision making to reach decisions that produce collective action	improves quality of instruction, student performance, and school operations
providing support for "help-seeking" as well as "help-giving"	makes a strong statement of shared responsibility and commitment to one another's learning
sharing the responsibility for making and/ or collecting materials	helps learning community members feel secure in asking for help and advice; enables the giving of assistance and advice without establishing one-up/one-down relationships
*Note: Most of these learning community activities cost nothing to implement.	

Reprinted with permission from Collins, David. (1997). *Achieving Your Vision of Professional Development.* Tallahassee, FL: Southeastern Vision for Education (SERVE), pp. 31-32.

Enhancing English Language Learning in Elementary Classrooms
Study Guide Section 11: Putting It All Together

Study Groups for Professional Development

What are Study Groups?

Study groups are small groups of three to six teachers or administrators who meet regularly to research, discuss, and design and implement strategies to improve the teaching and learning in their school. The purpose of study groups is professional development for teachers which results in improved student learning in the classroom.

Why are Study Groups necessary?

Teachers are bombarded with new ideas, materials, and instructional methods from staff development workshops and other sources, but they rarely get the time to learn about a particular topic in depth or to work with colleagues to try out these ideas in their classrooms. Michael Fullan, a leader in professional development and school change, says that there are not too few innovations in schools, but too many. Teachers need time and support to choose the innovations that are appropriate to their teaching and to their students, and time and support to learn about the innovations and to integrate them into their classroom practice. Fewer than ten percent of teachers are able to do this without support.

Study groups also change the culture of the school. Study groups implemented schoolwide, reduce teacher isolation and help the school become a community of learners (teachers as well as students). Study groups can be focused to implement curricular innovations (e.g., a new reading program) or implement instructional school improvement goals. But, study groups are *not* the same as committees. The purpose of a study group is teacher professional development which results in improved student learning. For example, determining that improved writing scores are a school improvement goal is committee work, but teachers studying how to assess writing, practicing with samples of student work, and designing new writing instruction are appropriate for a study group.

How are Study Groups implemented in a school?

When can we possibly meet as a study group is usually the first question teachers and administrators ask. Research on study groups suggests that each group meet one hour per week or one hour every two weeks at the least. Study groups may be grade-level groups or cross-grade groups. Cross-grade groups have two advantages: they are less likely to discuss administrative details and they support "vertical" integration of the faculty and curriculum. Study groups generally stay together for the school year.

Some study groups meet before or after school, especially if teachers can be paid for their time or earn required staff development credits. Sometimes the school schedule is adjusted for slightly longer days, four days a week, and then early dismissal and study groups on the remaining day. One innovative school uses its Title I funds to purchase substitute teachers on the day that study groups meet. The subs are hired for the full day, but rotate to different classes to free the teacher for his/her hour or hour and a half study group meeting.

How are topics chosen?

Again, there are options: the faculty could choose a single topic for the school (e.g., literacy) and study groups could choose aspects of that topic for their in-depth study; the faculty could develop a list of priorities and grade-level teams could choose from this list or individual teachers could choose from the list if cross-grade groups are possible; or study groups could select topics on their own. Sample topics for study groups include: effectively using cooperative learning, integrating phonemic awareness and phonics activities into literature, integrating technology into the classroom, using brain-based learning methods, improving conflict resolution methods, using visualization as a comprehension strategy, grant writing to meet student and teacher learning needs, and implementing multi-age classrooms. Topics should reflect faculty/school priorities and student needs.

What do study groups actually do?

Study groups research, discuss, and design and implement strategies to improve teaching and student learning. They may read a few current articles (for help in identifying good articles, ask district/state specialists, exemplary teachers, other schools, university professors), attend workshops and share information, conduct action research, examine student work, and plan and implement improved lessons and units. Study groups may wish to set a goal related to student achievement at the beginning of their work and report outcomes and impacts at the end.

Study groups generally decide how to conduct their own meetings. Some groups assign roles, such as facilitator and recorder, and others do not. Some groups rotate roles. Each group must complete a one-page summary of each meeting which records the most important learnings and lists the next steps to be taken. Summaries are kept in a log or binder and one copy is turned in to the principal. Some schools post summaries in the faculty lounge so that other teachers may ask about what different groups are learning. Other schools share the findings from study groups for five to ten minutes at the beginning of faculty meetings.

What are the benefits of Study Groups?

Study groups reduce teacher isolation and return learning and excitement to teaching; they increase the ability of the faculty to work together to improve the school; they help both teachers and schools to become more effective; and they improve student learning.

SECTION 11

What lessons have been learned from experience?

Research on study groups demonstrates that, once the majority of the faculty decides to participate, all teachers must join a study group. Participation cannot be voluntary. In many schools, administrators, paraprofessionals, and support staff also join a study group, either a faculty group that interests them or their own group, e.g., office staff could study the cultures of the ELL students and parents that they serve.

Experience also shows that many teachers are not used to working collegially and may expect to experience conflict and confusion in study groups. First, teachers should recognize that this is a new way of working, try to make it work, and remember the benefits. Carlene Murphy also recommends focusing on the *content* being studied (e.g., talking about what you are learning, how you might use it in your classroom, what seems difficult or unclear) to help personality issues recede in importance.

Administrative support at both the school and district level is critical. Teachers need to know that their efforts are recognized and valued. Schools and districts should also make every attempt to schedule study groups on paid time; professional development is part of the job, not an optional extra.

Finally, schools should periodically evaluate the study group process and ask for faculty feedback for improvement. In one school, teachers left their classrooms with substitutes for one hour every other week to attend study groups. The second year, the faculty asked to change the schedule to after school meetings so that they did not have to leave their classes.

References for more information on Study Groups:

Murphy, Carlene. Study groups foster schoolwide learning. *Educational Leadership*, November, 1992. A good, basic overview.

Study groups in practice. *Journal of Staff Development*, 16 (3), Summer, 1995. Several teachers report their experiences in study groups.

Enhancing English Language Learning in Elementary Classrooms

Study Guide

Appendix

Study Guide Appendix

Table of Contents

- Cooperative Learning Structures

- References

- Resources: Organizations and Journals

- Participation and Portfolio Checklist

APPENDIX

Cooperative Learning Structures

1. Think-(Write)-Pair-Share

- Teacher chooses a topic or question.
- Students individually think, then may write a few notes to record their thoughts.
- Pairs of students discuss their ideas and may agree on a response to share with the whole class.
- The whole class shares ideas.
* Advantages for ELLs: Gives students time to think in their new language and then to try out communicating their ideas with a partner before sharing with the whole class; "recycles" language and content at least three times.

2. Numbered Heads Together

- Teacher divides students into groups with equal numbers.
- Students in each group number off.
- Teacher asks a question.
- Students in each group "put their heads together" to decide on an answer. All students are responsible for knowing the answer.
- Teacher chooses a number at random. Students with that number raise their hands. Teacher calls on one or more to answer.
* Especially good for reviewing material and checking comprehension.

3. Paraphrase Passport

- Students form pairs.
- Teacher poses question or problem.
- Students individually think.
- The first partner begins speaking while the second partner listens without commenting.
- The first partner stops talking.
- The second partner paraphrases what the first partner says while the first partner listens silently.
- The partner confirms the accuracy of the paraphrasing.
- The roles reverse.
* Advantages for ELLs: Students hear the language needed to express ideas. They have a more focused opportunity to develop their listening and restating skills. Especially good for expressing opinions, judgements, values, and descriptions.

4. Inside/Outside Circle

- Students stand in two concentric circles. One circle faces *in*. The other circle faces *out*.
- Students form pairs by facing another student in the other circle.
- Students in one circle begin speaking while the students in the other circle listen.
- The speaking and listening roles reverse.
- The circles rotate so each student has a new partner. Speaking and listening resumes.
* Especially good for sharing (for example, sharing what they liked best about a recent field trip,

about their vacations, about their families), describing (for example, describing a picture they just drew), or explaining (for example, explaining how they arrived at an answer to a problem). Easily combined with Paraphrase Passport. Advantages for ELLs: increases focused speaking and listening time; offers multiple opportunities to express meaning on a given topic.

5. Mix & Match

- Teacher prepares a set of cards.
- Students stand in an open space where movement is possible.
- Each student receives a card. All cards should be used. (If there is an odd number of students, teacher should participate.)
- Students begin walking around "mingling." As they mingle, they greet each other appropriately.
- Each time a student greets a classmate, they exchange cards.
- Students continue mingling and exchanging cards until the teacher asks them to stop.
- Students look at the card in their hand.
- Students work together to find the person with the card that matches theirs.
- * Advantages for ELLs: All ELLs at all levels of language proficiency can participate since strategies both verbal and non-verbal can be used to find pairs. Increased appropriate interaction with class members is promoted.

6. Rotating Review

- Teacher posts charts. Each chart is labeled with a different topic.
- Groups of students are assigned to each posted chart. Each group is assigned a different color and has one marker in that color.
- Groups discuss the topic orally without writing.
- Groups write about the topic.
- Groups rotate to the next topic, discuss it, then a new person in the group writes about it.
- Rotating continues until the groups return to the chart where they began. Groups review and discuss what other groups added to that chart.
- * Advantages for ELLs: increases focused speaking and listening time; increases focused reading time; ELL must paraphrase in writing what group members are saying.

7. Sticky Note Charts

- Teacher prepares charts. Each chart has a different topic and is divided with a "Y" shape (3 division spaces; for example, looks like, sounds like, feels like) or a "T" shape (2 division spaces; can be looks like, sounds like).
- Students work in small groups. Each member of the group has a different color pen/pencil.
- Groups are provided with a chart.
- Groups discuss the topic of the chart without writing.
- Teacher instructs group members to begin completing the chart in writing.
- Groups pass their chart to the next group.
- Group members review and discuss the topic and what is written on the chart without writing.
- Teacher instructs group members to write comments, questions, additions, changes, feedback, or suggestions on sticky papers. Sticky papers are then stuck to the chart.

APPENDIX

- Groups continue passing charts until they return to their original writers.
- Groups review their charts and the comments that have been stuck to them. They discuss the content of the comments and decide whether or not to amend their original chart. They may send a scout to seek out members of other groups (using the pen color as a guide) for clarification or additional information.
* Focuses listening, speaking, reading, and writing on a limited topic with group input. Thinking skills include evaluation of others' ideas.

Things To Remember When Using Cooperative Learning

1. Vary grouping strategies.

2. Plan for positive interdependence and individual accountability.

3. Teach and model activities before asking students to do them.

4. Recognize and reward effective group work.

References

Section 1: Introduction

Flores, J.L., Ed. (1996). *Children of la frontera: Binational efforts to serve Mexican migrant amd immigrant students.* Charleston, WV: ERIC Clearinghouse on Rural Education and Small Schools.

Section 2: Learning to Read

Adams, M.J. (1996). *Beginning to read: thinking and learning about print.* Cambridge, MA: MIT Press.

Clay, M. (1991). *Becoming literate: The construction of inner control.* Portsmouth, NH: Heineman.

Fielding, L., & Pearson, D. (1994). Reading comprehension: What works. *Educational Leadership,* 51 (5), 62-68.

Learning to read and write: Developmentally appropriate practices for young children. (1998). Joint Position Statement between the National Association for Education of Young Children and the International Reading Association.

Sutton, C. (1989, May). Helping the nonnative speaker with reading. *The Reading Teacher,* 42 (9), 684-688.

Strickland, D. (1998). *Teaching phonics today: A primer for educators.* Newark, DE: International Reading Association.

Thonis, E. (1980). *Teaching reading to the non-English speaker.* New York: Collier McMillan.

Section 3: Language Acquisition

ASCD Update. (1994, March). Teaching language minority students: Role of native-language instruction is debated. Vol. 36, No. 5. Alexandria, VA: Association for Supervision and Curriculum.

August, D. and Pease-Alvarez, L. (1996). *Attributes of effective programs and classrooms serving English language learners.* Washington DC, Santa Cruz, CA: National Center for Research on Cultural Diversity and Second Language Learning.

Chamot, A.U. (1993, May). Effective instructional practices enhance student achievement. *Forum,* 16 (4).

Collier, V.P. (1995). *Acquiring a second language for school* (Directions in language and education, Vol.1, No. 4). Washington, DC: National Clearinghouse for Bilingual Education.

Crandall, J. (1994). *Content-centered language learning. ERIC Digest.* Washington DC: ERIC Clearinghouse on Languages and Linguistics.

Cummins, J. (1984). *Bilingualism and special education: Issues in assessment and pedagogy.* San Diego, CA: College-Hill.

Cummins, J. (1987). *Empowering minority students.* (Teacher Training Monograph No. 5). Gainesville, FL: The University of Florida.

APPENDIX

Empowering ESOL teachers: An overview. (no date). Volume I, Section V. Tallahassee, FL: Florida Department of Education.

Genesee. F., Ed. (1999). *Program alternatives for linguistically diverse students* (Educational Practice Report 1). Washington DC and Santa Cruz, CA: Center for Research on Education, Diversity and Excellence.

Hamayan, E.(1993). Current trends in ESL curriculum. In S. Hudelson et al (Eds.). *English as a second language curriculum resource handbook.* Millwood, N.J.: Kraus International Publications.

Krashen, S.D. (1996 June). A gradual exit, variable threshold model for limited English proficient children. *NABE News.* 19(7):1-18.

Krashen, S.D. (1981). Bilingual education and second language acquisition theory. In *Schooling and language minority students: A theoretical framework.* Los Angeles: Evaluation, Dissemination, and Assessment Center, California State University.

Law, B. and Eckes, M. (1990). *The more-than-just-surviving handbook: ESL for every classroom teacher.* Winnipeg, MB, Canada: Peguis Publishers Limited.

Long, M.H. and Porter, P.A. (1985). Group work, interlanguage talk, and second language acquisition. *TESOL Quarterly*, 19(2), 207-228.

National Center for Research on Cultural Diversity and Second Language Learning. (1992, Dec.). Myths and misconceptions about second language learning. *ERIC Digest.* (EDO-FL-92-10).

Pinker, S. (1994). *The language instinct.* New York: HarperCollins.

Saville-Troike, M. (1984). What really matters in second language learning for academic achievement? *TESOL Quarterly* 18 (2).

Short, D.J. (1991) *Integrating language and content instruction: Strategies and techniques* (Program Information Guide No. 7). Washington, DC: National Clearinghouse for Bilingual Education.

TESOL (Teachers of English to Speakers of Other Languages). (1996). *ESL standards for preK-12 students.* Alexandria, VA: TESOL.

Thomas, W.P., and Collier, V. (1996, May). Language minority student achievement and program effectiveness. *NABE News.*

Thomas, W.P., and Collier, V. (1995). *Research summary of study in progress: Language minority student achievement and program effectiveness.* Fairfax, VA: George Mason University.

Thomas, W.P., and Collier, V. (1997). *School effectiveness for language minority students.* Washington, D.C.: National Clearinghouse for Bilingual Education.

Section 4: Culture

Bennett, C.I. (1998). *Comprehensive multicultural education*. Boston: Allyn and Bacon.

Damen, L. (1987). *Culture learning: The fifth dimension in the language classroom.* Reading, MA: Addison-Wesley.

Fradd, S.H. and Lee, O. (1998). *Creating Florida's multilingual global workforce: Educational policies and practices for students learning English as a new language.* Tallahassee, FL: Florida Department of Education.

Matiella, A.C. (1991). *Positively different: Creating a bias free environment for young children.* Santa Cruz, CA: ETR Associates.

Menkart, D. (1993). *Multicultural education: Strategies for linguistically diverse schools and classrooms*. Washington, DC: National Clearinghouse for Bilingual Educations.

Section 5: Writing

Samway, K.D. (1992). *Writers' workshop and children acquiring English as a non-native language* (Program Information Guide No. 10). Washington, DC: National Clearinghouse for Bilingual Education.

Section 6: Math

Franco, Lynda. Interactive math activities for ELLs. Unpublished document.

Section 7: Integrated Instruction

Chamot, A.U. and O' Malley, J.M. (1986). *A cognitive academic language learning approach: An ESL content-based curriculum*. Roslyn, VA: National Clearinghouse for Bilingual Education.

Chamot, A.U. and O' Malley, J.M. (1994). *The CALLA handbook: Implementing the cognitive academic language learning approach.* Reading, MA. Addison-Wesley.

CREDE. (1998, Nov.). Developing language proficiency and connecting school to students' lives: Two standards for effective teaching. (*ERIC Digest*). Santa Cruz, CA: Center for Research on Education, Diversity and Excellence.

Drake, S.M. (1993). *Planning integrated curriculum: The call to adventure.* Alexandria, VA: Association for Supervision and Curriculum Development.

Fogarty, R. (1991). *The mindful school: How to integrate the curricula.* Palatine, IL: IRI/Skylight Publishing, Inc.

APPENDIX

Gianelli, M.C. (1991). Thematic units: Creating an environment for learning. *TESOL Journal:* 13-15.

Jacobs, H.H. (1991). An interdisciplinary curriculum: A conversation with Heidi Hayes Jacobs. *Educational Leadership* 49 (2): 24-26.

Perkins, D. (1993). The connected curriculum. *Educational Leadership,* 51(2): 90-91.

Short, D.J. (1991a). *How to integrate language and content instruction: A training manual.* Washington, DC: The Center for Applied Linguistics.

Short, D.J. (1991b). *Integrating language and content instruction: Strategies and techniques* (Program Information Guide No. 7). Washington, DC: National Clearinghouse for Bilingual Education.

Section 8: Reading to Learn

Olson, M.W., and Gee, T.C. (1991). Content reading instruction in the primary grades: Perceptions and strategies. *The Reading Teacher,* 45 (4), 298-307.

Section 9: Assessment

Eastern Stream Center on Resources and Training (ESCORT), Region IV Comprehensive Center at AEL and Region XIV Comprehensive /Center for Applied Linguistics. (1998). *Help! They don't speak English starter kit for primary teachers,* Third Edition. (Copies may be obtained from ESCORT, 1-800-451-8058.)

Education Update. (1997, June*).* Assessment that serves instruction. Vol. 39, No. 4. Alexandria, VA: Association for Supervision and Curriculum Development.

Education Update. (1996, June). On the cutting edge of assessment: Testing what students can do with knowledge. Vol. 38, No. 4. Alexandria, VA: Association for Supervision and Curriculum Development.

Education Update. (1998, June); Matching assessment with curriculum. Vol 40, No.4. Alexandria, VA: Association for Supervision and Curriculum Development.

Empowering ESOL teachers: An overview. (Revised 1996 edition). Volume II, Section IX. Tallahassee, FL: Florida Department of Education.

Herman, J.L. (1992). What research tells us about good assessment. *Educational Leadership,* 49 (8), 74-78.

Jameson, J. (1999) *Issues in grading limited English proficient students.* From Theory to Practice, No. 9. Tampa, FL: Region XIV Comprehensive Center at ETS.

O'Malley, J.M. and Pierce, L.V. (1996). *Authentic assessment for English language learners: Practical approaches for teachers*. Addison-Wesley Publishing Company.

Solis, A. (1995). Grading LEP students: Developing sound practice. *NABE News.* pp. 21-44.

Wiggins, G. and McTighe, J. (1998). *Understanding by design*. Alexandria, VA: Association for Supervision and Curriculum Development.

Section 10: Family/Parent Involvement

Derrick-Mescura, M. (1999). *Working with families*. From Theory to Practice, No. 10, Tampa, FL: Region XIV Comprehensive Center at ETS.

Olsen, L., et. al. (1994). *The unfinished journey: Restructuring schools in a diverse society.* San Francisco, CA: California Tomorrow.

Violand-Sanchez, E., Sutton, C., and Ware, H. (1991). *Fostering home-school cooperation: Involving language minority families as partners in education* (Program Information Guide No. 6). National Clearinghouse for Bilingual Education.

Section 11: Putting It All Together

Fullan, M. (1998). Leadership for the 21st century: Breaking the bonds of dependency. *Educational Leadership* 55(7), 6-10.

Goldenberg, C. and Sullivan, J. (1994). *Making change happen in a language minority school: A search for coherence* (Educational Practice Report No. 13). Washington DC and Santa Cruz, CA. National Center for Research on Cultural Diversity and Second Language Learning.

McLeod, B. (1996). *School reform and student diversity: Exemplary schooling for language minority students.* Washington, D.C.: The George Washington University, Institute for the Study of Language and Education.

Resources: Organizations and Journals

<u>Organizations</u>

1. TESOL (Teachers of English to Speakers of Other Languages)
    700 South Washington, Ste. 200
    Alexandria, VA 22314
    703-836-0774 fax: 703-836-7864
    www.tesol.org

2. National Clearinghouse for Bilingual Education (NCBE)
    The George Washington University
    2121 K Street, NW, Suite 260
    Washington, DC 20037
    202-467-0867
    www.ncbe.gwu.edu (includes an on-line library)

3. Eastern Stream Center on Resources and Training
    (ESCORT) (For Migrant Education Inquiries)
    SUNY at Oneonta
    Oneonta, NY 13820
    800-451-8058

4. National Association for Bilingual Education (NABE)
    1030 15th Street , NW, Suite 470
    Washington, DC 20005-1503
    202-898-1829
    www.nabe.org

5. Center for Applied Linguistics (CAL)
    4646 40th Street NW
    Washington, D.C. 20016-1859
    202-362-0700
    www.cal.org

6. Association of Supervision and Curriculum Development (ASCD)
    1703 North Beauregard Street
    Alexandria, VA 22311-1714
    800-933-ASCD(2723)
    703-578-9600
    www.ascd.org

Journals and Newsletters

ERIC/CLL News Bulletin (free)
ERIC Clearinghouse on Languages and Linguistics
Center for Applied Linguistics
4646 40th Street, NW
Washington, DC 20016-1859
202-362-0700

Bilingual Research Journal
National Association for Bilingual Education
1030 15th Street , NW, Suite 470
Washington, DC 20005-1503
202-898-1829

NCBE Program Information Guides
NCBE Occasional Papers
NCBE Forum
National Clearinghouse for Bilingual Education
The George Washington University
Center for Language and Education
2121 K Street, NW, Suite 260
Washington, DC 20037
202-467-0867

Phi Delta Kappan
408 N. Union
P.O. Box 789
Bloomington, IN 47402

The Reading Teacher
International Reading Association
800 Barksdale Road
 P.O. Box 8139
Newark, DE 19714-8139

TESOL Journal, TESOL Matters, TESOL Quarterly
TESOL Incorporated
700 South Washington St., Ste. 200
Alexandria, VA 22314
703-836-0774; fax: 703-836-7864

Participation and Portfolio Checklist

Enhancing English Language Learning in Elementary Classrooms

Name: _____

School: _____

Identification #: _____

Part A. Participation

In order to receive credit for a section, the participant must attend and actively participate in all discussions unless alternate arrangements are approved in advance.

	Yes	No
Section 1: Introduction		
Section 2: Learning to Read		
Section 3: Language Acquisition		
Section 4: Culture		
Section 5: Writing		
Section 6: Math		
Section 7: Integrated Instruction		
Section 8: Reading to Learn		
Section 9: Assessment		
Section 10: Family/Parent Involvement		
Section 11: Putting It All Together		

Part B. Products as Listed on Checklist

Complete all products as assigned in the Study Guide and document their completion on the next page. Place outside assignments and your journal in a folder to be evaluated by the facilitator. Only completed products are acceptable.

Participation and Portfolio Checklist

	Yes	No
Section 1: Introduction		
Summary Reading		
Think-Pair-Share Worksheet		
Section 2: Learning to Read		
Developing Reading Skills for ELLs		
Phonemic Awareness		
Concepts of Print		
When is the ELL Ready to Begin Reading?		
Section 3: Language Acquisition		
Adapting a Lesson Using The Three Principles		
Adapting a Lesson for Stages of Language Development		
Pros and Cons of Program Models		
Section 4: Culture		
Culture Study Group		
Adapting Lessons to Include Multicultural Strategies		
Section 5: Writing		
Creating and Using a Writing Rubric		
What does Julio Know About Writing?		
Talking to Julio		
Section 6: Math		
Learning to Speak Math		
Making Math More Comprehensible		
Making Math More Interactive		
Including Higher Order Thinking skills		
Section 7: Integrated Instruction		
Lesson Plan Checklist: Sample Lesson 1		
Integrated Instruction: Personal Priorities		
Developing An Integrated Lesson		
Section 8: Reading to Learn		
Comparing Lessons		
Content Reading Instruction in the Primary Grades: Perceptions and Strategies		

(continued, next page)

APPENDIX

	Yes	No
Section 9: Assessment		
Corn Lesson Assessment		
Corn Lesson Rubric		
Section 10: Family/Parent Involvement		
Family Involvement "Y" Charts		
Section 11: Putting It All Together		
Praise-Question-Polish		
Creating a Learning Community at Your School		
Other:		
Journal		
OA #1: ELL Student Interview		
OA #2: Outside Reading by K.D. Samway		
OA #3: Poster Session Preparation		
OA #4: Assessment for Poster session		
OA #5: Parent Interview		

APPENDIX